THE
EVERYTHING®

QUICK MEALS
COOKBOOK

Delicious meals
—from appetizers to desserts—
that don't take long to prepare

Barbara Doyen

Adams Media Corporation
Holbrook, Massachusetts

An Everything® Series Book. Everything® is a
registered trademark of Adams Media Corporation.

Published by Adams Media Corporation
260 Center Street, Holbrook, MA 02343. U.S.A.
www.adamsmedia.com

ISBN: 1-58062-488-X

Printed in the United States of America.

J I H G F E D C B A

Library of Congress Cataloging-in-Publication Data

Doyen, Barbara.
    The everything quick meals cookbook / by Barbara Doyen.
        p.   cm.
    ISBN 1-58062-488-X
    1. Quick and easy cookery. I. Title
    TX833.5 .D69 2001
    641.5′55—dc21   00-066355

Illustrations by Barry Littmann

This book is available at quantity discounts for bulk purchases.
For information, call 1-800-872-5627.

See the entire Everything® series at everything.com

Contents

Chapter 1 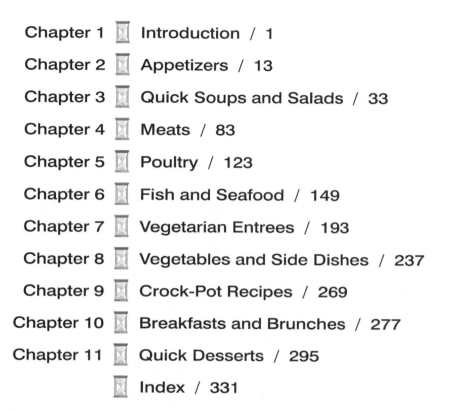 Introduction / 1

Chapter 2 Appetizers / 13

Chapter 3 Quick Soups and Salads / 33

Chapter 4 Meats / 83

Chapter 5 Poultry / 123

Chapter 6 Fish and Seafood / 149

Chapter 7 Vegetarian Entrees / 193

Chapter 8 Vegetables and Side Dishes / 237

Chapter 9 Crock-Pot Recipes / 269

Chapter 10 Breakfasts and Brunches / 277

Chapter 11 Quick Desserts / 295

Index / 331

Charts

Emergency Substitutions / iv

Weights and Measures / 10

How to Measure It / 12

Cutting Techniques / 32

Yields and Equivalents / 82

Internal Meat Temperature When Roasting / 122

Wash Those Veggies! / 236

Steaming Tips / 268

How to Cook It / 294

Cake Pan Tips / 330

Emergency Substitutions

Baking Powder: 1 teaspoon: $1/2$ teaspoon cream of tartar + $1/4$ teaspoon baking soda

Balsamic Vinegar: Sherry or cider vinegar (not white)

Beer: Apple juice or beef broth

Broth: 1 teaspoon granulated or 1 cube bouillon dissolved in 1 cup water

Brown Sugar, Packed: Equal amount of granulated sugar

Buttermilk: 1 teaspoon lemon juice or vinegar plus milk to make 1 cup; let stand 5 minutes

Cajun Seasoning: Equal parts white pepper, black pepper, ground red pepper, onion powder, garlic powder, and paprika

Chocolate: For 1 square, unsweetened: 3 tablespoons cocoa plus 1 tablespoon butter

For 1 square, *semisweet*: 1 square unsweetened + 1 tablespoon sugar

For 2 squares, *semisweet*: $1/3$ cup semi-sweet chips

Corn Syrup: *For light or dark:* 1 cup sugar + $1/4$ cup water

For dark: 1 cup light corn syrup or 1 cup maple syrup, or $3/4$ cup light corn syrup + $1/4$ cup molasses

Cornstarch: For 1 tablespoon: 2 tablespoons all-purpose flour

Cream of Mushroom Soup: For 1 can: 1 cup thick white sauce + 4-ounce can mushrooms, drained and chopped

Dates: *For chopped:* equal amount raisins, prunes, currants, or dried cherries

Eggs: For 1 egg: 2 egg whites or 2 egg yolks or $1/4$ cup liquid egg substitute

Flour: For cake flour: 1 cup minus 2 tablespoons all-purpose flour

Self-rising flour: 1 cup all-purpose flour + 1 teaspoon baking powder and $1/2$ teaspoon salt

Honey: $1^{1}/4$ cups sugar + $1/4$ cup water

Leeks: Equal amount green onions or shallots

Lemon Juice: For 1 teaspoon: 1 teaspoon cider vinegar or white vinegar

Milk: $1/2$ cup evaporated (not condensed) milk plus $1/2$ cup water

Molasses: Equal amount honey

Mushrooms: For 1 cup cooked: 4-ounce can, drained

Poultry Seasoning: For 1 teaspoon: $3/4$ teaspoon sage + $1/4$ teaspoon thyme

Prunes: Dates, raisins, or currants

Pumpkin Pie Spice: For 1 teaspoon: $1/2$ teaspoon cinnamon + $1/4$ teaspoon ground ginger + $1/8$ teaspoon ground allspice + $1/8$ teaspoon ground nutmeg

Red Pepper Sauce: For 4 drops: $1/8$ teaspoon ground cayenne (red) pepper

Sour Cream: Plain yogurt

Tomato Products: For 1 cup juice: $1/2$ cup sauce + $1/2$ cup water

For $1/2$ cup paste: simmer 1 cup sauce till reduced to $1/2$ cup

For 2 cups sauce: $3/4$ cup paste + $1^{1}/4$ cup water

Wine: For white: apple juice, apple cider, white grape juice, chicken or vegetable broth, water

For red: apple cider, chicken, beef or vegetable broth, water

Yogurt: Sour cream

Chapter 1

Introduction

Quick Meal Strategies

We all have such active lives that the last thing we want to do is to return home from a busy day and have to spend a lot of time preparing a meal. To solve this problem, some people hire a personal chef. Others support their local fast-food restaurants. The first solution costs us financially and takes more money than most care to spend; the second costs us nutritionally and can get quite boring.

The answer? Cooking quick meals at home! You really can serve delicious home-cooked meals for your family in less time than it takes to load up the kids, travel to the nearest drive-up window, wait in line, and return home with fast food in a sack. All you have to do is follow some simple strategies.

Strategy #1

When planning quick meals, start by deciding on the main dish or entree first. What will it be? Then decide on the vegetables. What would go well with the main dish? From there you can figure what else you might need or want, like a salad, other side dishes, soup, or dessert. The entree or main dish is the heart of the meal and everything else should complement it in flavor, texture, and color.

Strategy #2

When preparing meals, have a game plan. Start making the recipe that takes the longest or that will give you time breaks while the food is baking or simmering or cooling, so you can get a start on another part of the meal. With a little practice, this becomes second nature to most home chefs so that everything is done and ready to eat at the same time.

Strategy #3

Prepare food in advance. This is not only a time-saver, but it reduces stress when you are rushed or entertaining. Many recipes in this book can be prepared ahead of time, and some should be prepared in advance for maximum flavor and texture. Some can be made ahead and frozen or refrigerated until needed. Others can be placed in a Crock-Pot in the morning for an evening meal.

Strategy #4

Cook for leftovers. Do not bake enough roast or meatloaf or chicken or even dessert for only one meal. Let's say it takes you eight minutes to stir up a main-course casserole and nine minutes to make a double batch. That additional minute buys you a second meal with little or no additional clean up time. The leftovers are great time-savers for the next day or for the freezer and can often be converted into a new dish with a little imagination so that it won't seem like you're having leftovers.

Strategy #5

Plan menus in advance. Really organized people decide on what they'll be serving for all their at-home meals one or even two weeks or two months in advance. Why? To insure good nutrition. To have food variety. To help stick to a particular diet. To better organize grocery lists. To save money by buying large quantities, using coupons before they expire, and taking advantage of sales. To plan around your own schedule, so that you can make extra meat on Tuesday to throw into a quick salad on Wednesday. To relieve stress because you'll avoid the anxiety of deciding what to fix and of finding you're out of something. But most of all, to save time.

Strategy #6

Know what you'll be preparing that day. If you don't want to be rigidly locked into a preplanned menu, at least have one or two possible ideas of what you could fix for the meals you'll have at home that day. I usually have one specific thing in mind, with one or two alternates based on the food on hand. Then you can be thinking about your choices and which you most prefer as you return to your kitchen after your day's activities.

Strategy #7

Keep a well-stocked pantry. If you're building your home and have a choice, go for a walk-in pantry. Mine is a room ten feet square and has floor to ceiling shelving on all the walls. It's actually cheaper than buying the same number of cabinets, and everything is in view, but also hidden behind a closed door.

Strategy #8

Keep a well-stocked freezer with plenty of meat, fish, poultry, and other items that become the building blocks for quick meals. Having a freezer separate from your refrigerator is really worthwhile. I have two stand-alone units, and keep both quite full even though I'm usually cooking for only two people. It's a huge time-saver, and it can be a money-saver as well if you are able to buy items cheaper in bulk or on sale or if you grow your own produce.

Strategy #9

Keep emergency food on hand. Keep the basic ingredients for your favorite recipes in your pantry and freezer. For instance, place cooked and sliced or cut up meats or poultry in the freezer for those days when you'll be really harried. It's so helpful if you can grab leftover chicken or roast in premeasured quantities from your freezer for quick thawing in the microwave, and retrieve canned items, like tuna or broth, from your pantry. These can be added to vegetable stir-fries, soups, or lettuce salads for ultra quick meals. Since we often have guests drop by when I don't

have time to bake, I keep a supply of frozen cookies and pies to serve my visitors with coffee or tea.

Strategy #10

Don't buy groceries more than once a week, or better yet, once every two weeks, if possible. Think how much time you'll save if you don't drop by to pick up a few things on your way home from work—driving to the store, finding a parking place, locating the items, standing in the checkout line, loading the groceries in the car, driving home. It all adds up to quite a lot.

Strategy #11

Don't go shopping without a list. Some people are so extremely well organized that they plan out their meals for several days or weeks, check the recipes, and formulate their list. I'm more the creative type and don't like to be locked into a rigid meal plan. But I don't want to forget anything important that would require an extra trip to the store, either. So I keep a running list of any ingredients I'm low on in my pantry, freezer, or fridge, add any items I need for the recipes I want to do

soon, and then check out store specials and look at the featured items in the produce and meat departments. If I find anything new that's interesting, I work it into my menu.

Strategy #12
Buy groceries when the store is not full of customers. This can vary by area, but most grocery stores are swamped between 4:00 P.M. and 6:00 P.M. when people are getting off of work, from 11:30 A.M. and 1:00 P.M. during lunch hour, and the day before a holiday. In my area 8:00 A.M. is usually a good time to go shopping (although one store has the aisles blocked with pallets at this time as the stockers replenish the shelves—which is very irritating!). I find Friday mornings are often busy; Monday mornings are not. One local store is open 24 hours and we usually find it's not crowded after 7:00 P.M., although sometimes there aren't enough checkout people. By making mental notes about your own store, you can avoid crowded aisles and lengthy checkout lines that take more time than it did to fill your cart.

Strategy #13
Buy multiples, especially when the items are on sale. I try to have at least two of everything in my pantry and freezers—more when the price is reduced; when I'm down to the second to the last item, I add it to my grocery list.

Strategy #14
Rewrite your grocery list in order. Of course your running list will be haphazard, because you're writing down the items as you find you need them. But before you go shopping, take a few moments to rewrite the list so the items appear in the order you'll be walking through the store. Sometimes large supermarkets will give you a store map, which is very useful as you create this revised list. If you can at least have the items organized by the row you'll find them in, you'll save lots of time—and frustration—as you locate them. Take along a pen or pencil so you can cross off each item as you place it in your cart. Circle the items you can't find so you can ask for help, and if they aren't available, immediately add them to your new running grocery list at home so you

can try again the next time you shop. By stocking at least two of every item and putting it on the list when you're down to one, you won't feel pressured to go from store to store when something is unavailable—because you'll have a spare. And you'll have a system to insure that you purchase the item on your next shopping trip.

Strategy #15
Have your groceries delivered if you're really busy and can afford it. This option is becoming available in more and more cities. You phone or fax in your order, or place it via the Internet, and the items are delivered to your home. Some delivery services provide a locked refrigerator in your garage or in a small storage room accessible from outside.

Strategy #16
Have a well-organized kitchen. Store everything near the area where it will be used the most and arrange your kitchen so that the most-used things are within easy reach. Items used less frequently should be stored in the back of the cupboard or drawer or else very

high or low, or perhaps in the pantry on the harder-to-reach shelves. For example, pots and pans used daily should be close to the stove, but large kettles or roasters might be located on the top shelf of the cupboard or pantry. Potholders should be kept near the oven and the utensils used to stir, whisk, or flip food should be near the stove. Try to organize all the equipment needed for mixing and assembling food in one area; this includes measuring cups and spoons, spices, electric mixer and food processor, etc. Dishes, flatware, and napkins should be easily accessible to the area where you eat. Place dividers in drawers to keep drawers from becoming a jumbled mess you have to paw through to find a tool. Store everything where it will be most used, assigning everything a place, and always returning it to its assigned place so you'll never have to waste time searching or digging for an item. You'll be able to grab things almost automatically as you prepare speedy meals.

Strategy #17
Buy great cooking equipment. Settling for cheap quality costs you in

time, and in the long run, money. Everything (with the exception of nonstick pans) should be dishwasher-safe for quick cleanup. Essentials include:

- An *electric mixer* with enough power to mix meatloaf and bread dough. If possible, buy an extra beater and an extra mixing bowl for convenience when cooking quick meals.
- A *food processor* that makes quick work of slicing, chopping, puréeing, shredding, etc. Good ones eliminate the need for a traditional blender. Mine is used for nearly every meal.
- A *cordless hand blender* to make quick soups, purées, and whipping cream and to chop or grind small quantities.
- Quality *pots and pans* with well fitting lids will save you cooking time and cleanup time. My favorite pan is high-quality stainless steel, which is almost as easy to clean as the nonstick pans. If the budget allows, I do recommend having one high-quality (which means it's rather expensive) nonstick skillet—the inexpensive ones are not worth buying. The downside to nonstick is that the pan can't be used on high heat or placed in the dishwasher; the plus side is that it's great for egg dishes like omelets, which can't be cooked on high heat anyway.
- Plenty of *dishes and covered casseroles* that go from freezer to oven to table. Before buying them, check that the lids fit tightly; too often I've found gaps after I've gotten the casserole home and out of the box. Gaps allow the food to dry out.
- A set of *mixing bowls* in graduated sizes. Or better, get a couple sets or more. You don't want to stop food preparation to wash out a bowl.
- An electric *slow cooker* so you can come home to a ready-to-serve one-pot meal. The heating element should be on the bottom and up the sides and the pot and lid should be removable for ease in cleaning. The pot and lid can go into the dishwasher if the heating elements are not attached.
- A *salad spinner* is indispensable when cleaning lettuce because it spins the leaves dry quickly. The inner bowl can also be used as a vegetable colander. When finished, just rinse the spinner

bowls and allow it to air dry. No more patting lettuce leaves dry with towels!

- A reliable *convection oven* that has a "pure convection" setting as well as "convection bake" and "bake." This not only speeds up baking time by 25 percent or more, but you are baking faster at a 25 percent lower temperature and do not have the typical microwave problem of parts of the food becoming really hot and parts staying cold. You can pack the oven, for example, with three pans of cookies, and all three will be done at the same time without having the top rack of cookies being underbaked and the bottom rack being burnt. A terrific time-saver!

- A high-quality *dishwasher* that is reliable and ultraquiet and does not require you to scrape or rinse the dishes. Yes, such a machine does exist and it's well worth the cost! The only exceptions to the no-scraping and no-rinsing requirement are dried-on raw eggs or burnt-on food, which might require soaking. If you buy quality stainless pots and pans (without the nonstick coating) you only need to soak the pan in hot

water about three minutes, and the burnt food readily releases.

Strategy #18
Have duplicates of often-used utensils like rubber scrapers, stirring spoons, measuring cups and measuring spoons, paring knives, etc. This eliminates another time-waster, cleaning a dirty utensil, during quick meal preparation.

Strategy #19
Choose easy-care appliances and kitchen appointments like flooring, countertop materials, cooktops or stoves, self-cleaning ovens, self-defrosting freezers, scrubbable cabinets, etc. Whenever you have a choice, search for the easiest-to-clean products available. You'll be glad you did—the time savings are enormous!

Strategy #20
Try to see meal preparation as a joy. By following the advice from this book, you will find creating meals to be so easy and enjoyable it will never be a dreaded chore again. Have fun trying garnishes to give even the most ordinary food pizzazz and make your

meals look beautiful with little effort. Give yourself and your family a boost by occasionally changing serving styles (buffet, formal, family), locations (dining room, breakfast room, deck, even the family room), by switching the dishes and table linens (all machine washable, of course), and using imaginative centerpieces that might be "found" objects from elsewhere in the house. Your positive approach will be translated into a life of happy mealtime memories with your family and friends.

About Quick Meals

This book was assembled with three basic approaches to quick home-cooked meals:

Many of these recipes are *fast*—you can prepare them and be eating them in minutes, usually with a minimum of ingredients.

Others are *easy*—you quickly assemble something that cooks or bakes without your attention. The time requirement is minimal, so you can be doing other things, like setting a pretty table or tossing a salad. Sometimes the food

cooks all day while you're gone, as in Crock-Pot cookery.

Still others are *made-ahead*—things that take the pressure off when you need to save time for a later meal. These can be stored in the refrigerator for use in the near future, or many will go into the freezer for later use. When entertaining or facing a busy week, plan at least some recipes that can be made well in advance.

Think through your menu's preparation sequence and you will find ways to multitask, perhaps by using all three approaches in one meal.

Apply these strategies to put together three or four menus that you have tried (and your family likes) and that work well for you to prepare in a short time. These become your personal standards or specialties that you fall back on regularly.

Do you owe dinner to two groups of friends? Why not invite them to visit on two consecutive nights and serve each group the same menu from your personal standards? You will save lots of prep time by doubling the quantities of the foods you buy and preparing them in advance.

Are you entertaining, but find yourself in a serious last-minute time pinch? Don't

panic! For those times you absolutely do not have time to make an entire quick meal, have your guests gather at your house for appetizers, take them to a restaurant for dinner, then bring them back to your home for dessert. Your preparation time—and stress level—is greatly reduced and you have still entertained them with two home-cooked courses.

As you use *The Everything® Quick Meals Book,* do not hesitate to write comments in the margins, perhaps highlighting the titles of the recipes that you enjoyed and putting asterisks by those recipes that you find worked well for entertaining. Make this book your personal reference for quick meals!

Cooking Quickly Means Cooking Safely

Follow these guidelines for safe meal preparation:

- Wash your hands often and well with soap and water, both before beginning meal preparation and often thereafter, whenever your hands get dirty.
- Dry your hands completely before plugging or unplugging electrical appliances.
- Store clean and dry potholders within easy reach for pans on the stove or in the oven.
- If you spill something on the floor, wipe it up immediately to prevent falls.

Weights and Measures

a dash = less than $\frac{1}{8}$ teaspoon	4 quarts = 1 gallon
3 teaspoons = 1 tablespoon	8 ounces = 1 cup liquid
4 tablespoons = $\frac{1}{4}$ cup	8 ounces = $\frac{1}{2}$ pound
$\frac{1}{3}$ cup = 5 tablespoons + 1 teaspoon	16 ounces = 2 pints or $\frac{1}{2}$ quart liquid
$\frac{1}{2}$ cup = 8 tablespoons	16 ounces = 1 pound
$\frac{2}{3}$ cup = 10 tablespoons + 2 teaspoons	32 ounces = 1 quart
$\frac{1}{2}$ pint = 1 cup	64 ounces = $\frac{1}{2}$ gallon
1 pint = 2 cups	1 liter = 1.06 quarts
1 quart = 4 cups	1 quart = .95 liter

- Aim pot handles toward the back of the stove rather than over the floor to prevent dangerous spills.
- Always practice food safety. Keep hot foods hot and cold foods cold. Thaw meats, poultry, and fish in the refrigerator or microwave. Never refreeze foods that have thawed without cooking them first. Use a meat thermometer.

Quick Measuring

Sticks of butter are easy to measure if the wrapper has markings on it. One pat of butter is 1 tablespoon, half a stick is $1/4$ cup, the whole stick is $1/2$ cup, and you can count off 5 $1/3$ tablespoon marks for $1/3$ cup of butter.

It's handy to have measuring cups in all sizes, including $1/8$, $1/4$, $1/3$, $1/2$, $2/3$, $3/4$, and 1 cup, because it saves time. If they are dishwasher safe, cleanup time is minimized.

Staples to Have On Hand

In the Freezer: Fresh and precooked meat and poultry, fish, bread, pound cake, pies, cookies, vegetables and fruits, shredded cheeses, green and red pepper, butter or margarine, nuts, prepared casseroles, coffee beans, etc.

In the Pantry: Canned vegetables and fruits, meats, chicken and beef broth, pasta, rice, couscous, flour, sugar, baking soda, baking powder, cocoa, chocolate chips, salt, pepper, herbs, spices, seasoning mixtures, coffee, tea, olive oil, vanilla, mayonnaise (unopened), prepared mustard, catsup, Worcestershire sauce, instant bouillon granules, minced dried onion, minced dried garlic, etc. Store multiples of anything, providing space isn't a problem and you're able to use them by their expiration date.

In the Refrigerator: Eggs (which keep a long while in their original carton with the large end up); milk; lettuce plus other seasonal fresh vegetables and fruits; whipping cream; fresh meats, poultry, and fish; condiments like pickles and prepared mustard; onions, leftovers; plus the meat, poultry, and fish that you are thawing for future quick meals.

How to Measure It

How to Measure Liquid Ingredients
1. Use a liquid measuring cup—a glass or plastic cup with graduated markings on the side.
2. Place the cup on a flat, level surface.
3. View the liquid at eye level.

How to Measure Dry Ingredients
1. Use graduated nesting measuring cups (dry measuring cups).
2. Spoon the ingredient into the appropriate cup, or dip the cup into the container of a dry ingredient.
3. Level it off with a knife or spatula.

EXCEPTION: Brown sugar must be packed into the measuring cup, pressing firmly with the fingers. The sugar should retain the shape of the measuring cup when it is dumped.

How to Measure Soft Ingredients
1. Use graduated dry measuring cups.
2. Soft bread crumbs, coconut, shredded cheeses, and similar soft ingredients should be lightly pressed down into the selected measuring cup.

EXCEPTION: Solid shortening must be firmly packed down into a dry ingredient measuring cup. Scoop it into the selected cup, pack with a spatula or the back of a spoon, then level it off with a spatula or knife.

How to Use Measuring Spoons
1. Use graduated measuring spoons for both liquid and dry ingredients.
2. For dry ingredients, level with a knife or spatula.
3. For liquid ingredients, pour carefully, near but not over the mixing bowl.

Chapter 2

Appetizers

Are the people in your house clamoring for food, yet you're running late and your meal isn't quite ready? Or perhaps you have guests arriving and need an icebreaker for everyone to feel comfortable and to buy yourself additional prep time?

Just hand each person a beverage and invite them to enjoy your quick and delicious appetizers. This will take the edge off your guests' hunger while encouraging them to enjoy themselves and chat a little, giving you a few additional moments to get the meal organized. And your guests will feel relaxed and welcome!

Appetizer Quick Fixes, Part 1

- Stuff celery segments with cheese spread or cream cheese seasoned with chives. Serve on a plate, perhaps on a bed of lettuce leaves or kale.
- Open a jar of black or green olives or cocktail onions or pickles. Drain and serve.

- Slice cheeses (Brie, Monterey Jack, Gouda, Gorgonzola, Gruyère, Colby, etc.) and summer sausage. Serve on a tray or platter.
- Prepare a relish tray of plain celery, carrot sticks, cauliflower segments, green onions, radishes or kohlrabi slices, perhaps served with a dip.
- Set out baskets filled with finger foods like nuts, crackers, pork rinds, potato chips, or pretzels.

Appetizer Quick Fixes, Part 2

- Offer fresh fruits or fruit combinations like grapes, strawberries, chunks of pineapple, slices of pears or kiwi, etc. Place in a bowl or on a tray. If the fruits are cut into bite-sized pieces, use a serving spoon and provide guests with toothpicks or cocktail forks and plates.
- Make an arrangement of dried fruits like peaches, apricots, raisins, or prunes, perhaps garnished with nuts like pecans, walnuts, or macadamias.

Eggplant Caviar

Prep Time: 10 minutes ⧗ Cook: 15 minutes

Yield: 2 cups

1 cup finely chopped onion
1 cup finely chopped bell pepper
2 tablespoons olive oil
1 large eggplant, cooked and innards scooped
   out and mashed
1 tomato, finely chopped
salt and pepper to taste

In a large skillet, brown the onion and green pepper in the olive oil. Add eggplant and tomato and stir often. Cook until the mixture is well done. Add more oil if it begins to stick. Add salt and pepper to taste. Transfer the mixture to a serving dish and chill.

Serve as a spread for crackers or as a vegetable dip.

With Appetizers, Presentation Is Key

Since it is served first, an appetizer will set the tone of a meal. For example, to create a festive atmosphere, serve a dip in the center of a colorful plate and surround it with lots of different crunchy vegetables. Or to help party guests break the ice and forget their nervousness, set out appetizers buffet style so they can help themselves. Appetizers also make for a casual beginning at the dinner table with children and make it easier for everyone to talk about their day at school or work.

Ham Roll-Ups

Prep Time: 15 minutes ⧗ Chill: 3 hours

Yield: about 24 appetizers

3 9-inch flour tortillas
3-ounce package cream cheese
¼ cup sour cream
6 rectangular slices boiled ham (about 6" × 4")
¼ cup chopped fresh chives or sliced green onions
*¼ cup shredded Cheddar, Swiss, or Monterey Jack
    cheese*
tomato salsa (optional)

Have the tortillas at room temperature. Soften the cream cheese, and combine with the sour cream. Spread on the tortillas. On each tortilla, place two slices of ham. Sprinkle with the chives and cheese. Roll up, wrap in plastic wrap, and chill for at least 3 hours.

To serve, cut into 1-inch slices. If desired, serve with tomato salsa.

Freezing Cheese

Placing a leftover hunk of cheese into the freezer not only conserves all those odd bits that are too small to use in another recipe, but also hardens up the soft cheeses enough for grating. Be sure to freeze soft cheeses when they have ripened; semisoft and harder cheeses can be frozen as is, or sliced or grated beforehand.

Hot Dungeness Crab Appetizer

Prep Time: 10 minutes ⌛ Heat: 8 minutes

Yield: about 2 cups

1 14-ounce can artichoke hearts
½ pound Dungeness crabmeat
2 cups mayonnaise
1 small yellow onion, sliced thinly
1 cup shredded Parmesan cheese
minced fresh parsley

Preheat the oven to 350°F. Drain the artichoke hearts and chop into ¼-inch pieces. Drain the crab well. Combine all ingredients except the parsley and mix well. Place in a shallow baking dish and heat in the oven for 6 to 8 minutes or until the internal temperature is at least 140°F. Garnish with minced parsley. Serve with assorted breads.

When making this dish ahead of time, do not cover with aluminum foil, as the crab will discolor.

Quick Tip: Kitchen Helpers

Consider asking some of your guests to assist in the meal preparation during the appetizer course. Nowadays, people don't mind tossing the salad or stirring a kettle of soup as you mastermind the whole affair. Most people gravitate to the kitchen anyway, so why not let them assist with small tasks?

Low-Fat Tortilla Chips

Prep Time: 15 minutes ⧖ Bake: 10 minutes

Yield: 2 cups chips

6 8-inch flour tortillas
1 teaspoon ground cumin
2 teaspoons garlic powder
¹/₂ teaspoon salt

Preheat oven to 350°F.

Spray one side of each tortilla with nonstick cooking spray. Mix the cumin, garlic powder, and salt together in a small bowl. Sprinkle over the sprayed side of the tortillas. Cut each tortilla into 6 wedges and arrange on a baking sheet. Bake until crisp, about 10 minutes.

Thawing Frozen Dishes

One of the best ways to quickly thaw meals that have been frozen is to place the container into warm or even simmering water. First loosen the top, and then check it every five minutes or so to determine the status of the frozen food.

Parmesan Crisps

Prep Time: 10 minutes ⧗ Bake: 9 minutes

Yield: about 40 crisps

1 loaf French bread baguette (about 12 inches)*
1 cup butter
1 cup grated Parmesan cheese

Preheat oven to 400°F.

Slice the baguette into ¼-inch slices, discarding the heels. In a small flat-bottomed baking dish, melt the butter. In a similar bowl, place the grated cheese. Quickly dip each side of the bread slices in butter (do not soak!), then in the cheese. Place in a jellyroll pan (do not substitute a cookie sheet because some butter may drain off in cooking).

Bake 5 minutes, then turn slices over. Bake an additional 4 minutes or until browned.

*A baguette is smaller in diameter than a regular loaf of French bread.

Balancing Your Menu

If you're leafing through this book in order to find the perfect dessert to balance a particular menu, keep in mind that opposites attract. In other words, if your entrée is rich, go for a light fruit-based dessert. Or if you are serving a light salad or sandwiches, choose a calories-be-damned chocolate dessert.

Seafood Roll-Ups

Prep Time: 12 minutes ⧖ Refrigerate: 3 hours

Yield: about 24 appetizers

5 9-inch flour tortillas
1 8-ounce package cream cheese
1/4 cup mayonnaise salad dressing
1 can crabmeat or 1 can shrimp, well drained and
    chopped, **or** 5 ounces fresh crabmeat, imitation
    crabmeat, or cooked shrimp, chopped
2 tablespoons chopped fresh chives
1/4 cup chopped red bell pepper
tomato salsa (optional)

Have the tortillas at room temperature. Soften the cream
cheese and combine with the salad dressing. Blend in the
chopped seafood. Spread on the tortillas, dividing evenly.
Sprinkle the vegetables evenly over the tortillas. Roll each up
tightly and wrap with plastic wrap. Refrigerate at least 3 hours.

To serve, cut in diagonal slices about 3/4 inch thick. If desired,
serve with tomato salsa.

Sour Cream Dip

Prep Time: 8 minutes ⧗ Chill: 1 hour

Yield: about 2 ½ cups

2 cups sour cream
¼ cup mayonnaise
2 tablespoons chopped fresh dill or 1 tablespoon dried,
*   crumbled dill*
2 tablespoons chopped fresh green onion
2 tablespoons chopped chives
1 tablespoon chopped parsley
salt
freshly ground pepper

Mix the sour cream, mayonnaise, dill, onion, chives, and parsley. Season to taste with salt and pepper. Chill.
Serve with fresh raw garden vegetables.

Full-Flavor Herbs

Crushing dried herbs before you add them to a recipe will result in a stronger flavor. You can pinch them between your fingers or use a spoon to crush them on a plate before adding to the dish.

Spinach Balls

Prep Time: 15 minutes

Yield: about 20 balls

2 packages frozen spinach, thawed
2 cups dry herb-seasoned bread stuffing mix
6 eggs
1 cup finely chopped onion
³/₄ cup butter, melted
³/₄ cup grated Parmesan cheese
1 cup chopped fresh parsley
1¹/₂ teaspoons garlic powder
¹/₂ teaspoon thyme
¹/₂ teaspoon pepper
1 teaspoon salt

Drain the spinach well by squeezing in several thicknesses of paper towels. Chop the spinach finely. In a large bowl, combine all ingredients and mix well. Form into small (1¹/₄-inch-diameter) balls; place on a cookie sheet and freeze solid.

When frozen, place in plastic freezer bags and store in the freezer until needed.

To bake: Preheat the oven to 375°F. Place the frozen balls on a cookie sheet and bake for 20 minutes.

Stuffed Celery Stalks

Prep Time: 10 minutes ⧗ Chill: 1 hour

Serves: 12

12 long celery stalks with leaves attached
6 ounces cream cheese, at room temperature
½ cup nonfat cottage cheese
¼ onion, cut up (optional)
2 tablespoons nonfat milk (if needed)
*12 large pimiento-stuffed green olives, cut into ¼-inch-
   thick slices*
paprika

Set the celery stalks on a cutting board, hollow side up. In small blender or food processor, combine the cream cheese, cottage cheese, and the onion, if using. Process at high speed for 4 minutes until smooth. If the mixture is very thick, add the milk, a few drops at a time, to thin to spreading consistency.

Using a knife, spread the mixture in the hollows of the celery stalks, dividing it evenly among the stalks. Push olive slices into the spread along the entire length of each stalk. Wrap in plastic wrap and chill well. Just before serving, unwrap and sprinkle with paprika.

Sweet Summer Cucumbers

Prep Time: 10 minutes ⧗ Refrigerate: 2 days

Yield: about 6 cups

2 cups thinly sliced white onions
8 cups thinly sliced cucumbers
2 cups sugar
1 cup cider vinegar
2 tablespoons salt
2 teaspoons celery seed

Stir the onions gently into the cucumbers in a large glass or plastic container. Mix together the sugar, vinegar, salt, and celery seed. Pour the liquid mixture over the cucumbers and onions. Cover and refrigerate. Let the mixture marinate for a couple of days before eating.

Fat Facts

The average American diet contains far too much fat, but all fats are not alike. Unsaturated fats are better for your body than saturated fats. Animal fats are saturated fats, and most vegetable fats are unsaturated fats. But remember . . .

- Coconut and palm oil are *saturated* vegetable fats and are used in most bakery and processed snack foods.
- All oils are 100 percent fat.
- Both butter and margarine are 100 percent fat.

Taco Scoop

Prep Time: 10 minutes

Serves: 8

1 8-ounce container sour cream
½ teaspoon chili powder
2 medium ripe tomatoes
2 cups shredded lettuce
1 tablespoon chopped fresh cilantro, parsley, or chives
    (optional)
8 ounces shredded sharp Cheddar cheese
nacho-flavor tortilla chips

Blend together the sour cream and chili powder. Seed and chop the tomatoes, draining on paper towels if necessary. Spread the sour cream in a 13 × 9-inch glass baking dish or on a serving platter. Sprinkle the lettuce, herbs, cheese, and tomatoes on top. Serve with nacho chips for dipping.

Leftover Roasts

Whenever you make a roast and get tired of leftovers, cut up the remaining meat in slices or cubes and freeze for future use in salads, sandwiches, or stir-fries.

Tamari Cashews

Prep Time: 8 minutes　　Bake: 20 minutes

Yield: about 3 cups

1 tablespoon canola or sunflower oil
1 pound broken cashews
2 tablespoons soy sauce

Preheat the oven to 350°F. Pour the oil into a baking dish and add the nuts, turning them in the oil. Roast in the oven for about 15 minutes, turning occasionally, until golden.

Sprinkle the soy sauce over the nuts, turning and coating them. Return to the oven for an additional 5 minutes. Cool and store in a sealable container.

Did you know?

To prevent fruits, like apple or pear slices, from turning brown, coat them in lemon juice mixed with an equal amount of water.

Tomato Bruschetta

Prep Time: 10 minutes ⧖ Broil: 1 minute

Serves: 8

8 slices French bread
2 cloves garlic, halved
1 teaspoon olive oil
2 tablespoons minced onion
1 diced tomato
pinch of oregano, crumbled
pinch of pepper
2 tablespoons grated Parmesan cheese

Toast the bread on both sides. Rub one side of each piece of toast with the cut side of the garlic. Keep the toast hot.

Heat the oil in a nonstick skillet over medium-high heat. Add the onion and cook, stirring until tender, about 10 minutes. Remove from the heat and stir in the tomato, oregano, and pepper. Spoon the tomato mixture over the garlic-rubbed side of the toast, dividing evenly. Sprinkle with the cheese, and brown slightly under a preheated broiler for 1 minute. Serve immediately.

Veggie Roll-Ups

Prep Time: 10 minutes ⧗ Chill: 3 hours

Yield: about 24 appetizers

5 9-inch flour tortillas
1 8-ounce package cream cheese
$1/4$ cup sliced green onion
$1/4$ cup chopped black olives
$1/2$ cup chopped bell pepper—green, red, yellow, or
    mixed
tomato salsa (optional)

Have the tortillas at room temperature. Soften the cream cheese and spread on the tortillas, dividing evenly. Sprinkle the vegetables evenly over the tortillas. Roll each up tightly and wrap with plastic wrap. Refrigerate at least 3 hours.

To serve, cut in diagonal slices about $3/4$-inch thick. If desired, serve with tomato salsa.

Quick Tip: No-Prep Vegetables

You can purchase precleaned and precut fresh vegetables in plastic bags or even prearranged on a platter. Just add a special dip for quick appetizers!

Apple Dip

Prep Time: 15 minutes   Chill: 1 hour

Yield: about 2 cups

1 8-ounce package cream
    cheese
1/2 cup mayonnaise salad
    dressing, regular or light

1/2 cup finely shredded Cheddar
    cheese
Yellow Delicious apples* or
    crackers

Allow cream cheese to stand at room temperature for 15 minutes. Blend cream cheese thoroughly with the salad dressing. Mix in the cheese, and chill.
Serve with wedges of apples or spread on crackers.

*When cut, Yellow Delicious apples do not brown as rapidly as other varieties.

Black Bean Dip

Prep Time: 15 minutes

Yield: 2 cups

2 cans (15 ounces each) black
    beans, drained
2 jalapeño peppers, seeded, if
    desired, and chopped
2 cloves garlic, chopped

1 large tomato, chopped
2 tablespoons minced fresh cilantro
1/2 teaspoon salt
1/2 teaspoon freshly ground pepper

Combine the beans, jalapeños, and garlic in a food processor. Purée until smooth.
Transfer to a bowl and add the tomato, cilantro, salt, and pepper. Mix well and serve with raw vegetables and/or pita bread triangles.

Creamy Garlic—Red Pepper Dip

Prep Time: 10 minutes

Yield: 2/3 cup

1 7-ounce jar roasted red peppers, drained
1 tablespoon balsamic vinegar
1/3 cup low-fat cottage cheese
2 cloves garlic, minced
salt and pepper to taste

Combine the roasted peppers and vinegar in a food processor. Purée until smooth. Add the cottage cheese, garlic, salt, and pepper, and process until smooth. Serve with raw vegetables and/or pita triangles.

Easy Mustard Dip

Prep Time: 8 minutes   Chill: 1 hour

Yield: about 1 1/2 cups

1 cup mayonnaise
1/2 cup Dijon mustard
1 tablespoon prepared horseradish
cut up vegetables
pretzels (optional)

Blend well the mayonnaise, mustard, and horseradish. Chill at least 1 hour. Serve as a dip with vegetables and, if desired, pretzels.

Spinach Dip

Prep Time: 15 minutes

Serve: 6

1 10-ounce package frozen spinach, thawed
2 cups sour cream
1 cup mayonnaise
1 envelope vegetable soup mix (Knorr brand)
1 small white onion, chopped
1 8-ounce can water chestnuts, drained and chopped
2 tablespoons grated Parmesan cheese

Squeeze out water from thawed spinach (do not cook). Add all other ingredients and mix. Serve with raw vegetables, crackers, or a round sourdough bread loaf that has been hollowed out and cut into bite-sized pieces. Spinach dip can be served inside the hollowed out loaf of bread.

Yogurt Dip

Prep Time: 8 minutes

Yield: 1 ½ cups

1 cup (8 ounces) plain yogurt
½ cup shredded cucumber
⅓ teaspoon dried dill, crumbled

Combine all the ingredients in a bowl and mix well. Serve with vegetables for dipping.

Cutting Techniques

Slice   Julienne   Dice, Step 1   Dice, Step 2

Slice a tomato   Chop a tomato   Chop   Core an apple

Julienne

1. Make thin slices.
2. Stack the slices a few at a time.
3. Cut into matchstick-like pieces.

Cube or Dice

1. Cut into strips the width of the desired cube or dice.
2. Stack a few of the strips or lay them side by side.
3. Cut into cubes or dice.

Chop or Mince

1. Position a chef's knife or other large knife over the food.
2. Lightly hold the knife down near the pointed end and chop by raising and lowering the handle end.

Snip

1. Place herb into a small measuring cup or bowl.
2. Cut quickly with repeated strokes of a kitchen scissors.

Section

1. Peel the citrus fruit and remove any additional white inner skin with a paring knife or parer.
2. Working over a bowl or plate, cut the peeled fruit in half.
3. Holding one half and using a paring knife, slice the top pulp section away from its bottom membrane, then slice the membrane away from the pulp on the top side of the next section.
4. Continue until each pulp section has been removed.

Chapter 3

**Quick Soups
and Salads**

Soups can be the first course in a formal dinner, following the appetizers. Soups can accompany a quick lunch or supper as a side dish. Or heartier soups with proteins and vegetables can be the main course all in one pot. No matter how they are used, soups are simple and soothing and an important component of quick menus.

When serving formally, a salad can be a separate course following the soup course. A salad can provide the vegetables for a quick lunch or supper. Or a salad can become the main course all in one dish, by adding protein.

Soup Quick Fixes

To quickly make an ordinary soup special, especially if it's a leftover, top each serving with grated or shredded cheese, a small chunk of cream cheese, or even a dollop of plain, unsweetened whipping cream, to name just a few possibilities. A creative topper not only adds color, texture, and flavor, but also makes each bowl irresistibly appealing!

Soup Toppings

- Chives
- Fresh or dried parsley
- Chopped nuts
- Sliced green onions plus their tops
- Sliced black or green olives
- Diced red or green sweet pepper
- Sliced avocado
- Shredded carrots or zucchini
- Chopped hard-boiled eggs
- Mung beans or alfalfa sprouts
- Paprika
- Lemon slices
- Whipped cream (can be piped into an attractive dollop)
- Sour cream
- Cream cheese
- Diced fresh celery
- Bacon bits
- Grated or shredded cheeses, such as Parmesan, Cheddar, or three-cheese blends
- Croutons or popcorn

To freeze a soup for later use:

First chill the soup thoroughly. Pour it into rigid containers, leaving at least ½ inch of space on top for expansion, and tightly seal. Label each container with the type of soup and also the date it is frozen. (Soups with potatoes in them often do not freeze well.)

Thaw the soup in the refrigerator, or remove the soup from the freezer container, place in a saucepan, and reheat gently.

Quick soup ideas

Combine two different flavors of canned soup for a taste twist. For example:

- Mix one can of condensed tomato soup with one can of condensed beef noodle soup plus one can of milk and one can of water.
- Mix one can of condensed tomato soup with one can of condensed Cheddar soup plus one can of milk and one can of water.

For a quick main course soup:

Combine a can of condensed soup with a can of protein. For example, try a can of condensed chicken noodle soup plus one soup can of water, with one can of chicken plus the liquid in the can. Add any leftover cooked vegetables you might have on hand. Mix together, heat, and serve.

Tips for buying lettuce:

Leaf lettuce is far more nutritious than the iceberg variety, but it doesn't keep as long. How do you manage to keep a supply on hand when you only buy groceries every week or two? Buy one bunch of the loose leaf type, one bunch of the butter type (if it's available), and one bunch of romaine lettuce. Use the loose leaf type first, because it's the first to go bad, then the butter type, then the romaine.

Tips for keeping lettuce fresh:

At the first sign of wilting, separate and immerse the leaves in a sink or bowl of water to get them well hydrated. Then dry the leaves in a salad spinner, and place them loosely in a plastic bag but do not seal the bag. Store the unsealed lettuce in the vegetable drawer of your refrigerator.

To extend the storage life of the lettuce:

Purchase cartridges or disks in the produce section of the grocery store; you place these in the vegetable and fruit drawer in your refrigerator. They slow

down deterioration for about three months by absorbing the ethylene gas that causes spoilage. They really do work and are worth the investment, saving you from more frequent trips to the store for perishable produce.

Did you know?

Lettuce leaves will stay fresh longer without browning at the edges if you tear them up by hand or cut them with a special plastic knife for lettuce rather than using a metal knife.

Quick green salad ingredients

- Water cress, chicory, endive, red or green cabbage, spinach, Swiss chard, dandelion greens
- Tomatoes
- Cucumbers
- Celery
- Carrots
- Onions, green onions, shallots
- Peas
- Beets
- Cauliflower
- Kohlrabi
- Green, red, or yellow sweet bell peppers
- Asparagus
- Avocado
- Zucchini
- Bean sprouts
- Mushrooms
- Radishes
- Black or green olives
- Crumbled bacon bits
- Fresh herbs like chervil, mint, parsley, sorrel, tarragon, dill, chives
- Fruits like oranges, bananas, apples, cherries, grapes, peaches, pears, pineapple, pomegranate kernels
- Cooked proteins like eggs, beef, pork, ham, chicken, turkey, salmon, tuna and other fish, and shellfish
- Cheeses like Cheddar, mozzarella, farmer cheese, and blends
- Croutons
- Nuts like pecans, walnuts, almonds and macadamias

Avgolemono with Orzo

A Greek soup

Prep Time: 15 minutes ⧖ Cook: 15 minutes

Serves: 6 to 8

8 cups chicken stock
4 eggs
juice of 2 lemons
³/₄ cup orzo

1 teaspoon salt
salt and freshly ground pepper
* to taste*

In a large soup pot, bring the stock to a boil. Remove from the heat.

Beat the eggs with a beater until frothy. Gradually beat in the lemon juice. Remove 2 cups of broth from the pot and little by little add it to the egg and lemon mixture, stirring constantly until well combined. Return the egg and broth mixture to the soup pot. Stir to combine well.

Meanwhile, in a medium saucepan, bring at least 2 quarts of water to a boil. Add 1 teaspoon salt. Add the orzo, stir to separate, and cook about 6 minutes or until al dente. Drain and stir into the soup. Heat the soup through, and add salt and pepper to taste. Do not let soup boil or it will curdle. Serve at once.

Quick Tip: Eggs

Always hard-boil extra eggs. These can be added to soups, salads, and casseroles. They can also be gently heated in the microwave and topped with a pat of butter and lightly salted and peppered for a quick protein. Hard-cooked eggs can be stored in the refrigerator for a week.

Beer Soup

Prep Time: 15 minutes ⧖ Cook: 7 minutes

Serves: 4

1 1/2 tablespoons all-purpose flour
3 1/2 tablespoons butter
1 12-ounce bottle beer
1 small piece of cinnamon
sugar to taste
2 egg yolks
1/2 cup milk
toasted white French bread

In a large stockpot, brown the flour in the butter, then add beer. Add cinnamon and sugar and bring to a boil. Whisk together the egg yolks and milk and stir into the hot (but no longer boiling) beer. Strain, and serve with toasted slices of bread.

Quick Fix: Green Salads

Keep a supply of the basics on hand in your refrigerator at all times: lettuce, celery, carrots, shredded cheeses, prepared salad dressings, etc. Chop up whatever leftover cooked meat you might have, add chopped or sliced hard-cooked eggs if you like, and toss with the salad, and you have a nutritious, nearly instant meal. (See Quick Green Salad Ingredients on page 36 for more ideas.)

Broccoli Soup

Prep Time: 15 minutes ⧗ Cook: 15 minutes

Serves: 5

1 medium-sized broccoli bunch
1 onion, chopped
2 cups peeled and diced potatoes
1 clove garlic, minced
1 1/2 cups vegetable stock or water
1/2 teaspoon dried thyme
1/4 teaspoon pepper
pinch of nutmeg
1 1/2 cups milk
salt

Separate the broccoli into florets. Set 2 cups aside for garnish. Peel the stems and chop coarsely. In a saucepan, combine the stems and remaining florets, onion, potatoes, garlic, stock, thyme, pepper, and nutmeg. Bring to a boil. Reduce the heat, cover, and simmer for 10 minutes or until potatoes are tender. Steam the reserved florets for 5 minutes or until tender.

In a blender or food processor, purée the soup, in batches if necessary, until smooth. Return to the saucepan. Add the milk. Heat through without boiling. Season with salt to taste.

Cheeseburger Soup

Prep Time: 15 minutes ⧗ Cook: 15 minutes

Serves: 6

1 ½ tablespoons olive oil
1 large onion, chopped
2 ribs celery, chopped
1 green pepper, chopped
1 pound lean ground beef
3 packets beef bouillon
3 tablespoons flour
4 cups milk
8 ounces grated Cheddar cheese

Heat oil in a soup pot. Sauté onion, celery, and green pepper until tender. Add the meat and brown. Mix in the beef bouillon and flour. Slowly add the milk, stirring constantly; do not boil. Add the cheese. Stir until melted and serve immediately.

Storing Greens

- Iceberg and Romaine lettuce and cabbage will keep up to a week with proper refrigerator storage, but most other lettuces and greens will wilt within 2 or 3 days. Bibb, leaf lettuce, and radicchio will keep up to 5 days.
- Greens can be refrigerated unwashed in their original plastic bag, then washed just before use. Greens washed earlier must be well dried and stored in an airtight plastic bag or container.
- Dressed leftover salad can be safely refrigerated and saved, but the greens will become very limp quickly.

Chinese Chicken Corn Soup

Prep Time: 15 minutes ⧗ Cook: 15 minutes

Serves: 6

3 cups chicken broth
1 8¼-ounce can creamed corn
1 cup diced, cooked, and skinned chicken
1 tablespoon cornstarch
2 tablespoons cold water
2 egg whites
2 tablespoons finely minced fresh parsley

Combine chicken broth, corn, and chicken pieces in a large saucepan. Bring mixture to a boil over medium heat, stirring occasionally. Blend cornstarch with cold water and add to soup. Continue cooking, uncovered, for 3 minutes.

Beat egg whites until foamy; stir into soup. Reduce heat to a simmer and cook until foamy. Ladle soup into individual bowls and garnish with parsley. Serve hot.

Parsley Hints

Lots of fruit and vegetable salads benefit from a couple of sprigs of parsley. The problem is that you need to buy a whole bunch to get those few sprigs. Parsley, however, will stay crisp and fresh for up to a week if you store it standing in a glass of ice water in the refrigerator. Change the water every couple of days, and give some parsley to the dog to freshen his breath.

Hearty Bean Soup

Prep Time: 15 minutes ⧖ Cook: 20 minutes

Serves: 4

2 tablespoons buttery, reduced-fat margarine
1/2 cup chopped celery
1/4 cup diced onions
2 tablespoons all-purpose flour
1 cup water
2/3 cup 1% low-fat milk
2 16-ounce cans white beans, drained
1 16-ounce can whole kernel corn with liquid
1 8-ounce can crushed tomatoes
3/4 cup low-fat shredded jack cheese
1/4 teaspoon salt
1/8 teaspoon pepper
dash of Tabasco sauce
sourdough bread

In a saucepan, melt the margarine over medium heat. Add the celery and onion and sauté until onion is translucent, about 10 minutes. Stir in the flour until well blended. Slowly pour in the water and milk while stirring constantly, then cook, stirring, for 5 minutes, or until thickened and smooth.

Add the beans, corn (with liquid), tomatoes, and cheese. Heat through, stirring often, but do not boil. Season to taste with salt, pepper, and Tabasco sauce. Serve with wedges of sourdough bread.

Hearty Corn Chowder

Prep Time: 10 minutes ⌛ Cook: 25 minutes

Serves: 8

4 cups cut-up potatoes (large chunks)
1 large onion, chopped
1 green bell pepper, chopped
2 cups frozen corn kernels
1 cup evaporated milk

In a saucepan, combine the potatoes, onion, and bell pepper with water to cover. Bring to a boil; reduce the heat to low, and simmer for 10 minutes. Add the corn and cook until vegetables are tender, about 10 more minutes.

Stir in the milk and bring to serving temperature, stirring well. Ladle into bowls and serve.

A Salad a Day . . .

Nothing beats a salad for low fat and high nutritional eating. And sometimes the very best salads are very simple recipes. For example consider how good thick slices of juicy tomatoes sprinkled with fresh basil, coarsely ground black pepper, and freshly chopped chives taste.

Salads can also be meals unto themselves. Start with fresh greens including dark-green spinach leaves, soft Bibb lettuce, curly red-tipped leaf lettuce and add crisp carrots, thinly sliced cucumbers, tomatoes, fresh mushrooms, green peppers, fresh zucchini, or even broccoli, and cauliflower. Add cold pasta or rice and serve with a hearty bread! A crunchy, crispy, delicious low-fat meal!

Hearty Ground Turkey and Vegetable Soup

Prep Time: 15 minutes ⧗ Cook: 25 minutes

Serves: 4

1 pound ground turkey
1 small onion, chopped
1 small green pepper, chopped
1 16-ounce can green beans
1 16-ounce can diced potatoes
1 16-ounce can stewed tomatoes
1 can tomato soup
salt and pepper to taste

Brown turkey in a Dutch oven until cooked through. Add chopped onion and chopped green pepper. Mix in green beans, diced potatoes, stewed tomatoes, and the tomato soup. Heat until warmed through, about 15 minutes. Add salt and pepper to taste.

Green Salad Tips

- Tear greens into bite-sized pieces by hand rather than using a knife. Lettuce cut with a knife browns much more quickly, so if you must cut, do so a short time before serving.
- Use a variety of greens, including the "reds" of cabbage and radicchio (say ra-DEE-keyo). But taste greens first, because some are more bitter than others.
- Greens should be thoroughly dry before adding dressing, to enable it to stick to the leaves.
- Don't dress a salad until you are ready to serve it. Use only enough to coat the greens lightly. If desired, you can serve additional dressing at the table.

Miso Soup

Prep Time: 15 minutes ⧗ Simmer: 10 minutes

Serves: 4 to 5

1/4 cup red miso*
3 1/2 cups chicken stock
8 ounces tofu (bean curd), cubed
4 sprigs parsley, finely chopped
2 large shiitake mushrooms, sliced

Whisk the miso into 2 tablespoons of slightly warmed stock and blend well. Gradually ladle the miso liquid into the remaining stock. Bring the soup to a simmer. Add the tofu cubes, parsley, and mushrooms. Maintain at a simmer until the mushrooms and tofu are heated. Do not boil or soup will become bitter and cloudy. Ladle the soup into individual bowls and serve immediately.

*Note: Miso is a fermented soybean paste, which can be found in most well-stocked supermarkets. Red miso is pungent and quite salty, while white miso is mellow and slightly sweet. Miso paste can be left at room temperature for a year or more, since its flavor improves with age. It should not be frozen.

Pea Soup

Prep Time: 12 minutes ⧖ Cook: 15 minutes

Serves: 4

2 10-ounce packages frozen peas
2 cups water
2 14½-ounce cans chicken broth
juice of 1 lemon
1 clove garlic, minced
1 small onion, chopped
salt and pepper to taste
small handful mint leaves, chopped
¼ cup plain yogurt

Cook the peas in 2 cups of boiling water for just a few minutes. Drain, reserving water for use later in the recipe.

Purée the peas in a food processor. Mix 2 cups of the cooking water, broth, and lemon juice in a saucepan. Add the puréed peas and bring to a simmer. Add garlic, onion, salt, and pepper. Turn off heat. Add the mint to the soup. Serve with a dollop of yogurt.

Peanut Butter Soup

Prep Time: 15 minutes ⧖ Cook: 10 minutes

Serves: 4

2 tablespoons minced onion
3 tablespoons butter
1 tablespoon flour
1 cup peanut butter, plain or crunchy
4 cups chicken broth
salt and pepper to taste
1 cup heavy whipping cream
1 tablespoon Madeira wine

Cook onion in butter until soft in 2-quart saucepan. Add flour and cook, stirring, until smooth. Stir in peanut butter; add chicken broth. Season to taste with salt and pepper. Cook, stirring, over low heat until thickened and smooth. Add cream. Just before serving, add Madeira.

Quick Tip: Crowd buffet

Add a soup and/or salad to a do-it-yourself sandwich buffet for a fast and easy way to serve a crowd.

Pinto Bean Soup

Prep Time: 15 minutes   Cook: 15 minutes

Serves: 4

4 tablespoons butter
¼ cup finely chopped onions
2 tablespoons finely chopped green bell pepper
2 tomatoes, finely chopped
1 teaspoon finely chopped garlic
1 teaspoon finely chopped fresh cilantro
1 teaspoon red chili powder
1 pinch cayenne pepper
1 tablespoon tomato paste
1 10-ounce can pinto beans
3 quarts chicken stock
salt and pepper to taste
4 teaspoons sour cream

Heat the butter in a large saucepan over medium heat until it melts. Add the onions, green bell peppers, tomatoes, and garlic. Cover the pan with a lid and simmer for 4 minutes.

Add the cilantro, red chili powder, cayenne pepper, and tomato paste. Stir the ingredients together and simmer for 3 minutes.

Add the pinto beans, chicken stock, salt, and pepper. Bring to a boil and cook vigorously for 4 minutes, or until the beans are heated through. Garnish each serving with a dollop of sour cream.

Quick Borscht

Prep Time: 10 minutes

Serves: 6

1 *16-ounce jar pickled beets, drained*
2 *cups buttermilk*
1 *tablespoon sugar*
2 *tablespoons lemon juice*
$1/4$ *cup snipped fresh chives*

Place the beets, buttermilk, sugar, and lemon juice in a blender or food processor. Purée until smooth. Ladle into bowls and top with the chives.

Straciatella à la Romana, or Raggedy Cheesy Egg Soup

Prep Time: 15 minutes

Serves: 4

3 eggs
3 tablespoons freshly grated Parmesan cheese
6 cups chicken stock

Beat the eggs until frothy and stir in the cheese. Bring the broth to a gentle boil. Pour in the egg mixture, and stir gently until eggs are set.

Tuna Chowder

Prep Time: 15 minutes ⧗ Cook: 20 minutes

Serves: 6

2 tablespoons butter
3 stalks celery, chopped
1 large onion, chopped
1 large potato, diced
3 tablespoons flour
3 cups milk
2 6½-ounce cans water-packed tuna
4 ounces Cheddar cheese, grated
1 teaspoon thyme
1 teaspoon dillweed
salt and pepper
¼ cup chopped fresh parsley for garnish

In a large stockpot, melt the butter. Sauté the celery, onion, and potato until the potato is done. Add the flour and milk and blend thoroughly. Cook for 5 minutes, stirring, until the mixture thickens.

Add the tuna, cheese, thyme, and dill. Season with salt and pepper to taste. Heat over medium-low heat for 5 to 10 minutes. Garnish each serving with chopped fresh parsley.

Quick Fix: Tuna Salad

Drain canned tuna, flake the meat into a bowl, stir in some mayonnaise, and add a little diced pickle or celery or onion. Mound on lettuce and serve.

Very Quick Sausage and Vegetable Soup

Prep Time: 15 minutes ⧗ Cook: 20 minutes

Serves: 4

1 14½-ounce can beef broth
1 14½-ounce can Italian stewed tomatoes
1½ cups water
2 cups frozen hash brown potatoes
1 10-ounce package frozen mixed vegetables
8 ounces smoked sausage, sliced
⅛ teaspoon pepper
2 tablespoons grated Parmesan cheese

Combine beef broth, undrained stewed tomatoes, and water in a large saucepan. Bring to a boil. Stir in hash brown potatoes, mixed vegetables, sausage, and pepper. Return to boiling. Reduce heat and simmer, covered, for 5 to 10 minutes. Ladle into soup bowls and sprinkle with Parmesan cheese.

Quick Fix: Bouillion

Beef bouillion cubes will work in place of canned broth. For a lighter taste, try vegetable bouillion cubes.

Black-Eyed Pea and Chickpea Salad

Prep Time: 15 minutes ⧖ Chill: 5 hours

Serves: 12

1 ½ tablespoons vinegar
¾ teaspoon salt
3 tablespoons olive oil
dash hot pepper sauce
1 clove garlic, crushed
2 16-ounce cans black-eyed peas, rinsed and drained
  well
1 16-ounce can chickpeas, rinsed and drained well
¼ cup chopped pimientos
¼ cup chopped green onions
lettuce leaves

In a large bowl, beat vinegar and salt until salt is partially dissolved. Add the oil, pepper sauce, and garlic until well blended. Stir in the black-eyed peas, chickpeas, pimientos, and green onions. Toss to coat. Cover, and chill for several hours, stirring occasionally. Serve on a lettuce-lined bowl or platter.

Caesar Salad

Prep Time: 15 minutes

Serves: 6

3 tablespoons extra virgin olive oil
2 tablespoons mayonnaise
juice of 1/2 lemon
1 teaspoon anchovy paste
1 teaspoon Worcestershire sauce
1 teaspoon Dijon mustard
1/4 teaspoon coarsely ground black pepper
1 head romaine lettuce, washed, dried, and torn into bite-size
  pieces
1/2 cup grated Parmesan cheese
1 10-ounce package thick croutons

Pour olive oil into a large wooden salad bowl. Add mayonnaise, lemon juice, anchovy paste, Worcestershire sauce, mustard, and pepper. Stir with a fork until well blended. Add lettuce and toss well to coat evenly with dressing. Add cheese and croutons and toss again.

Quick Fix: Cottage Cheese Salad

Cottage cheese can become an instant salad or side dish if you top each serving with a canned peach or apricot half, drained of liquid. The whole thing can be served on a lettuce leaf for added color.

California Black Bean Salad

Prep Time: 20 minutes · Chill: 30 minutes

Serves: 8

1 15-ounce can black beans, drained and rinsed
1 12-ounce can corn kernels, drained
1 tomato, chopped
½ cup chopped red onion
½ cup chopped green bell pepper
2 cloves garlic, minced
¾ cup low-fat Italian dressing
2 teaspoons minced fresh parsley
¾ teaspoon Tabasco sauce
½ teaspoon pepper
½ teaspoon garlic powder
½ teaspoon chili powder

In a bowl, mix together all the ingredients. Cover and chill for 30 minutes before serving.

Quick Meal: Onions

Red onions tend to be sweeter than white or Spanish onions, but a sweet Vidalia will make a good substitute.

Chicken Pasta Salad

Prep Time: 10 minutes ⧗ Chill: 1 hour

Serves: 6

1 head broccoli, chopped
¼ teaspoon salt
3 cups diced cooked chicken
½ pound pasta shells, cooked and drained
2 large tomatoes, cubed
½ cup coarsely chopped red onion
½ teaspoon pepper
1 cup Italian dressing

Steam the broccoli over boiling water for about 5 minutes. Drain, place in a large bowl, and sprinkle with the salt. Chill by rinsing in cold water. Add the chicken, pasta, tomatoes, and onion, and sprinkle with the pepper. Pour the dressing over the salad and mix gently but thoroughly. Cover and chill before serving.

Quick Meal: Eggs

Eggs round out a quick supper, and can be fried, poached, scrambled, or made into omelets. Have them with your soup or salad for a quick meal. (Have you heard? Eggs are one of the most nutritious protein foods around and experts now recommend that they be part of a healthy diet.)

Chinese Coleslaw

Prep Time: 20 minutes 　 Chill: 1 hour

Serves: 6

4 cups shredded Chinese cabbage
1 8¼-ounce can crushed pineapple, drained
1 8-ounce can water chestnuts, drained and sliced
1 cup chopped fresh parsley
¼ cup sliced scallions
¼ cup low-fat mayonnaise
1 tablespoon mustard
1 teaspoon peeled and grated fresh ginger

In a bowl, combine the cabbage, pineapple, water chestnuts, parsley, and scallions. Toss to mix. Cover and chill. In a small bowl, whisk together the mayonnaise, mustard, and ginger. Cover and chill.

To serve, spoon the mayonnaise dressing over the cabbage mixture and toss to coat thoroughly.

Quick Fix: Salad Ingredients

Save time slicing vegetables by buying them pre-cut from the salad bar at your grocery store, or dicing them in a food processor.

Classic Waldorf Salad

Prep Time: 10 minutes   ⧗   Chill: 1 hour

Serves: 6

½ cup mayonnaise
1 tablespoon sugar
1 teaspoon lemon juice
salt to taste
2 cups diced red-skinned apples
1 cup finely sliced celery
½ cup coarsely chopped walnuts

Blend the mayonnaise with the sugar, lemon juice, and salt. Combine the apples, celery, and nuts, and fold in the dressing mixture. Chill before serving.

Quick Fix: Apple Salad

Cut apples into bite-sized chunks in a bowl and stir in mayonnaise, plain yogurt sweetened with a little honey, or whipped cream. If desired, you can add some finely diced celery and even a few small marshmallows.

Cool Bean Salad

Prep Time: 15 minutes   ⧗   Chill: 30 minutes

Serves: 4

1 15-ounce can white beans, drained and rinsed
¼ cup cubed cooked lean pork
1 red bell pepper, chopped
2 cloves garlic, chopped
½ teaspoon dried sage, crumbled
½ tablespoon olive oil
1 tablespoon red wine vinegar

In a medium bowl, combine the beans, pork, bell pepper, garlic, and sage. Add the oil and vinegar and toss well. Chill for 30 minutes before serving.

Creamy Dill Parsley Dressing

Prep Time: 5 minutes

Yield: 1 cup

1 cup plain yogurt
1 teaspoon crumbled dried dill
½ teaspoon lemon juice
1 teaspoon chopped parsley

In a bowl, mix all ingredients well. Serve with mixed fresh greens.

Easy Greens with Spicy Lemon Dressing

Prep Time: 10 minutes

Serves: 4

1/4 cup olive oil
2 tablespoons lemon juice
2 cloves garlic, minced or pressed
1 tablespoon Dijon or other spicy mustard
10 to 12 ounces mixed greens
grated Parmesan cheese
salt and freshly ground black pepper

Whisk the olive oil, lemon juice, garlic, and mustard together in a large salad bowl (not wooden). Add the fresh greens; sprinkle with Parmesan cheese and salt and pepper to taste. Toss until the dressing thoroughly coats the greens.

Five-Cup Salad

Prep Time: 8 minutes   Chill: Overnight

Serves: 8

1 cup drained mandarin oranges
1 cup drained crushed pineapple
1 cup coconut
1 cup miniature marshmallows
1 cup sour cream

Combine all ingredients and refrigerate overnight.

Fresh Tomato and Wild Rice Salad

Prep Time: 15 minutes ⧗ Let stand: 20 minutes

Serves: 4

3 large vine-ripened tomatoes
1 clove garlic
2 cups cooked wild rice
3 green onions, chopped
3 tablespoons chopped fresh basil
2 tablespoons olive oil

Peel, seed, and chop the tomatoes. Peel and cut the garlic; rub the salad bowl well with it and discard. Place the rice, tomatoes, onion, and basil in the bowl; drizzle the olive oil over all and toss well to combine. Let stand at room temperature about 20 minutes before serving, to combine the flavors.

Blanching Vegetables

One way to make sure that vegetables are well cooked before you add them to a soup and to ensure that they don't turn soggy during cooking is to blanch them ahead of time. In a saucepan, bring about 4 cups of water to a boil. Add the vegetables, cook for 3 minutes, then remove and immediately rinse under cold water. This last step prevents the vegetables from absorbing excess liquid, in essence forming a seal on the skin.

Fruity Chicken Salad

Prep Time: 15 minutes ⧗ Chill: 1 hour

Serves: 8

2 ½ cups shredded cooked chicken
1 ½ cups peeled melon chunks
1 ½ cups peeled cucumber chunks
1 ½ cups seedless green grapes
½ cup mayonnaise
2 tablespoons plain yogurt
1 ½ teaspoons cider vinegar
⅛ teaspoon salt
⅛ teaspoon pepper
⅓ cup chopped fresh coriander
2 tablespoons lime juice

In a medium bowl, combine the chicken, melon, cucumber, and grapes. In a larger bowl, whisk together the remaining ingredients to make a dressing. Add the chicken-fruit mixture to the dressing and toss to mix. Cover and chill for at least an hour before serving.

Hot Red Cabbage and Apple Salad

Prep Time: 20 minutes ⧗ Cook: 30 minutes

Serves: 4

1 small head red cabbage, shredded
1 medium onion, finely sliced
1 apple, peeled and shredded
3 tablespoons apple cider vinegar
¼ cup apple juice
¼ cup water
2 teaspoons sugar, or to taste
salt and pepper to taste
1 tablespoon chopped fresh parsley for garnish

Put the cabbage, onion, apple, vinegar, juice, water, sugar, salt, and pepper into a large saucepan. Cover and cook on medium-low heat for about 30 minutes, or until cabbage is soft, stirring occasionally. Serve with parsley sprinkled on top.

Quick Tip: Eliminate some prep work

Serve foods whole or in larger portions when possible. For example, serve individual wedges of lettuce and allow people to cut it as they eat it, or serve whole apples rather than taking time to cut them into slices and core them.

Minnesota Wild Rice Salad

Prep Time: 10 minutes ⧖ Chill: 1 hour

Serves: 8 to 10

2 12-ounce packages frozen cooked diced chicken*
6 bay leaves
1 small jar artichoke hearts
3 cups cooked wild rice (1 cup raw)
3 cups halved red grapes
salt and pepper to taste
½ to 1 cup mayonnaise

Thaw the chicken in a bowl with the bay leaves, stirring occasionally. Drain the artichokes well and quarter. Combine the rice with the thawed chicken (discard the bay leaves), artichokes, and grapes. Season to taste with salt and pepper. Add the mayonnaise, beginning with ½ cup, and adding more if needed; combine well. Salad should be moderately dry rather than creamy. Chill thoroughly before serving.

*3 cups cooked, cubed chicken can be substituted.

Mixed Greens with Honey and Oranges

Prep Time: 20 minutes

Serves: 6

¼ *cup water*
¼ *cup honey*
¼ *cup white vinegar*
2 heads butter lettuce
2 heads radicchio
3 oranges

In a small saucepan, bring the water, honey, and vinegar to a boil; reduce the heat and simmer for 2 minutes. Remove from the heat; let cool.

Arrange the butter lettuce and radicchio on 6 salad plates. Using a sharp knife, peel the oranges, removing all the bitter white membrane, then free the sections from the membranes by cutting along either side of each section. Remove any seeds and divide the orange sections among the salad plates. Drizzle each salad with the cooled dressing and serve.

Quick Fix: Vinegar

Keep staples like red and white vinegar in your pantry. If you're in a pinch, try substituting rice vinegar for white vinegar.

Oriental Noodle Salad

Prep Time: 15 minutes ⏳ Sauté: 15 minutes

Serves: 4

2 packages ramen noodles
2 tablespoons peanut oil
¼ cup sliced almonds
¼ cup sesame seeds
8 green onions, minced
1 head cabbage, minced
¼ cup sugar
1 teaspoon salt
1 teaspoon pepper
½ cup peanut oil
6 tablespoons rice vinegar

Break noodles into 1-inch pieces. Heat the oil in a large skillet and sauté the almonds and sesame seeds until lightly browned. Add the onions and cabbage and sauté for 5 minutes, or until translucent. Add the noodles. In a cup, mix the sugar, salt, pepper, oil, and vinegar together, and add to the mixture. Toss until heated through.

Peach-Spinach Salad

Prep Time: 15 minutes

Serves: 6

1½ cups spinach, stems removed and leaves torn
1 cup cucumbers, scored and sliced
1 fresh peach, pitted, peeled, and sliced
2 fresh plums, pitted and sliced
¼ cup sliced scallions
1 cup plain yogurt
1 tablespoon lemon juice
1 tablespoon water
¼ teaspoon dried dill, crumbled

In a large bowl or on 6 salad plates, combine the spinach, cucumber, peach, plums, and scallions. In a small bowl, whisk together the yogurt, lemon juice, water, and dill until smooth. Toss with the salad and serve.

Quick Fix: Canned Fruit

Sliced, canned peaches will work in place of fresh ones, and the juice they're stored in can often be incorporated into the recipe as well.

Red-Leafed Greek Salad

Prep Time: 10 minutes

Serves: 4

*4 to 6 handfuls red-leafed
  salad greens*
1 large tomato cut into wedges
1 large red onion, sliced thinly
4 ounces feta cheese, crumbled

2 tablespoons balsamic vinegar
2 cloves garlic, pressed
5 tablespoons extra virgin olive oil
*salt and freshly ground pepper
  to taste*

Carefully sort through the greens and then wash and dry them well. Toss the greens with the tomato wedges, onion slices, and feta cheese. Mix the vinegar, garlic, olive oil, and salt and pepper well, whisking in a small bowl. Pour over the greens mixture and toss. Serve immediately with a fresh loaf of French bread.

Do you cry over onions?

Some people have a terrible time skinning and chopping onions because their eyes tear up, while others aren't bothered at all. Unfortunately, I'm in the former group and react so badly I can't even see. Here's what I've found that helps: store two or three whole onions in a tightly sealed container in the refrigerator—I like to use a plastic ice cream carton. When I need an onion, I take it chilled from the refrigerator and peel it under cold running water at the sink. If I need a larger quantity of onion, I usually slice and chop it quickly in my food processor. If I need a smaller quantity, I usually chop it by hand, near the downdraft exhaust fan of my cooktop. (This does not work if your stove is exhausted up because it will draw the onion fumes toward your eyes.)

Rotini Salad Alfredo

Prep Time: 15 minutes ⧖ Refrigerate: 2 hours

Serves: 8

2 cups plain yogurt
1 cup mayonnaise
1 cup grated Parmesan cheese
1 tablespoon dried basil leaves or dill
2 cloves garlic, minced
1 teaspoon salt
½ teaspoon white pepper
4 large red bell peppers, chopped
3 cups blanched peas
½ cup chopped green onions
1 pound rotini, cooked and chilled

In a large bowl, blend the yogurt, mayonnaise, Parmesan cheese, basil or dill, garlic, salt, and pepper. Add the bell peppers, peas, and green onions and stir well. Add the pasta and stir gently.

Cover and refrigerate for at least 2 hours.

Salmon Tortellini Salad

Prep Time: 15 minutes ⧗ Refrigerate: 5 hours

Serves: 4

1 8-ounce package frozen or fresh cheese tortellini
4 carrots, thinly sliced
1 zucchini, sliced
1 red bell pepper, cut into narrow strips
2 6½-ounce cans salmon, drained and flaked
1 cup plain yogurt
¼ cup grated Parmesan cheese
¼ cup chopped fresh parsley
1 tablespoon milk
1 teaspoon dried oregano, crumbled

Cook the tortellini as directed on the package. Drain, rinse under cold water, and drain again. In a medium bowl, gently toss together the pasta, carrots, zucchini, and bell pepper. Add the salmon and mix. In a small bowl, stir together the yogurt, cheese, parsley, milk, and oregano until well mixed. Add to the pasta mixture and toss gently to coat evenly. Cover and refrigerate for several hours before serving.

Seafood Pasta Salad

Prep Time: 15 minutes ⧖ Chill: 30 minutes

Serves: 4

2 cups cooked pasta, tri-colored spirals
1 cup shrimp, cooked, or tuna
1 green pepper, diced
$1/4$ cup sliced carrots
$1/2$ cup sliced zucchini
$1/3$ cup Worcestershire sauce
$1/3$ cup mayonnaise
salt and pepper to taste

In a mixing bowl, combine pasta, shrimp or tuna, green pepper, carrots, and zucchini. Add Worcestershire sauce, mayonnaise, salt, and pepper, and toss lightly to combine. Refrigerate at least 30 minutes before serving.

Cooking Pasta for Salad

When preparing a cold pasta salad, you can save time by cooking a batch of pasta in advance. Once cooked, rinse immediately under cold water and drain thoroughly, then pat with paper towels to absorb the excess moisture. Place in a large lock-top plastic bag and store in the refrigerator. The pasta will keep for up to 3 days.

Simple Vinaigrette Dressing

Prep Time: 8 minutes

Yield: ³/₄ cup

¹/₄ cup red wine vinegar
1 tablespoon fresh lemon juice
1 teaspoon prepared Dijon mustard
salt and freshly ground pepper to taste
¹/₂ cup extra-virgin olive oil

Mix together the vinegar, lemon juice, mustard, salt, and pepper. Add the olive oil a little at a time, beating with a whisk until the mixture emulsifies.

This dressing can also be made in the blender. Put all ingredients into the blender and blend at a high speed for a very short time.

Quick Fix: Lemon juice

Bottled lemon juice is much easier to use than fresh, and will keep well in the refrigerator.

Smoked Fish Salad with Cilantro Dressing

Prep Time: 15 minutes

Serves: 4

Dressing:

2 tablespoons plain yogurt
1 tablespoon fresh lemon juice
1 tablespoon white wine vinegar
1 tablespoon minced cilantro
1/4 teaspoon salt, or to taste
1/8 teaspoon freshly ground pepper
dash ground red pepper

Salad:

1 head romaine lettuce
1/3 to 1/2 pound smoked fish (salmon or whitefish)
    flaked into bite-sized pieces
1 cup small ripe olives
1 15-ounce can chickpeas, drained
1/2 medium red onion, thinly sliced
1/2 cup olive oil

Combine all the dressing ingredients in a small bowl. Set aside.
Trim the romaine and discard the stem ends. Slice the
remaining inner leaves into 1½-inch pieces. Wash and dry. Place
in a large bowl with the smoked fish, olives, chickpeas, and
onion. Whisk the olive oil into the dressing; adjust the seasoning.
Pour over the salad and toss.

Strawberry Chicken Salad

Prep Time: 15 minutes ⧗ Chill: 1 hour

Serves: 4

½ cup mayonnaise
2 tablespoons chutney
1 tablespoon lemon juice
1 teaspoon grated lemon zest
1 teaspoon salt
1 teaspoon curry powder
2 cups diced cooked chicken
1 cup sliced celery
¼ cup chopped red onion
1½ pints strawberries, stemmed
4 lettuce leaves
fresh mint sprigs

In a large bowl, stir together the mayonnaise, chutney, lemon juice, lemon zest, salt, and curry powder, mixing well. Add the chicken, celery, and onion. Toss well, cover, and chill.

Just before serving, slice 1 pint of the strawberries. Add to the chicken mixture and toss gently. Line a platter or individual serving plates with the lettuce leaves. Mound the chicken mixture on the lettuce. Garnish with the whole strawberries and mint. Serve at once.

Szechuan Noodle Salad

Prep Time: 12 minutes

Serves: 4

1/4 cup white wine vinegar

1/4 cup water

2 tablespoons soy sauce

2 tablespoons minced fresh
  ginger

1 tablespoon sesame oil

2 cloves garlic, minced

1 teaspoon sugar

1 teaspoon Tabasco sauce

1 pound thin spaghetti, cooked

1 cup grated carrot

1 cup frozen peas, thawed

1 red pepper, cut into strips

2 cups bean sprouts

1/4 cup chopped fresh parsley

In a large bowl, stir together the vinegar, water, soy sauce, ginger, oil, garlic, sugar, and Tabasco. Add the cooked noodles and toss. Add the carrots, peas, red pepper, bean sprouts, and parsley; toss again.

Asian Sesame Oil

Asian sesame oil, which is widely available in supermarkets, is not like the big bottles of vegetable oils that line the market shelves. Because sesame oil is generally used only in small amounts, it is typically available in glass bottles holding 10 ounces or less.

Asian sesame oil is made from roasted seeds, and it has an intense nutty taste that brings out the earthy flavor of a brown rice or wild rice. Indeed, whenever you want to add a nutty taste to a dish without using nuts that are rich in fats, choose sesame oil. You'll get robust flavor with a minimum of fat and calories.

Taco Salad

Prep Time: 10 minutes 　Cook: 30 minutes

Serves: 8

2 pounds ground beef
2 2-ounce packages taco seasoning mix
2 large onions, chopped
10 ounces Cheddar cheese, grated
1 8-ounce bag corn chips, crushed
1 large head lettuce, torn
2 tomatoes, cut into chunks

Prepare taco mix with ground beef according to package directions, adding the onions.

In a big serving bowl, combine the cheese, chips, torn lettuce, and tomatoes. Just before serving pour taco meat mixture in the bowl and toss with other ingredients. Serve warm.

Quick Tip: Storing onions

Chop more onions than needed and store the remainder in a tightly-lidded jar in the refrigerator, or freeze, using double or triple wrappings. These precautions keep the onion from flavoring the nearby food.

Tangy Greek Salad

Prep Time: 20 minutes ⌛ Cook: 12 minutes

Serves: 4

2 cups red wine vinegar
1/3 cup extra virgin olive oil
2 cups white wine
2 pounds button mushrooms, sliced
16 green olives
24 Greek olives
12 cloves garlic, chopped
12 small shallots, chopped
2 teaspoons fresh tarragon, finely chopped
1/2 teaspoon salt
8 large leaves butter lettuce
4 green onions, sliced and cut into 2-inch pieces
2 carrots, julienned
4 parsley sprigs for garnish
2 lemons, cut into wedges, for garnish

In a large saucepan combine the red wine vinegar, olive oil, and white wine. Cook on medium-high heat for 4 to 6 minutes, or until the liquid is caramel colored and reduced by half.

Add the mushrooms, green olives, Greek olives, garlic, shallots, tarragon, and salt. Simmer for 4 to 6 minutes, or until the liquid is reduced by half. Let the mixture cool.

On each of 4 individual serving plates, place 2 of the lettuce leaves. Spoon on the cooked vegetables with the juice. Sprinkle on the onions and carrots. Garnish the dish with the parsley and the lemon wedges.

Traditional Three-Bean Salad

Prep Time: 10 minutes ⧗ Chill:4 hours

Serves: 6 to 8

1 16-ounce can French-cut green beans
1 16-ounce can yellow (wax) beans
1 16-ounce can red kidney beans
1 onion
$^1/_2$ cup sugar
$^2/_3$ cup vinegar
$^1/_3$ cup vegetable oil
$^1/_2$ teaspoon salt
$^1/_8$ teaspoon pepper

Drain the beans. Slice the onion thinly, then cut the slices in quarters. Whisk together the sugar, vinegar, oil, salt, and pepper. Combine the beans, onions, and dressing, mixing well. Chill at least 4 hours or overnight, stirring occasionally. If desired, the salad can be drained before serving.

Quick Fix: Marinades

Prepare dishes that need to marinate for several hours the night before. The dish will be more flavorful by the time you serve it.

Tuna Rice Salad

Prep Time: 15 minutes

Serves: 4

Salad:

1 6-ounce can chunk tuna
2 cups cooked white rice
1 cup cooked green beans
1 medium tomato, seeded and chopped
½ cucumber, peeled and chopped
1 tablespoon chopped fresh mint
2 tablespoons black olives, sliced

Dressing:

2 tablespoons lemon juice
1 tablespoon water
1 tablespoon olive oil

Drain the tuna well. In a large bowl, toss all the salad ingredients to combine. In a separate bowl, combine the lemon juice and water; drizzle the oil into the mixture while whisking to combine. Pour over the salad and toss well.

Waldorf-Style Fruit Salad

Prep Time: 12 minutes

Serves: 6

2 unpeeled Red Delicious apples, cored and cubed
24 red grapes
24 green grapes
2 oranges, sectioned
1 cup plain yogurt
1 tablespoon honey
lettuce leaves
2 bananas, sliced
¼ cup walnuts, chopped

In a bowl, toss together the apples, grapes, and oranges. In a small bowl, stir together the yogurt and honey. Mix into the fruit, tossing to coat evenly. To serve, place lettuce leaves on each plate and place the fruit mixture on the lettuce. Place the bananas around the edge of the plate, and sprinkle the walnuts over all.

Quick Tip: Assembling green salads for serving later

Put the salad dressing in the bowl, then throw in the ingredients (other than lettuce) that would taste good marinated in the dressing—things like mushrooms, green onions, etc. Then place the lettuce on top. Refrigerate the whole thing until just before serving, then toss and it's ready in no time! This is especially convenient when having guests.

Warm Orzo Salad

Prep Time: 10 minutes

Serves: 6

2 cups fresh basil leaves, minced
½ cup minced fresh parsley
4 cloves garlic, minced
½ teaspoon salt
¼ cup olive oil
*1 pound orzo pasta, cooked al dente and drained
    thoroughly*
1 red pepper, chopped

Combine the basil, parsley, garlic, salt, and oil in a serving bowl. Add the orzo and red pepper and mix well. Toss the salad before serving.

Quick Fix: Garlic

To save time, buy a jar of minced garlic and keep it in the refrigerator.

Warm Sweet Potato and Apple Salad

Prep Time: 15 minutes   Cook: 15 minutes

Serves: 12

$^3/_4$ cup mayonnaise

$^3/_4$ cup plain yogurt

1$^1/_2$ tablespoons curry powder

$^1/_2$ teaspoon salt

2$^1/_2$ pounds sweet potatoes (about 7 medium sized),
     cooked, peeled, cooled, and cut into $^3/_4$-inch chunks

2 medium-sized Granny Smith apples, cut in $^1/_2$-inch
     pieces

1 20-ounce can pineapple chunks, drained

$^1/_2$ cup raisins

In a large saucepan, whisk together the mayonnaise, yogurt, curry powder, and salt over low heat until well blended. Stir in the potatoes, apples, pineapples, and raisins. Toss gently to mix and coat. Cover and continue to cook over low heat for 7 to 10 minutes, until potato is heated through, stirring constantly.

Curry Powder

Curry powder is not one spice, but a combination of anywhere from 15 to 50 different spices. Madras curry has a fuller, richer flavor than national brands, but there are even differences between the kinds of curry powder you find in the supermarket. Become a curry connoisseur!

Yields and Equivalents

Apple
1 medium, chopped = about 1 cup
3 medium = 1 pound
3 medium = $2^3/_4$ cups pared and sliced

Beans, Dried
1 cup = $2^1/_4$ to $2^1/_2$ cups cooked

Butter
1 ounce butter = 2 tablespoons butter or margarine
1 stick butter or margarine = $1/_4$ pound or 8 ounces
1 cup butter or margarine = 2 sticks or $1/_2$ pound

Celery
2 medium stalks = $2/_3$ to $3/_4$ cup

Chocolate
1 ounce = 1 square
1 cup chips = 6 ounces

Cheese
1 pound American, Cheddar, Colby, Monterey Jack, Swiss, or similar cheeses = 4 cups shredded
1 cup shredded = $1/_4$ pound

Cranberries
1 cup fresh makes 1 cup sauce
1 pound = 4 cups

Crumbs
1 cup cracker crumbs = 28 saltine crackers or 14 square graham crackers or 24 rich round crackers
1 cup bread crumbs
  soft = $1^1/_2$ slices bread
  dry = 4 slices bread
1/4 cup dry bread crumbs = $3/_4$ cup soft bread crumbs or 1/4 cup cracker crumbs
1 cup vanilla wafer crumbs = 22 wafers

Eggs
1 cup = 4 large eggs
$1/_4$ cup liquid egg substitute = 1 egg
1 cup egg yolks = 10 to 12 egg yolks
1 cup egg whites = 8 to 10 egg whites

Fruits (see also Apples, Cranberries)
Bananas—3 large or 4 small = 2 cups sliced or $1^1/_3$ mashed
Cherries— $1/_2$ pound = 1 cup pitted
Grapes—1 pound = 2 cups halved
Peaches or Pears—1 medium = $1/_2$ cup sliced
Rhubarb— 1/2 pound = 2 to 4 stalks = 1 cup cooked
Strawberries—1 quart = 2 cups sliced

Garlic
1 clove fresh = $1/_2$ teaspoon chopped = $1/_8$ teaspoon garlic powder

Green Pepper
1 large = 1 cup diced

Herbs
1 tablespoon fresh, snipped = 1 teaspoon dried or $1/_2$ teaspoon ground

Lemon
Juice of 1 lemon = about 3 tablespoons
Grated peel of 1 lemon = about 1 teaspoon

Macaroni or Tube-Shaped Pastas
1 to $1^1/_4$ cups = 4 ounces = 2 to $2^1/_2$ cups cooked
16 ounces = about 8 cups cooked

Mushrooms, Fresh
8 ounces = about $2^1/_2$ cups sliced = about 1 cup cooked
1 cup sliced and cooked = 4 ounce can, drained

Mustard
1 teaspoon dry = 1 tablespoon prepared

Nuts
1 cup chopped = $1/_4$ pound or 4 ounces
1 cup whole or halved = 4 to 5 ounces

Olives
24 small = 2 ounces = about $1/_2$ cup sliced

Onion, Green top
1 sliced = about 1 tablespoon
8 sliced, whites only = about $1/_2$ cup
4 sliced, whites + 4 inches green top = about $1/_2$ cup
Regular
  1 medium, chopped = $1/_2$ cup
  1 medium = 1 teaspoon onion powder or 1 tablespoon dried minced

Orange
Juice of 1 orange = $1/_3$ to $1/_2$ cup
Grated peel of 1 orange = about 2 tablespoons

Potatoes
3 medium = 2 cups sliced or cubed
3 medium = $1^3/_4$ cups mashed

Rice
1 cup white rice (long grain) = about 7 ounces = 3 to 4 cups cooked
1 cup white rice (instant) = 2 cups cooked
1 cup brown rice = 3 cups cooked
1 cup wild rice = 3 to 4 cups cooked
1 pound cooked wild rice = about $2^2/_3$ cups dry

Spaghetti and Noodles
8 ounces = 4+ cups cooked
1 pound = 8+ cups cooked

Sugar, Powdered
1 pound = 4 cups

Tomatoes
1 cup canned = $1^1/_3$ cups fresh, cut up and simmered 5 minutes

Whipping Cream
1 cup = 2 cups whipped

Yeast
1 compressed cake = 1 package or $2^1/_4$ teaspoons regular or quick active dry

Chapter 4

Meats

Meat has always been a staple of the American diet, and beef, pork, and lamb are now better than ever due to careful breeding and feeding practices. Meat comes in such a variety of cuts and styles, and can be prepared using so many cooking methods and flavorings, there are sure to be enough varieties to please every palate.

To dress up beef or pork, try the following garnishes:

- Pickles: Make thin slices the full length, nearly to the stem end of a whole pickle. Press gently to create a fan.
- Raw cherry tomatoes are a tasty and colorful garnish with meat, but tend to squirt when stabbed with a fork, so slice them in half with a sharp knife before adding to the serving dish or individual plates.
- Celery: Cut narrow strips nearly the full length of celery chunks and plunge them into ice water to make brushes.

Other garnishes for meat platters include:

- Green, red, or yellow pepper rings
- Onion rings (raw or canned)
- Radishes or radish roses
- Stuffed olives
- Mint, basil, thyme, or oregano sprigs
- Mushrooms
- Sliced hard-cooked eggs, perhaps sprinkled with paprika
- Kiwi slices

California Tri-Tip

Prep Time: 15 minutes ⧖ Refrigerate: overnight ⧖ Grill: 40 minutes

Serves: 6

1 tablespoon cracked peppercorns (crush peppercorns
     with mortar and pestle)
2 teaspoons garlic salt
1 teaspoon dry mustard
¼ teaspoon cayenne pepper
2–3 pound tri-tip roast

Mix together pepper, garlic salt, mustard, and cayenne. Rub into the surface of the tri-tip. Cover with plastic wrap and refrigerate overnight.

Soak oak, mesquite, or hickory chips in water for at least 30 minutes and then add to coals. Sear the tri-tip directly over medium heat, turning once, to seal in juices (about 5 minutes total). Then grill the tri-tip indirectly over medium heat,* turning once, until the internal temperature is about 140°F (approximately 30 to 35 minutes). Remove from heat and let stand for 5 minutes. Slice diagonally against the grain.

Serve warm or at room temperature as an entrée or in a sandwich.

*This means turning off the center burner on a 3-burner gas grill or moving the coals to the outside of a charcoal grill. Position the meat in the center of the grill.

Chicken Fried Steak

Prep time: 12 minutes

Serves: 2

1 egg
¼ cup milk
1 cup bread crumbs
1 teaspoon oregano
1 teaspoon seasoned salt
2 6-ounce cube steaks
¼ cup vegetable oil
cheese (optional)

In a shallow bowl, beat egg and milk together. In another dish, combine bread crumbs, oregano, and seasoned salt. Dip cube steaks in egg mixture; turn to coat well. Dip steaks in seasoned mixture, turning once to cover.

In a heavy skillet, heat oil. Brown steaks in oil. Reduce heat, cover with lid slightly ajar, and cook for 10 to 15 minutes. Cook longer if necessary, until tender. If desired, melt cheese on top of steaks to add flavor.

Quick Fix: Butter toppings for beef

To quickly dress up steaks or burgers, serve them topped with herb butter. Soften several tablespoons of butter and add your favorite herbs (fresh are best, but dried herbs also work), like parsley, thyme, basil, oregano, or finely chopped onion, snipped chives, minced garlic, etc. It's absolutely wonderful! (In case you haven't heard, many experts now believe real butter is better for your health than any margarine.)

Chili Mac

Prep time: 15 minutes Cook:30 minutes

Serves: 4

½ pound ground beef
¼ cup chopped onion
¼ cup chopped green pepper
29-ounce can whole tomatoes
1½ teaspoons chili powder
1 teaspoon salt
dash pepper
4 ounces elbow macaroni

Spray a large skillet with cooking spray, or add about 1 teaspoon vegetable oil, and heat over medium-high heat. Brown the meat along with the onion and pepper. Drain the fat.

Add the tomatoes, chili powder, salt, and pepper, mixing well, and breaking up the tomatoes slightly. Bring to a boil and stir in the macaroni. Cover, reduce heat, and simmer about 20 minutes, or until macaroni is done.

Classic Reuben Sandwich

Prep time: 12 minutes   ⧗   Fry: 10 minutes

Serves: 4

1 cup sauerkraut, very well drained
2 tablespoons unsalted butter, divided
8 slices rye bread
³⁄₄ cup Thousand Island or Russian dressing
¹⁄₂ pound Swiss cheese, thinly sliced
¹⁄₂ pound corned beef, thinly sliced

Be sure the sauerkraut is well drained, using a paper towel if necessary. Heat 1 tablespoon of the butter in a large skillet over medium to medium-high heat. While butter is melting, spread one side of 4 pieces of bread with dressing. Lay the bread, dressing side up, in the skillet, moving the bread around to fully coat with butter. Layer the cheese, sauerkraut, and corned beef on the bread in the skillet.

With the remaining bread slices, butter one side and spread the other with dressing. Top the sandwiches in the skillet, placing the bread butter side up. Press down firmly. After the sandwiches have cooked for about 5 minutes on one side, carefully flip with a spatula. Press down firmly again. Cover the skillet for about 3 to 4 minutes, or until the cheese has melted and the second side is golden. Serve hot with kosher dill pickles, if desired.

Easy Ground Beef Stroganoff

Prep time: 12 minutes ⧖ Cook: 25 minutes

Serves: 4

1 pound ground beef
2 tablespoons dried minced onion
1 package or cube beef bouillon
$\frac{1}{8}$ teaspoon garlic powder
1 tablespoon ketchup
1 teaspoon Kitchen Bouquet or Gravy Master
1 can condensed cream of mushroom soup
1 4-ounce can mushrooms, drained
$\frac{1}{2}$ cup sour cream
*1 9-ounce package wide egg noodles, cooked and kept
    warm*

In a large skillet, brown beef. Drain. Stir in remaining ingredients, except sour cream and noodles, and heat to boiling. Cover and simmer 10 to 15 minutes.

Remove from heat and stir in sour cream. Serve hot over egg noodles.

Did you know?

Cooked meat can be frozen for two or three months. Freeze in 1 or 2 cup measures. Thaw in the refrigerator or microwave. Do not freeze cooked meats a second time, and do not refreeze thawed meats that have not been cooked.

Easy Pepper Steak

Prep time: 15 minutes ⧖ Cook: 20 minutes

Serves: 4

2 tablespoons oil
1 onion, sliced
2 green peppers, sliced
1 clove garlic, minced
1 cup beef bouillon
1 cup + 2 tablespoons soy sauce
1 tablespoon cornstarch
1 1/2 teaspoons ginger
1 1/2 cups cooked roast beef, julienned
3 cups cooked white rice

Heat oil in a large skillet over medium high heat. Sauté onions and peppers until almost softened. Add garlic and cook for another minute. Stir together remaining ingredients, except beef and rice. Add to skillet along with beef. Cook and stir until sauce is thick and meat is hot. Serve over hot white rice.

Quick Tip: Combo plate

If you choose a combination meat and vegetable main dish, all you need to do is add a salad and maybe a dessert and you have a meal. An added benefit is not only the preparation time that is saved, but also cleanup time is minimized because you've used fewer dishes in preparation and serving.

Easy Stovetop Chili

Prep time: 10 minutes ⧖ Cook: 50 minutes

Serves: 4

1 pound ground beef
1 cup chopped onion
1 cup chopped celery
1 1/2 teaspoons sugar
1/2 teaspoon salt
3/4 teaspoon garlic powder
1 1/2 tablespoons chili powder
3/4 teaspoon oregano leaves
1/4 teaspoon pepper
1 15-ounce can tomato sauce
1 6-ounce can tomato paste
2 1/2 cups water (may need more)
1 15 1/2-ounce can kidney beans, drained

In a large heavy skillet, brown beef and onions. Drain juices. Add all remaining ingredients except kidney beans. Mix well. Bring mixture to a boil. Reduce heat and simmer, covered, for 30 minutes.

Add the beans and simmer, uncovered, for 10 minutes to heat beans. Add more water if needed.

Filet Southwestern

Prep time: 15 minutes ⧗ Broil: 12 minutes

Serves: 4

*4 1-inch tenderloin steaks or
  filets mignons (if cut to
  order, have the butcher
  flatten them)*
¼ cup butter
1 tablespoon lime juice

3 tablespoons minced shallots
*1 tablespoon minced fresh
  cilantro*
*2 teaspoons puréed chipotle
  peppers in adobo sauce**
vegetable oil

Preheat the broiler and adjust the rack so the filets will be 4 inches from the heating element.

Soften the butter and beat the butter and lime juice with an electric mixer until light and fluffy. Mix in the shallots, cilantro, and peppers. Remove the filets from the refrigerator about 15 minutes before you are ready to begin cooking them. If the butcher did not flatten the filets, flatten them slightly by pressing with a plate.

Oil one side of the filets lightly and place on the broiler pan oiled-side down. Spread about 1 teaspoon of the butter mixture on each filet. Broil 4 minutes (for rare) or 6 minutes (for medium).

Turn the filets; top each with another teaspoon of the butter mixture, and broil an additional 4 to 6 minutes. To serve, top each filet with a quarter of the remaining butter mixture.

*Chipotle peppers canned in adobo sauce are available at many groceries. Purée the entire contents in the blender, and store what you do not use in this recipe tightly covered in the refrigerator for seasoning other Southwestern dishes.

Garlicky London Broil

Prep time: 15 minutes ⧗ Marinate: 1 hour ⧗ Broil: 10 minutes

Serves: 4

1 ½ pound beef flank steak
³/₄ teaspoon cracked black pepper
2 cloves garlic, crushed separately
¼ cup olive oil
3 tablespoons lemon juice
salt and pepper to taste

Score the flank steak on both sides in a diamond-shaped pattern with cuts about ¼-inch deep. Combine ³/₄ teaspoon pepper and 1 clove crushed garlic, and rub onto meat. Make the marinade by combining the remaining crushed garlic with the olive oil and lemon juice. Place the meat and marinade in a glass dish or sealed plastic food bag and turn to coat. Marinate in the refrigerator about 1 hour, turning several times.

Preheat the broiler and adjust the rack so the top of the steak will be 3 inches from the heating element. Place the steak on the broiler pan, broil about 5 minutes, season the top with salt and pepper, then turn. Broil 5 minutes more for medium-rare, or a few minutes longer if medium is desired. Remove, season, and slice very thinly diagonally across the grain to serve.

Grilled Rib-Eye Steaks with Onions

Prep Time: 12 minutes   Grill: 8 minutes

Serves: 4

4 large onions, sliced
2 tablespoons olive oil
4 boneless rib-eye steaks (about 1-inch thick)
4 cloves garlic, split in half
salt and pepper
4 teaspoons dry vermouth

In a large skillet, cook onions in oil until golden brown (about 10 to 15 minutes). Cover and keep warm.

Rub both sides of the steaks with the cut side of the garlic and season with salt and pepper. Grill the steaks for 3 to 4 minutes on each side, or to the desired degree of doneness. Pour 1 teaspoon vermouth over each steak immediately before removing from the grill. Serve with grilled onions.

Quick Tip: Frozen meat

Want to roast frozen meat but don't have time to thaw it first? No problem! Just add a third to a half more time than it would take for fresh or thawed meat.

London Broil with Mushrooms

Prep Time: 15 minutes ⧗ Marinate: overnight ⧗ Grill: 7 minutes

Serves: 4 to 6

½ cup dry red wine
¼ cup olive oil
2 cloves garlic, minced
2 tablespoons red wine vinegar
1 green onion with green top, finely chopped
1 teaspoon Worcestershire sauce, plus an extra dash
1 London broil (about 2 pounds)
2–3 cloves garlic, slivered
salt and black pepper to taste
1 pound fresh mushrooms, sliced
1 tablespoon butter

In a small mixing bowl, combine red wine, oil, minced garlic, vinegar, green onion, and Worcestershire sauce. Poke several small holes in the London broil and place the garlic slivers in the holes. Place the meat in a shallow baking pan and pour the wine mixture over the meat. Cover and refrigerate, turning once, for several hours (or overnight if possible).

Grill the London broil for 3 to 4 minutes. Turn and sprinkle cooked side with salt and pepper to taste. Cook for another 3 minutes or until cooked to your liking. During the last few minutes of cooking, sauté the sliced mushrooms in butter. Add a dash of Worcestershire sauce and remove from heat. To serve, slice the meat against the grain. Top with mushrooms.

Mom's Meatloaf

Prep Time: 12 minutes   Bake: 1 hour

Serves: 6

*1 ½ pounds lean ground beef
   or meatloaf mix*
1 cup soft bread crumbs
½ cup chopped celery
⅓ cup chopped onion
½ teaspoon dry mustard
*1 tablespoon dried parsley
   (optional)*

salt and pepper to taste
1 egg
¼ cup milk
*1 tablespoon Worcestershire
   sauce*
¼ cup ketchup

Preheat the oven to 350°F.

Combine the meat, bread crumbs, celery, onion, mustard, parsley, salt, and pepper. Beat the egg lightly and add the milk and Worcestershire sauce; add the liquid ingredients to the meat mixture. Combine well. Turn into a lightly greased 8 × 11-inch baking dish, patting into a loaf shape.

Bake 45 minutes, then top with ketchup, spreading to cover. Return to the oven for an additional 15 minutes.

Quick Tip: Meatloaf

Make a meatloaf, but instead of shaping it into one big loaf, place individual portions in muffin tins. This reduces baking time and makes serving easy.

Open-Face Beef Stroganoff Sandwiches

Prep Time: 8 minutes   Heat: 10 minutes

Serves: 4

1 4-ounce can mushroom stems and pieces, drained
1 1/2 cups leftover beef gravy or 18-ounce jar prepared
   beef gravy
1/2 cup sour cream
8 thin slices roast beef
4 slices bread

In a large skillet over medium heat, stir mushrooms and gravy until hot. Stir in sour cream until smooth. Add roast beef slices and cook until heated through. Top each slice of bread with two roast beef slices and some gravy.

Meat Safety

In cooking:
- Thaw meat in the refrigerator. Do not refreeze.
- Marinate meat in the refrigerator.
- Wash cutting boards thoroughly after handling meat on them.
- Use separate utensils and plates for cooked and uncooked meats.

In storing:
- Never leave cooked meat at room temperature more than 2 hours before refrigerating.
- Reheat leftovers until very hot.
- Use leftovers within 3 days.

Pepper Pesto Pasta

Prep Time: 15 minutes ⧗ Sauté: 12 minutes

Serves: 4

1 9-ounce package refrigerated angel hair pasta, or 8
  ounces dry pasta
1 red bell pepper
1 pound sirloin steak
¼ cup olive oil
2 cloves garlic, minced
1½ teaspoons seeded and crushed red chili peppers
½ cup pesto
salt to taste

Cook the pasta according to package directions, cutting or breaking into thirds before cooking, and drain. Seed the red pepper and cut into lengthwise strips. Slice the beef into pieces ⅛- to ¼-inch thick and 2 to 3 inches long.

In a large skillet, heat the oil over medium-high heat; sauté the garlic and chili peppers for 1 minute, then add the beef and brown until no longer pink. Add the pepper strips and sauté for about 2 minutes more, or until peppers are crisp-tender. Stir in the pesto and salt to taste. Toss with the pasta and serve.

The Perfect Basic Burger

Fry: 12 minutes

Allow ¹/₄ pound ground meat per burger. Thaw meat in the refrigerator, if frozen; make sure it is completely thawed in the middle as well as on the surface. Gently shape into patties that are about 4 inches in diameter and ¹/₂-inch thick. If patties are not to be cooked immediately, separate with waxed paper and refrigerate.

If using ground beef that is 90 percent or more lean, spray the skillet lightly with cooking spray or wipe lightly with oil. Do not add additional fat or water. Preheat the skillet over medium heat for about 5 minutes. Add the burgers and cook 10 to 12 minutes, until the juices run clear and the center is no longer pink or is very slightly pink. Turn once during cooking, but to preserve the juiciness do not press to flatten with a spatula. Season after cooking is completed.

Cheeseburgers: Top with a slice of cheese after turning.

Basic Burger Mix: To 1 pound of ground beef add ¹/₃ cup fine bread crumbs, ¹/₄ cup finely chopped onion, 1 tablespoon Worcestershire sauce, and ¹/₂ teaspoon pepper. Mix before shaping into patties. Do not overmix or the texture will become too compact.

Burger Dress-Ups

Pinwheel Burger: Cut four slices of different kinds and colors of cheese into diagonal quarters. After turning burgers, top each with four quarters of different cheeses in a pinwheel shape.

Pepper Burger: Before shaping into patties, mix 2 tablespoons chopped jalapeño peppers and ¹/₄ cup chopped onion into the ground beef. Top with Jack cheese.

Blue Burger: Before shaping into patties, mix ¹/₄ cup chopped, well-drained canned mushrooms and ¹/₄ teaspoon pepper into the ground meat. After removing from the skillet, top with crumbled blue cheese.

Earth 'n' Turf Burger: After cooking, top burger with a slice of cheese, sliced tomatoes, sliced cucumbers, and sprouts; spread the bun with creamy Italian salad dressing.

Quick Microwave Beef Stew

Prep Time: 15 minutes ⧗ Microwave: 25 minutes

Serves: 3 to 4

*2 to 2½ cups cut-up cooked stew beef (about 1 pound
  cooked beef)*
4 medium carrots cut into 2½-inch strips
3 medium potatoes, pared and cut into 1½-inch pieces
1 cup sliced celery
1 envelope onion soup mix
3 tablespoons unbleached flour
2¼ cups water

Mix all ingredients in a 2½-quart casserole. Cover and microwave
on high to boiling, 10 to 12 minutes; stir. Cover and let stand 5
minutes. Microwave again until vegetables are tender, 10 to 12
minutes more, stirring every 5 minutes.

Quick Tip: Potatoes

Store potatoes in a cool, dark place to keep them fresh longer.

Sassy Sirloin

Prep Time: 12 minutes 　 Broil: 8 minutes

Serves: 4

1 tablespoon black pepper
½ teaspoon onion powder
1 teaspoon ground thyme
¼ teaspoon red pepper
1½ pounds boneless sirloin steak

Combine spices in a small bowl; stir well.

Trim fat off the steak. Press the spice mixture into the meat on both sides. Place the steak on a rack coated with cooking spray. Place the rack in a shallow baking pan. Broil 5 inches from the heat for 4 minutes on each side, or till desired doneness is reached. Cut the steak diagonally across the grain into ½-inch-thick slices.

To Preserve Juiciness

When broiling or pan-broiling meat, salt each side after it has cooked, not before. Salt draws moisture out of meat when it is added before cooking. It also inhibits browning.

Use tongs to turn steaks; do not pierce them with a fork. Use a spatula to turn ground beef patties and do not flatten them, which will cause the flavorful juices to run out.

Sloppy Joe Stew

Prep Time: 12 minutes ⧖ Cook: 30 minutes

Serves: 4

1 tablespoon olive oil
1 pound ground beef
½ cup chopped onions
½ teaspoon salt
dash of pepper
1½ cups canned tomatoes
2 large potatoes, peeled and sliced
1 cup fresh sliced carrots
½ cup chopped celery

Heat the oil in a large, heavy skillet over low heat. Add the hamburger, and cook the meat until it browns. Drain the fat.

Add the onions, salt, and pepper and stir. Add all the remaining ingredients. Stir, cover the skillet, and bring to a boil. Reduce the heat, and simmer until the potatoes are tender.

Spicy Chinese Beef

Prep Time: 15 minutes ⧖ Stir-fry: 7 minutes

Serves: 12

1 tablespoon peanut oil
2 onions, sliced
4 cloves garlic, minced
4 teaspoons peeled and minced fresh ginger
1 pound extra-lean beef, thinly sliced
2 tomatoes, cut into chunks
2 green bell peppers, cut into long, narrow strips
¼ cup oyster sauce
2 tablespoons soy sauce
2 teaspoons chili paste
2 cups bean sprouts
4 cups cold cooked white rice
3 tablespoons peanuts
5 scallions, chopped

In a wok or large, deep skillet, heat the oil over high heat for 30 seconds. Add the onions and stir-fry for 2 minutes. Add the garlic, ginger, and beef, and stir-fry until beef is browned, another 2 minutes.

Add the tomatoes, bell peppers, oyster sauce, soy sauce, and chili paste. Stir-fry for another 2 minutes. Add the bean sprouts and stir well. Add the rice and toss with the beef mixture. Sprinkle with the peanuts and scallions and serve.

Steak and Cheese Wraps

Prep Time: 15 minutes ⧗ Cook: 15 minutes

Serves: 4

4 tortillas (herb or pepper flavor recommended)
8 ounces Monterey Jack or Cheddar cheese, thinly sliced
2 large white onions
2 large green peppers
1 pound sirloin steak
3 tablespoons olive oil
2 to 3 teaspoons black pepper

Preheat the oven to 350°F. On a baking sheet, layer the tortillas with cheese; do not put cheese closer than 1 inch from the edges. Set aside.

Slice the onions and green peppers thickly. Slice the steak into strips about 1/4-inch thick and 2 inches long. Heat the olive oil in a grill pan or large skillet over medium-high heat. Add the onions, green peppers, and black pepper. Stir and cook for about 3 to 4 minutes. Push the vegetables to the sides of the pan and add the steak strips in the middle. Cook to the desired doneness, stirring occasionally. When about 4 minutes are left in cooking time, put the tortillas in the oven. Mix together the steak and onion/pepper mixture in the pan.

Remove the tortillas when the cheese is close to melted, and layer each tortilla with the steak mixture. Roll the tortilla halfway from bottom to top, fold one side in about an inch so that no ingredient can slip out that side, and continue to roll the rest of the way. Continue with the remaining tortillas. Serve hot.

Steak Stroganoff

Prep Time: 15 minutes ⧖ **Cook: 25 minutes**

Serves: 6

1 pound round steaks, thinly sliced
3 tablespoons butter, divided
½ cup chopped onions
½ pound mushrooms, sliced
2 tablespoons tomato paste
2 tablespoons water
½ teaspoon basil
1 tablespoon cornstarch
1 cup plain yogurt
¼ cup sherry or beef broth
3 cups cooked noodles

Trim the fat off the meat and slice into strips. Melt 2 tablespoons of the butter in a skillet. Sauté the onions until soft. Add the beef. Brown for about 5 minutes. Remove the beef and keep warm. Add the remaining tablespoon of butter and sauté the mushrooms in the butter. Stir in the tomato paste, water, and basil. Return the meat to the pan and simmer briefly.

In a separate pan mix the cornstarch with 1 tablespoon of the yogurt, then stir in the remaining yogurt and cook over medium heat until thickened. Add to the meat mixture and heat thoroughly. Thin with sherry or broth as desired. Serve over cooked noodles.

Texas Hash

Prep Time: 15 minutes   Bake: 45 minutes

Serves: 6

1 pound ground beef
2 stalks celery, chopped fine
2 large onions, diced
2 green peppers, chopped fine
1 16-ounce can chopped tomatoes
½ cup uncooked white rice
1 tablespoon chili powder

Preheat oven to 350°F. In a large ovenproof skillet, brown the meat; add the celery, onion, and peppers and cook slightly, stirring with the meat. Add the tomatoes, rice, and chili powder; stir. Cover and bake for 45 minutes.

Cappelletti Carbonara

Prep Time: 20 minutes ⧖ Cook: 25 minutes

Serves: 4 to 6

¹/₄ pound bacon, cut into 1-inch pieces
2 medium onions, chopped
3 tablespoons olive oil
5 tablespoons chopped parsley
2 tablespoons chopped fresh basil
¹/₂ cup chopped prosciutto
¹/₂ pound freshly grated fontina cheese
salt and freshly ground pepper to taste
1 tablespoon salt
1 pound cappelletti
4 eggs, beaten
freshly grated Parmesan cheese

Sauté the bacon in a large, deep skillet until crisp. Drain well and pour off the fat. In the skillet, sauté the onions in the olive oil until softened. Add the parsley, basil, prosciutto, and cheese with salt and pepper to taste. Cover and simmer over low heat, stirring often, 5 to 10 minutes.

Meanwhile, in a large pot, bring at least 4 quarts of water to a rolling boil. Add 1 tablespoon salt. Add the pasta, stir to separate, and cook until al dente. Drain.

Place the pasta in a warm serving bowl. Add the eggs and toss well. Transfer to the skillet and heat and stir well to heat through. Sprinkle with Parmesan and serve at once.

Farmer's Supper

Prep Time: 15 minutes ⧖ Cook: 25 minutes

Serves: 6

1 ½ tablespoons olive oil
5 medium potatoes, peeled and thinly sliced
salt and freshly ground pepper to taste
½ cup chopped onion
½ cup chopped green pepper
2 cups ham cut in julienne strips
6 eggs
½ cup grated Cheddar cheese

Heat oil in a large skillet. Spread half of the potato slices in the skillet and sprinkle with salt and pepper to taste. Top with half the onion and green pepper; sprinkle with seasonings again. Arrange half of the meat on top; repeat layers. Cover and cook over low heat 20 minutes, or until potatoes are tender.

Break eggs on top; cover and cook until eggs are desired doneness, about 5 minutes. Remove from heat. Top with cheese and cover a minute or two until cheese starts to melt.

Grilled Ham Steaks with Pineapple

Prep Time: 12 minutes ⧖ Cook: 25 minutes

Serves: 4

1½ pound ham steak (cut 1-inch thick)
¼ cup frozen orange juice concentrate, thawed
4 canned pineapple slices (reserving 2 tablespoons juice)
¼ cup dry white wine
1 teaspoon mustard powder
¼ teaspoon ground ginger

Slice fat edges of ham to keep from curling. Combine the orange juice, pineapple juice, wine, mustard, and ginger. Brush the mixture generously over ham and pineapple slices. Grill the ham steak over medium heat for 10 to 15 minutes, brushing occasionally with the sauce. Grill the pineapple slices until warm, also basting with sauce.

Turn the ham, baste, and grill another 10 minutes. Place the pineapple slices on the ham steak during the last 10 minutes of cooking.

Quick Fix: Ham

A fully-cooked ham is a wonderful quick protein, because you only need to slice it. It makes great sandwiches, it can be cut up and served cold on top of a lettuce salad, or a slice can be heated in a skillet or the microwave for a hot meal. To serve a crowd, heat the entire ham in the oven according to package directions. Hot ham slices can be topped with mustard (plain, honey mustard, or Dijon), shredded or sliced cheese (try Cheddar), or fruit sauces (try pineapple or cherry).

Pasta Shells with Prosciutto, Peas, and Mushrooms

Prep Time: 15 minutes ⧗ Cook: 20 minutes

Serves: 4

2 tablespoons olive oil

2 ¼-inch-thick slices prosciutto,
  fat removed, cut into
  ¼-inch dice

½ cup chopped onion

2 cups sliced fresh mushrooms

1½ cups blanched young peas
  or frozen peas, thawed

1 teaspoon unsalted butter

2 cups chicken stock

salt and freshly ground pepper
  to taste

1 tablespoon salt

1 pound pasta shells

½ cup freshly grated Parmesan
  cheese

In a large, deep skillet, heat the oil over medium heat. Add the prosciutto and onion and cook, stirring, until the onion is wilted. Add the mushrooms and continue to cook until they lose all moisture, about 5 minutes. Add the peas, butter, and stock. Simmer until the liquid is reduced by half, about 10 minutes. Season with salt and pepper to taste.

Meanwhile, in a large pot, bring at least 4 quarts of water to a rolling boil. Add 1 tablespoon salt. Add the pasta, stir to separate, and cook until not quite al dente. Drain.

Transfer the pasta to the skillet and combine with the hot sauce. Cook briefly to heat through. Remove to a large warm bowl, toss with the Parmesan, and serve at once.

Pasta with Prosciutto and Walnuts

Prep Time: 15 minutes Cook: 15 minutes

Serves: 4

3 cloves garlic, minced
1/4 cup olive oil
1/4 pound thinly sliced prosciutto, chopped
1 cup chopped walnuts
1/2 cup chopped fresh parsley
1/4 cup chopped fresh basil
1 7-ounce jar roasted red peppers, chopped
1/2 cup pitted, chopped kalamata olives
1 pound linguine, cooked al dente, and well drained

In a large heavy skillet, sauté the minced garlic in olive oil. When the garlic starts to turn brown, add the chopped prosciutto and sauté until crisp. Add the walnuts and sauté until they are toasty brown. Add the parsley, basil, red peppers, and olives.

Add the linguine to the sauce and stir well. Heat over a low flame until the pasta is heated through.

Tortellini with Prosciutto and Mesclun

Prep Time: 15 minutes ⧖ Cook: 10 minutes

Serves: 4

2 tablespoons olive oil
½ cup onion, minced
¼ pound thinly sliced prosciutto, cut into narrow strips
½ cup peeled, seeded, and chopped tomato
2 tablespoons chopped fresh basil
½ teaspoon dried oregano
2 tablespoons balsamic vinegar
1 teaspoon salt
freshly ground pepper to taste
1 tablespoon salt
1 pound cheese tortellini
2 cups mesclun (mixture of young salad greens)
½ cup freshly grated Parmesan cheese

In a large skillet, heat the oil over high heat. Add the onion, prosciutto, tomato, basil, and oregano and sauté for 2 minutes. Stir in the vinegar and remove from the heat. Add the salt and pepper. Transfer to a large bowl.

In a large pot, bring at least 4 quarts water to a rolling boil. Add 1 tablespoon salt. Add the pasta, stir to separate, and cook until al dente. Drain. Rinse under cold water until cool and drain again. Immediately transfer to the bowl holding the prosciutto mixture.

Add the mesclun and the Parmesan to the bowl and toss well.

Greek-Style Lamb Patties

Prep Time: 10 minutes ⧖ Broil: 10 minutes

Serves: 6

1 pound ground lamb
½ cup dry bread crumbs
½ cup crumbled feta cheese
2 tablespoons finely chopped onion
2 tablespoons chopped fresh parsley
1 clove garlic, crushed
1 teaspoon dried mint

Preheat the broiler and adjust the rack so the patties will be 5½ to 6 inches from the heating element.

Combine all ingredients, mixing well. Divide the mixture into 6 portions and shape into 4-inch patties. Place on the rack of a broiler pan that has been lightly greased or sprayed with cooking oil. Broil 4 to 5 minutes per side, turning once, or to desired doneness.

Quick Fix: Butter topping for lamb

Dress up plain lamb by melting ½ cup butter and stirring in 1 teaspoon crushed dried mint or 1 tablespoon finely snipped fresh mint and pouring it over the meat.

Quick Tangy Veal Cubed Steaks

Prep Time: 12 minutes ⧖ Cook: 10 minutes

Serves: 4

2 tablespoons butter
1 pound cubed veal steaks
juice of 1 lemon
¹/₄ cup lemon or plain yogurt, or sour cream

In a large skillet, heat the butter over medium heat. Sauté the cube steaks until done, turning once (about 5 to 7 minutes). Remove to a serving platter. Reduce the heat to low and deglaze the skillet with the lemon juice. Add the yogurt or sour cream and stir in thoroughly, warming through. Pour over the cubed steaks and serve.

Meat Safety

At the supermarket:
- Check the sell-by date, if available.
- Select meat that feels firm, not soft.
- Avoid packages with holes or tears, or with excessive liquid, which indicates that the correct temperature and storage procedures have not been maintained.

At home:
- Refrigerate promptly on a plate so that juices do not leak onto other foods.
- Store meat unopened for up to 2 days. Freeze it if it will not be used within 2 days. Meat wrapped in butcher paper should be unwrapped and rewrapped in foil, freezer bags, or freezer paper. Meat in transparent film can be frozen in the package for up to 2 weeks, but rewrap it for longer periods to prevent freezer burn.

Easy Honey-Herb Chops

Prep Time: 10 minutes ⧖ Broil: 12 minutes

Serves: 4

2 tablespoons honey
¼ cup Dijon mustard
½ teaspoon rosemary
¼ teaspoon thyme
¼ teaspoon pepper
4 boneless pork chops, about 1-inch thick

Preheat the broiler.

Combine the honey, mustard, rosemary, thyme, and pepper, whisking to combine well. Brush over the chops and place on a broiler pan that has been lightly greased or sprayed with cooking spray. Broil the chops 4 inches from the heating element, turning once and basting two additional times on each side with the honey mixture. Total cooking time will be about 12 minutes.

Quick Tip: Herbs

Dried herbs will present a stronger flavor if they are crushed a bit before being added to a dish.

Pork Chops Dijon

Prep Time: 12 minutes ⧖ Cook: 30 minutes

Serves: 4

1 pound boneless lean pork chops
1 onion, chopped
3 tablespoons Dijon mustard
2 tablespoons Italian dressing
¼ teaspoon pepper

Spray a large skillet with nonstick cooking spray and place over medium-high heat. Add the chops and brown on both sides, turning once. Transfer the chops to a plate and set aside. Add the onions to the skillet and cook and stir over medium heat until soft, about 3 minutes. Push the onions to the side of the skillet and return the chops to the skillet.

In a small bowl, quickly stir together the mustard, dressing, and pepper. Spread the mixture over the chops. Cover and cook over medium-low heat until the meat is tender, about 15 minutes. Serve immediately.

Ham Facts

Fully-cooked hams are ready to eat when purchased. Often, they are heated or "baked" and served hot. They can be smoked or unsmoked. Fully-cooked hams are the most common variety today, but hams that are not fully cooked are sometimes available. They *must* be roasted or baked before eating.

A canned ham is ham meat with the bone and much of the fat removed. The meat is then re-formed into a hamlike shape.

Pork Chops in Wine Sauce

Prep Time: 10 minutes ⧗ Cook: 40 minutes

Serves: 4

1 teaspoon sage
1 teaspoon rosemary
2 cloves garlic, chopped
1 teaspoon salt
1 teaspoon freshly ground pepper
4 pork chops, about 1 inch thick
2 tablespoons butter
1 tablespoon olive oil
3/4 cup dry white wine

Combine the sage, rosemary, garlic, salt, and pepper. Press a little of this mixture firmly into both sides of each of the pork chops. Melt the butter and oil in a heavy 10-inch skillet. Brown the chops on both sides, turning carefully with tongs. Remove and pour off all but a small amount of fat from the pan. Add two-thirds of the wine and bring to a boil. Return the chops to the pan. Cover, reduce heat, and simmer until the chops are tender when pressed with the tip of a knife, about 25 to 30 minutes.

When ready to serve, remove chops to a heated plate. Add remaining wine to the skillet and boil down to a syrupy glaze. Pour over the chops.

Pork Schnitzel

Prep Time: 15 minutes ⧗ Cook: 3 minutes

Serves: 4

1 pound pork cutlets
1 teaspoon salt
1 teaspoon pepper
$\frac{1}{2}$ cup flour
2 eggs, beaten
1 $\frac{1}{4}$ cups dry bread crumbs
oil

Pound cutlets as thin as possible. Sprinkle with salt and pepper. Set up an assembly line with flour on one plate, eggs on another, and crumbs on a third. Coat each cutlet with flour, then egg, then bread crumbs.

Heat $\frac{1}{4}$ inch of oil in a large skillet over medium heat. Add as many cutlets as will fit without crowding. Cook until golden brown on each side, about 1 $\frac{1}{2}$ minutes. Drain cutlets on paper towels.

Quick Tip: Ham

Because my favorite brand of whole cooked ham is not always available, I buy a couple whenever I find them and store them in my freezer because they are so easy to heat and serve to a crowd—and delicious!

Lumache with Leek and Sausage Sauce

Prep Time: 15 minutes Cook: 15 minutes

Serves: 4

2 large leeks, coarse outer layers and tough green part
  removed
2 tablespoons olive oil
1 clove garlic, minced
2 sweet Italian sausages (casings removed)
1 cup chicken stock
1 10-ounce package frozen tiny peas, thawed
1 tablespoon salt
salt and freshly ground pepper to taste
1 tablespoon salt
1 pound lumache
¹/₂ cup freshly grated Parmesan cheese

Rinse the leeks well. Cut into ¹/₂-inch rounds and rinse again until all dirt is washed away.

In a large, deep skillet, heat the oil over medium heat. Add the leeks, garlic, and sausage, and cook until the leeks soften and sausage browns. Add the chicken stock and simmer 3 minutes. Stir in the peas, add salt and pepper to taste, and cook 2 minutes.

Meanwhile, in a large pot, bring at least 4 quarts of water to a rolling boil. Add 1 tablespoon salt. Add the pasta, stir to separate, and cook until just al dente. Drain.

Add the pasta to the skillet. Sprinkle with the Parmesan and toss to coat well. Transfer the pasta to a warm platter and serve.

Sausage Skillet

Prep Time: 15 minutes   ⧗   Cook: 25 minutes

Serves: 4 to 6

1 tablespoon oil
2 cups frozen shredded hash brown potatoes
½ pound sausage
2 tablespoons diced red or green bell pepper
6 eggs
salt and pepper to taste
⅓ cup shredded Cheddar cheese

Heat the oil in a medium skillet on medium-high heat. Add the hash browns and cook 8 to 10 minutes, stirring occasionally.

Meanwhile, brown the sausage in another skillet. The last minute of cooking, add the peppers and stir. Remove from the heat and drain well. In a bowl, beat the eggs well, then add the sausage and pepper mixture. Season with salt and pepper.

When the hash browns are cooked, spread to cover the bottom of the skillet evenly. Pour the egg mixture over the hash browns. Reduce the heat to medium-low and cover. Cook 10 minutes or until eggs are set. Remove from the heat and sprinkle with cheese.

Sausage Skillet Supper

Prep Time: 10 minutes ⧗ Cook: 30 minutes

Serves: 4

4 small red potatoes, cut in ½-inch cubes
4 Italian-style sausages, cut in ¼-inch slices
1 onion, diced
1 green bell pepper, cut in lengths
1 red pepper, cut in lengths

In a saucepan, cover the potatoes and sausage with water; simmer, covered, until sausage is fully cooked, about 20 minutes.

Drain off the water; add vegetables to the potatoes and sausage in the saucepan. Simmer 10 minutes, stirring occasionally.

How to Read a Meat Label

A standard meat label tells you what part of the animal the meat comes from (the primal, or wholesale, cut) and what the retail name of the cut is. (Retail names for certain cuts can vary slightly from region to region in the United States.) It will also tell you the weight, price per pound, and total price. Some supermarkets also provide sell-by dates and cooking instructions on labels.

The label sometimes states the grade of the meat as well. Usually, the more fat marbled in the meat, the higher its grade, because fat adds flavor, juiciness, and tenderness (as well as those pesky calories and health risks!). Prime meats have the most marbling and are the most expensive, choice has less marbling, and select has even less, making it leaner but not as flavorful. Meat grading is done by USDA inspectors if the meat processor chooses to have it done and to pay for it. Meat *safety inspection,* on the other hand, is required by law and is supported by your tax dollars.

Internal Meat Temperature When Roasting

Home economists recommend the use of a meat thermometer as the most foolproof way to test the doneness of meats.

A standard meat thermometer is inserted into meat or poultry and left in place during cooking. It is inserted into the center of thickest part of the meat, usually at a slight angle. To provide an accurate reading, it should not touch bone or fat or the pan.

An instant or rapid response thermometer is a more expensive tool, which takes a temperature reading within one minute. It should not be left in the meat or in the oven. It is easier to use than a standard thermometer for meat that is grilled or broiled, and it is particularly useful to gauge doneness when cooking steaks thicker than $1^1/_2$ inches.

MEAT	INTERNAL TEMPERATURE
Beef Roasts	145°F medium rare
	160°F medium
Other Beef Cuts	145°F medium rare
	160°F medium
	170°F well done
Veal Roasts	160°F medium
Pork Roasts	160°F medium
	170°F well done
Other Pork Cuts	160°F medium
	170°F well done
Ham (fully cooked)	140°F heated through
Lamb Roasts	145°F medium rare
	160°F medium
	170°F well done
Other Lamb Cuts	145°F medium rare
	160°F medium

Chapter 5

Poultry

C hicken, turkey, and other types of poultry have a delicate flavor that takes well to all manner of preparations and seasonings. You can buy poultry in many forms: the whole bird, the cut up bird complete with drumsticks and wings, quarters, breasts, thighs, and even ground meat. Turkey also comes as cutlets and breast fillets or tenderloins. All are suitable to many styles of cooking and are favorites in many kitchens.

Thawing Poultry

Uncooked frozen poultry should be thawed in the refrigerator or in cold water. It *should not* be thawed simply by leaving out at room temperature, because there is a danger that bacteria will grow in it. Poultry can also be thawed in a microwave oven; check the manufacturer's directions for your oven.

To thaw in the refrigerator: Place the poultry in a dish or pan so that it will not drip on other food as it thaws. A whole chicken will thaw in about 24 hours; cut up pieces will thaw in 2 to 8 hours, depending on how it is packaged. Thaw in the original wrapping.

A turkey under 12 pounds will take 1 or 2 days; a 12- to 16-pound turkey will take 2 or 3 days; a 16- to 20-pound turkey will take 3 or 4 days; and a turkey over 20 pounds will take 4 to 5 days.

To thaw on the countertop in cold water: Place the chicken or turkey, in its original wrap or in a sealed plastic bag, in a large pan or bowl of cold water. Change the water every 30 minutes. It will take about 30 minutes per pound of poultry. Allow up to 2 hours to thaw a whole chicken. For turkey, allow up to 6 hours for under 12 pounds; up to 8 hours for 12 to 16 pounds; up to 10 hours for 16 to 20 pounds; and up to 12 hours for over 20 pounds.

Cooked frozen poultry should be thawed in the refrigerator. Allow up to 8 hours for cubed chicken or turkey, and up to 24 hours for whole pieces.

Authentic Kung Pao Chili Chicken

Prep Time: 10 minutes Stir-fry: 15 minutes

Serves: 4

3 boneless chicken breast halves
1½ tablespoons peanut oil
1 dried red chili
⅓ cup shelled peanuts
2 tablespoons water
2 tablespoons dry sherry
1 tablespoon soy sauce
1 tablespoon chili bean sauce

1 teaspoon sugar
2 cloves garlic, minced
2 scallions, chopped
1 teaspoon grated ginger
2 teaspoons rice or cider vinegar
1 teaspoon sesame oil
4 cups cooked white rice

Dice the chicken into 1-inch cubes. Heat the oil in a wok or skillet and add the chili. Add the chicken and peanuts and stir-fry until the chicken is cooked. Add the remaining ingredients, except the sesame oil and rice, and bring to a boil. Cook for a few minutes. Add the sesame oil and serve over rice.

Cooking Chicken and Turkey

Poultry should always be cooked to "well done."

For **chicken**, a meat thermometer should read 180°F for a whole chicken, 170°F for bone-in parts, and 160°F for boneless parts.

To check visually for doneness, pierce chicken with a long-tined fork in its thickest part. Juices should run clear. An alternative method is to make a small cut with a thin, sharp knife into the thickest part of the chicken. Meat should no longer be pink.

For **turkey**, a meat thermometer should read 180°F in the thighs and 170°F in the breast for a whole turkey. Stuffing should read 165°F. Turkey breasts should read 170°F when cooked alone.

Broiled Chicken with Yogurt and Spices

Prep Time: 15 minutes ⧗ Refrigerate: overnight ⧗ Broil: 5 minutes

Serves: 6

1 teaspoon ground cumin
1 teaspoon ground coriander
1 teaspoon cayenne pepper
¼ teaspoon ground allspice
1 cup plain yogurt
1 teaspoon grated lemon zest
2 tablespoons lemon juice
3 cloves garlic, chopped
salt to taste
6 skinless, boneless chicken breast halves

In a shallow dish, combine the cumin, coriander, cayenne, and allspice. Stir well. Add the yogurt, lemon zest, lemon juice, garlic, and salt. Stir well again. Add the chicken and spoon the sauce over the chicken to coat. Cover and refrigerate overnight.

Preheat the broiler. Remove the chicken from the marinade and drain well. Place the chicken on the broiler pan. Slip under the broiler about 3 inches from the heat source. Broil, turning once, until nicely browned and cooked through, about 5 minutes. Serve immediately.

Busy Day Guadalajara Chicken and Rice Skillet

Prep Time: 10 minutes ⧖ Cook: 15 minutes

Serves: 4

3 boneless chicken breast halves
1 tablespoon oil
1 15-ounce jar salsa
³/₄ cup chicken broth
¹/₂ cup chopped green pepper
1 cup quick-cooking rice
¹/₂ cup shredded Cheddar cheese

Cut the chicken into 1-inch cubes. Heat oil in a large skillet and sauté chicken until cooked. Stir in salsa, chicken broth, and green pepper, and bring to a boil. Stir in the uncooked rice. Sprinkle with the cheese, cover, and remove from the heat. Let stand 5 minutes until rice is cooked.

Quick Fix: Chicken salad

For a quick salad or sandwich, drain canned chicken and stir in some mayonnaise and a little diced pickle or celery or onion. Mound on lettuce or spread on bread and serve.

California Chicken and Wild Rice Salad

Prep Time: 12 minutes   ⧗   Chill: 1 hour

Serves: 6

1 4.3 oz. package mixed white and wild rice
3 cups cooked chicken, cut into bite-sized pieces
4 scallions, chopped
1 cup Italian dressing
2 ripe avocados
1 tablespoon fresh lemon juice
½ cup toasted pine nuts or sliced almonds
1 cup cherry tomatoes

Prepare rice according to package directions. When the rice is ready, stir in the chicken and scallions; add the dressing and toss well. Pour into a serving dish and chill.

Dice the avocados and toss with the lemon juice. Garnish the salad with avocados, nuts, and cherry tomatoes.

Quick Garnish

Using a strawberry with the green cap and stem still on, make thin slices nearly up to the cap. Press gently to create a strawberry fan. The color and flavor complement poultry.

Chicken-'n-Chips Bake

Prep Time: 10 minutes ⧖ Bake: 15 minutes

Serves: 6

2 cups cubed cooked chicken
2 cups sliced celery
½ cup blanched almonds (optional)
½ teaspoon salt
½ teaspoon monosodium glutamate
2 teaspoons grated onions
2 tablespoons lemon juice
1 cup mayonnaise
½ cup shredded Cheddar cheese
1½ cups crushed or whole potato chips

Preheat oven to 425°F.

In a lightly greased shallow 1½-quart baking dish, combine the chicken, celery, almonds, salt, monosodium glutamate, onions, lemon juice, and mayonnaise. Sprinkle with cheese and potato chips. Bake for 15 minutes or until heated through.

Quick poultry on the grill

Coat turkey or chicken fillets or breasts liberally with olive oil and sprinkle with purchased chicken rotisserie seasoning (it's in the spice section of the store). Place the poultry on the grill on medium heat, turning it once or twice with tongs (don't prick with a fork) until done.

Easy Sunday Afternoon Chicken

Prep Time: 12 minutes ⧖ Bake: 1 hour

Serves: 6

4 boneless, skinless chicken breasts
1 10-ounce can cream of chicken soup
½ can water
1½ teaspoons curry powder
2 tablespoons lemon juice
1 cup grated Cheddar cheese
1 cup mayonnaise
1 8-ounce package herb stuffing mix

Preheat oven to 350°F. Lay chicken breasts in a 9 × 12-inch casserole. Combine the soup and water in a small bowl. Pour the soup mixture over chicken. Mix the remaining ingredients into the stuffing mix. Spread the stuffing mix over the chicken. Bake 1 hour. If the stuffing gets too brown, cover loosely with aluminum foil.

Safe Chicken Handling

Today, with everyone so aware of salmonella and other bacteria that can easily be transmitted through raw chicken, the following standards bear repeating:

- Always wash your hands before and after handling raw chicken.
- Thoroughly wash all cutting boards and utensils you've used to prepare raw chicken.
- Make sure chicken is thoroughly cooked (to 170°F) before serving.
- If chicken smells funny, throw it out.

Garlic and Sun-Dried Tomatoes with Chicken and Penne

Prep Time: 12 minutes ⧖ Cook: 20 minutes

Serves: 6

2 tablespoons virgin olive oil

6 cloves garlic, chopped

3 large boneless, skinless
  chicken breasts, about 6
  ounces each

3 cups chicken stock

1/2 cup oil-packed sun-dried
  tomatoes, diced

1/4 cup chopped parsley

8 scallions, white and half of
  green tops, chopped

salt and freshly ground pepper
  to taste

1/4 cup unsalted butter, softened

1 tablespoon salt

1 pound penne pasta

In a large, deep skillet, heat the oil over medium heat. Add the garlic and sauté until golden. Do not allow to burn. Add the chicken and sauté for 2 minutes on each side, or until cooked through. Remove the chicken from the pan, cut it into 1-inch cubes, and reserve.

Pour the chicken stock into a saucepan and add the tomatoes, parsley, and scallions. Add salt and pepper to taste. Bring to a boil and reduce over high heat 5 to 10 minutes. Add the chicken to the pan and whisk in the butter, a bit at a time, to thicken the sauce. Remove from the heat and keep warm.

Meanwhile, in a large pot, bring at least 4 quarts of water to a rolling boil. Add 1 tablespoon salt. Add the penne; stir to prevent sticking. Cook until al dente. Drain.

In a bowl toss the penne in the sauce, transfer to a warm platter, and serve.

Japanese Grilled Chicken

Prep Time: 10 minutes ⧖ Marinate: overnight ⧖ Grill: 20 minutes

Serves: 4 to 6

½ cup Italian dressing
½ cup teriyaki sauce
4 to 6 boneless chicken breast halves

Combine the Italian dressing and teriyaki sauce. Marinate the chicken in this mixture overnight. Grill over hot coals for about 20 minutes, turning chicken after 10 minutes. Cook until the meat is no longer pink and the juices run clear.

Types of Chicken

Broiler-fryers usually weigh from 3 to 3½ pounds. They are an all-purpose, tender chicken and can be broiled, fried, or roasted.

Roasting chickens are older and larger than broiler-fryers, usually weighing from 4 to 6 pounds. They are not as tender as broiler-fryers and should not be broiled or fried. But when cooked by a slow method like roasting, they become tender and flavorful.

Stewing chickens are also usually between 4 and 6 pounds. They are more mature and less tender birds, and should be cooked by simmering or stewing, as in soups or stews, or to make cut up chicken for recipes.

Cornish hens, also called Rock Cornish game hens, weigh only 1 to 1½ pounds and are all white meat.

Marinated Chicken Kebobs

Prep Time: 15 minutes ⧗ Marinate: 20 minutes ⧗ Grill: 8 minutes

Serves: 4

1 tablespoon lemon juice
1 tablespoon water
1 tablespoon olive oil
½ teaspoon dried tarragon,
    crumbled
¼ teaspoon Tabasco sauce
⅛ teaspoon salt
1 clove garlic, minced

4 skinless, boneless chicken
    breast halves, cut into 1-inch
    cubes
1 red bell pepper, cut into
    1-inch squares
2 medium zucchini, cut into
    1-inch-thick slices

In a small bowl, combine the lemon juice, water, oil, tarragon, Tabasco sauce, salt, and garlic. Place the chicken in a lock-top plastic bag and set in a deep bowl. Pour the lemon juice mixture into the bag, secure the top closed, and let the chicken stand for 20 minutes at room temperature, turning the bag frequently.

Preheat the broiler.

Drain the chicken, reserving the marinade. Thread the chicken, bell pepper, and zucchini alternately onto 4 10- to 12-inch long skewers. Arrange the skewers on a broiler pan. Slip under the broiler 4 to 5 inches from the heat source. Broil, turning once and brushing occasionally with the reserved marinade, until the chicken is tender and cooked through, about 8 minutes. Serve immediately.

Marinated Ginger Chicken

Prep Time: 12 minutes ⧖ Marinate: 4 hours ⧖ Grill or broil: 20 minutes

Serves: 4

1 2½ to 3 pound frying chicken, cut into serving pieces
½ cup lemon juice
½ cup vegetable oil
¼ cup soy sauce
1 teaspoon grated gingerroot or 1 tablespoon ground
  ginger
1 teaspoon onion salt
¼ teaspoon garlic powder

Place chicken in a shallow baking dish. In a small bowl, combine the lemon juice, oil, soy sauce, ginger, onion, and garlic powder. Pour over the chicken. Cover and refrigerate at least 4 hours or overnight, turning occasionally.

Grill or broil for about 20 minutes, turning after 10 minutes. Cook until the meat is no longer pink and the juices run clear, basting frequently with marinade.

Quick Fix: Butter sauce

Dress up plain chicken or turkey by melting ½ cup butter and stirring in 1 teaspoon crushed dried mint or 1 tablespoon finely snipped fresh mint and pouring over the meat.

Pasta Provençale

Prep Time: 15 minutes ⧗ Cook: 10 minutes

Serves: 4

1 tablespoon olive oil
3 yellow onions, sliced
3 green bell peppers, seeded
   and sliced
1 clove garlic, crushed
3 zucchini, cut into medium dice
3 yellow summer squash, cut
   into medium dice
4 tomatoes, cut into large pieces

$^1/_4$ cup fresh basil leaves, torn
salt and freshly ground pepper
   to taste
1 tablespoon all-purpose flour
1 cup heavy cream
$^1/_3$ cup chicken stock
1 tablespoon salt
1 pound rotini or other twist
   shape pasta

In a large, deep skillet, heat the oil over medium heat. Add the onions, bell peppers, and garlic, and sauté 3 minutes. Add the zucchini and yellow squash and sauté 1 minute. Add the tomatoes and basil and cook briefly, just until the tomatoes soften. Season with salt and pepper to taste.

Drain the vegetables in a colander set over a bowl to catch the juices. Let the juices cool, then add the flour. Stir well so that there are no lumps and the mixture is smooth. Add the cream and stock, stirring constantly. Stir the cream mixture into the vegetables. Bring to a simmer over low heat and cook 2 to 3 minutes. Do not boil.

Meanwhile, in a large pot, bring at least 4 quarts of water to a rolling boil. Add 1 tablespoon salt. Add the pasta, stir to separate, and cook until al dente. Drain. Transfer the hot pasta to a serving platter or to individual plates and spoon the vegetable mixture over the top.

Quick Chicken Piccata

Prep Time: 12 minutes ⧗ Cook: 20 minutes

Serves: 4

4 boneless chicken breast halves, skinned
salt and freshly ground pepper to taste
2 tablespoons butter
1 teaspoon olive oil
½ cup chicken broth
¼ cup vermouth
2 tablespoons fresh lemon juice
1 tablespoon capers, drained and rinsed
lemon slices for garnish

Pat chicken dry. Season with salt and pepper. Melt butter with oil in a large heavy skillet over medium-high heat. Add the chicken and cook until springy to the touch, about 4 minutes per side. Remove from the skillet; keep warm.

Increase heat to high. Stir the broth and vermouth into the skillet. Boil until reduced by half, scraping up any browned bits. Remove from the heat. Mix in the lemon juice and capers. Place the chicken on plates and pour the sauce over the chicken. Garnish the chicken with lemon slices.

Quick Chicken Vinaigrette

Prep Time: 10 minutes ⊠ Sauté: 10 minutes ⊠ Bake: 10 minutes

Serves: 4

4 boneless, skinless chicken breast halves
salt and pepper
1 clove garlic, crushed
2 tablespoons olive oil
2 tablespoons tarragon vinegar
1/3 cup dry sherry

Preheat oven to 350°F. Sprinkle the chicken with salt and pepper. Combine the garlic with the oil and vinegar in a skillet. Sauté the chicken breasts until golden brown, turning frequently. Remove and place in a baking dish. Pour the sherry over the chicken and bake for 10 minutes.

Reducing the Fat Even More

Since chicken is naturally low in fat, and even lower once you remove the skin, it's generally necessary to use a little bit of fat when cooking chicken in a skillet. Choose a nonstick skillet, or use a bit of water or chicken broth in place of the usual oil or butter. Or you might find that you can cut the amount of fat in a traditional recipe by half, without reducing the appeal of the dish. Cooking methods such as broiling, baking, poaching, and microwaving also use little fat in cooking.

Simmered Broccoli Lemon Chicken

Prep Time: 10 minutes ⧗ Cook: 20 minutes

Serves: 4

1 tablespoon oil
4 boneless chicken breast halves
1 10-ounce can cream of broccoli soup
$\frac{1}{4}$ cup milk
2 teaspoons fresh lemon juice
$\frac{1}{8}$ teaspoon pepper
4 thin lemon slices

Heat the oil in a skillet. Sauté the chicken breasts about 10 minutes, until browned on both sides. Pour off the fat. Combine the soup, milk, lemon juice, and pepper. Pour over the chicken. Top each chicken piece with a slice of lemon. Reduce heat to low and cover. Simmer 5 to 10 minutes until chicken is tender, stirring occasionally.

Where's the Fat?

Even though it's a pain to remove the skin from chicken, and you feel like you're missing out by not eating that crunchy, satisfying skin, consider these figures:

- A $\frac{1}{2}$-pound chicken breast—one serving—without the skin contains 9 grams of fat.
- A $\frac{1}{2}$-pound serving from a whole chicken with the skin removed contains 13 grams of fat.
- A $\frac{1}{2}$-pound serving from a whole chicken with the skin left on contains 38 grams of fat.

Souper Chicken

Prep Time: 10 minutes ⏳ Bake: 1 ½ hours

Serves: 4 to 6

1 can cream of mushroom soup
1 can cream of chicken soup
1 can cream of celery soup
²/₃ cup chopped celery
1 cup long-grain rice
3 to 3¹/₂ pound chicken, cut up, or 6 pieces chicken
¹/₄ cup butter, melted

Preheat oven to 350°F.

In a large bowl, combine the three soups, celery, and rice. Turn into a 9 × 13-inch baking dish. Arrange the chicken pieces on the soup and rice mixture, and drizzle the melted butter over the chicken pieces. Cover and bake about 1 ½ hours, or until the largest chicken pieces are no longer pink in the center.

Quick Tip: Boneless chicken

Buying chicken breasts that are already deboned and skinned is a great time-saver! They cost more, but one way to save money is to buy larger quantities when they are on sale and freeze them.

Stellar Stir-Fry

Prep Time: 15 minutes ⧗ Stir-fry: 10 minutes

Serves: 4

2½ tablespoons red wine
1 tablespoon soy sauce
½ teaspoon cornstarch
¼ teaspoon sugar
⅛ teaspoon salt
1 tablespoon peanut oil
2 cups blanched broccoli florets

1 cup blanched diagonally
  sliced carrots, thin slices
½ cup thin onion wedges
6 ounces skinless chicken
  breasts, cut into thin strips
2 cups hot cooked rice

In a small bowl, make the sauce by combining the red wine, soy sauce, cornstarch, sugar, and salt. Stir to dissolve the cornstarch. Set aside.

In a wok heat the oil; add the broccoli, carrots, and onion. Cook, stirring quickly and frequently, until vegetables are tender and crisp and onions are browned. Stir in the chicken and stir-fry 2 more minutes.

Add the sauce to the chicken mixture and cook, stirring constantly, until the sauce is thickened, 2 to 3 minutes.

Serve each portion over ½ cup cooked rice.

Easy Turkey Potpie

Prep Time: 15 minutes   Bake: 14 minutes

Serves: 6

1 potato, cut into cubes
1 tablespoon butter
¼ cup diced onion
½ cup sliced celery
1 10-ounce jar turkey or chicken gravy
¼ cup water
1 10-ounce package frozen mixed vegetables
2 cups cut-up turkey, white or dark meat or a
  combination
¼ teaspoon pepper
¼ teaspoon marjoram
1 can refrigerated biscuits

Preheat the oven to 400°F.

Boil or steam the potato cubes until just tender. In a medium ovenproof skillet, heat the butter over medium heat; and sauté the onion and celery in the butter about 3 minutes. Stir in the gravy, water, vegetables, turkey, and seasonings. Bring to a boil, then remove from the heat.

Arrange the biscuits on top of the mixture. Bake 12 to 14 minutes, or until the biscuits are golden brown.

Farfalle with Turkey and Sausage

Prep Time: 15 minutes ⧖ Cook: 20 minutes

Serves: 4

1 tablespoon olive oil
1 cup coarsely chopped onion
1 clove garlic, minced
1 green bell pepper, seeded
   and julienned
12 ounces boneless, skinless
   turkey breasts, cut into
   ½-inch-wide pieces
½ pound sweet or hot Italian
   sausages, cut crosswise into
   ½-inch-thick pieces

1 16-ounce can Italian plum
   tomatoes, with juice,
   chopped
¼ cup dry red wine
½ teaspoon dried oregano
¼ teaspoon dried basil
1 teaspoon sugar
1 tablespoon salt
12 ounces farfalle pasta
¼ cup heavy cream
salt and freshly ground pepper
   to taste

In a large, deep skillet, heat the oil over medium heat. Add the onion, garlic, and bell pepper and sauté until just softened. Add the turkey and sausage and sauté until slightly browned. Add the tomatoes with the juice, the wine, oregano, basil, and sugar. Bring to a boil, lower the heat, and simmer gently, stirring occasionally, for 10 minutes, or until the tomatoes cook down and thicken slightly.

Meanwhile, in a large pot, bring at least 4 quarts of water to a rolling boil. Add 1 tablespoon of salt. Add the farfalle and stir to prevent sticking. Cook until al dente. Transfer to a warm serving bowl.

Add the cream and salt and pepper to taste to the tomato sauce and simmer for 3 minutes, or until it thickens slightly. Pour the hot sauce over the farfalle, toss well, and serve.

Glazed Turkey Breast

Prep Time: 10 minutes ⧖ **Roast: 2 ½ hours**

Serves: 8 to 10

*4 to 6 pound turkey breast
glaze (see below)*

Preheat the oven to 325°F.

Place the turkey breast on a rack in a shallow roasting pan. Roast uncovered about 2 to 2½ hours, or until a meat thermometer reads 175°F. During the last 30 minutes of roasting, brush with one of the following glazes:

Honey Mustard Glaze: Combine ¼ cup honey and 2 tablespoons sweet or Dijon mustard.

Citrus Glaze: Combine ⅓ cup orange marmalade, 1 tablespoon lime juice, and ½ teaspoon dried mint leaves.

Types of Turkey

- *Turkey hens* are female turkeys and usually weigh up to 15 pounds.
- *Turkey toms* are male and usually weigh 15 pounds or more.
  The two are very similar in tenderness and ratio of white to dark meat. Choose on the basis of size.
- For holiday turkeys, allow about 1 pound per person if you want leftovers.

Herb-Roasted Turkey Breast

Prep Time: 12 minutes   ⧖   Roast: 2 ½ hours

Serves: 8 to 10

4 to 6 pound turkey breast
1 tablespoon chopped fresh sage
½ tablespoon chopped fresh thyme
½ tablespoon chopped fresh marjoram
vegetable oil
salt and pepper

Preheat the oven to 325°F.

Gently loosen the skin of the turkey breast on both sides, but do not detach it from the breast bone. Mix the chopped herbs together and gently spread them under the skin. Place the turkey breast skin-side up on a rack in a shallow roasting pan. Rub the turkey skin generously with oil, then sprinkle with salt and pepper.

Roast the turkey uncovered about 2 to 2½ hours, or until a meat thermometer reads 175°F. Baste with pan drippings or additional oil during the last half hour of roasting.

Did you know?

Turkey can be used for any recipe that calls for chicken and vice versa.

Linguine with Turkey, Tomatoes, and Olives

Prep Time: 20 minutes ⏳ Cook: 30 minutes

Serves: 4 to 6

2 teaspoons olive oil
1 cup finely diced onion
3 large cloves garlic, finely
   chopped
1 pound turkey breast, skin
   removed and cut into bite-
   sized pieces
1 tablespoon chopped fresh
   basil
1/2 teaspoon dried thyme
1/2 teaspoon dried rosemary

12 to 16 kalamata or other oil-
   cured olives, pitted and
   coarsely chopped
1 1/2 tablespoons capers, drained
2 ripe tomatoes, coarsely
   chopped
2 cups chicken stock
1 tablespoon salt
1 pound linguine
1 cup freshly grated pecorino
   Romano cheese

In a large, deep skillet, heat the oil over medium heat. Add the onion and garlic and cook until the onion is translucent. Add the turkey, basil, thyme, and rosemary and sauté until the turkey is lightly browned. Stir in the olives, capers, and tomatoes and cook briefly, until the tomatoes begin to give off liquid. Remove the turkey from the skillet. Add the chicken stock, bring to a boil, and simmer over medium heat until the broth is reduced by half. Return the turkey to the sauce and stir well.

Meanwhile, in a large pot, bring at least 4 quarts of water to a rolling boil. Add 1 tablespoon salt. Add the linguine, stir to separate, and cook until al dente. Drain.

Transfer the linguine to the skillet and toss with the sauce until the sauce is evenly distributed. Transfer to a warm serving dish, top with the cheese, and serve.

Turkey Cutlets, Indian Style

Prep Time: 12 minutes ⧖ Grill: 7 minutes

Serves: 6

2 large limes
1/3 cup plain yogurt
1 tablespoon vegetable oil
2 teaspoons minced, peeled ginger
1 teaspoon ground cumin
1 teaspoon ground coriander
1 teaspoon salt
1 clove garlic, crushed
1 1/2 pounds turkey cutlets
cilantro sprigs for garnish

Prepare a fire in a charcoal grill.

Grate the peel and extract the juice from 1 lime. Place 1 teaspoon of grated peel and 1 tablespoon juice in a large bowl. Cut the other lime into wedges and set aside. Add yogurt, vegetable oil, ginger, cumin, coriander, salt, and garlic to the lime peel and juice, and mix until blended.

Just before grilling, add the turkey cutlets to the bowl with the yogurt mixture, stirring to coat the cutlets. Do not let the cutlets marinate in the yogurt mixture, as their texture will become mealy.

Place the turkey cutlets on the grill over medium-hot coals. Cook the cutlets 5 to 7 minutes until they just lose their pink color throughout. Serve with lime wedges. Garnish with cilantro sprigs.

Jerky Turkey Kebobs

Prep Time: 20 minutes

Serves: 4

about 2 pounds turkey thighs, skinned, boned, and cut into 1-inch cubes (or 1 pound boneless, skinless turkey dark meat)

Jamaican Marinade:

¼ cup lime juice
1 tablespoon soy sauce
4 chopped green onions
1 jalapeño pepper, seeded
2 cloves garlic, peeled
1 teaspoon each ginger, allspice, thyme, cumin, ground black pepper
½ cup water

Combine the marinade ingredients in a blender and purée until smooth. Pour into a glass bowl, add the turkey cubes, and stir to coat well. Cover and refrigerate 4 to 5 hours, stirring occasionally.

When ready to cook, preheat the broiler. Remove the turkey from the marinade. Thread the turkey onto 4 metal skewers. Spray the broiler pan with cooking oil spray, place the skewers on it, and broil 5 inches from the heat a total of 10 to 12 minutes, turning once. Cook until turkey is no longer pink and juices run.

Turkey Tetrazzini

Prep Time: 10 minutes 　 Bake: 45 minutes

Serves: 5 to 6

8 to 10 ounces spaghetti or
  linguine
1 4-ounce can mushrooms
  (reserve the liquid)
2 or more cups cooked turkey
4 tablespoons butter

$^{1}/_{4}$ cup flour
salt and pepper to taste
1 16-ounce can chicken broth,
  or 1$^{3}/_{4}$ cups turkey broth
1 cup half-and-half
$^{1}/_{2}$ cup grated Parmesan cheese

Break the spaghetti into pieces, and cook according to
package directions, but undercook slightly. Drain. In a large bowl,
toss the noodles with the drained mushrooms and turkey.

Preheat oven to 350°F. Melt the butter over low heat. Stir in the
flour, salt, and pepper, and cook until the mixture is bubbly. Remove
the pan from the heat, and stir in the broth, half-and-half, and reserved
mushroom liquid. Stirring constantly, heat the sauce until it boils; boil 1
minute.

Pour the sauce over the noodle mixture and mix thoroughly. Place
mixture in an
8 × 11-inch baking dish. Sprinkle the Parmesan cheese on top. Bake
about 45 minutes, or until hot and bubbly in the center.

Chapter 6

Fish and Seafood

Fish is usually a good menu choice to serve guests, because all but the most austere vegetarian diets include fish and seafood. Many experts recommend eating fish at least once a week as it is rich in protein and other nutrients. Today, most types of fish and seafood are readily available fresh, but if not, you can do well with the frozen varieties.

There is no need to become bored with fish, because there are many preparation methods and garnishes available to you. Best of all, fish takes very little time to prepare and cook.

Fish and Seafood Garnishes, Part 1

- Drag fork tines the length of an unpeeled cucumber, scraping parallel lines into the skin. Repeat until the entire skin is striped. Cut 1/8-inch slices straight across the cucumber or on the diagonal. Overlap several slices on the serving platter or lay directly on each individual serving.
- Fresh parsley, rosemary, or chervil sprigs can be placed on serving plates with fish or seafood to add color.

Fish and Seafood Garnishes, Part 2

- Lemon, orange, and lime slices go well with fish and seafood. To dress them up, cut thin slices crosswise to make a wheel, then make another cut halfway into each slice. Twist these cut edges in opposite directions to make an attractive S-shaped garnish.
- A small wedge of fresh pineapple or cantaloupe is wonderful served with fish or seafood, and can be placed on a small green lettuce leaf for added color.

Did You Know?

- It's best to thaw fish in the refrigerator in its original wrapping. Place it in a baking pan to catch any drips that could contaminate other food in the refrigerator.
- Keep fish well chilled until just before cooking.
- Breaded fish should not be thawed; follow package directions.
- Do not thaw and refreeze raw fish.
- Fish is done when it readily flakes with a fork.

Fillets of Fish with Lime and Cumin

Prep Time: 10–12 minutes ⧗ Bake: 15 minutes

Serves: 4

12 fish fillets
2 tablespoons lime juice
1 teaspoon cumin
¼ cup plain yogurt
salt and freshly ground pepper to taste

Preheat the oven to 350°F. Arrange fish in a single layer in a baking dish. Combine the lime juice and cumin, and pour over the fish, turning to coat. Bake uncovered for 10 to 15 minutes or until the fish flakes easily when tested with a fork.

In a bowl, combine the yogurt with 1 tablespoon of the juice from the baking dish. Season with salt and pepper to taste and serve over the fish.

Lime Juice and Cumin

Any fresh fish fillet baked with a little lime juice and cumin makes a quick and tasty main dish. Serve with whole-grain rice.

Baked Fish Fillets

Prep Time: 10 minutes Bake: 15 minutes

Serves: 4

1 ½ pounds leeks, trimmed, washed, and chopped
½ cup fish stock or water
salt and freshly ground pepper to taste
1 tablespoon Dijon mustard
1 ½ pounds cod, halibut, or salmon fillets

Preheat the oven to 400°F. Combine the leeks in an ovenproof casserole with the fish stock, salt, pepper, and mustard. Spread the leeks out in the casserole. Place the fish on top of the leek mixture and sprinkle with salt and pepper. Cover the casserole and bake 10 to 15 minutes or until a knife meets no resistance when inserted into the thickest part of the fillet. Serve with the leek mixture spooned over the fish.

To Bake Fish:

- Use a 350°F oven.
- Coat the fish with melted butter or olive oil to prevent drying and brush on more while it's in the oven.
- Check after 12 minutes, but it could take up to 30 minutes if the fish is thick.

Grilled Fish Fillets with Herbed Mustard Sauce

Prep Time: 15 minutes ⧗ Grill: 8 minutes

Serves: 4

4 fillets gray sole, Pacific tuna, or gulf snapper
1 1/2 tablespoons olive oil
salt and freshly ground pepper to taste
2 tablespoons unsalted butter
1 clove garlic, minced
1/3 cup whipping cream
1 teaspoon Dijon mustard
1 tablespoon seasoned rice vinegar
1/4 cup minced fresh dill
1 tablespoon minced fresh mint

Heat the gas or charcoal grill until hot. Brush the fillets with olive oil and season with salt and pepper. Grill the fillets for 2 to 4 minutes per side. Grill until the fish flakes when tested with a fork at its thickest part. Remove to a serving platter and keep warm.

Melt the butter over medium heat in a skillet, add the garlic, and cook for 30 seconds. Add the cream and mustard. Heat to a boil and cook until thickened slightly, about 1 minute. Remove from the heat and stir in the vinegar, dill, mint, and salt and pepper to taste. Spoon the sauce over the fish just before serving.

Poached Cod with Spicy Buttermilk Sauce

Prep Time: 10 minutes   Cook: 20 minutes

Serves: 4

1 ½ pounds cod fillets
³⁄₄ teaspoon turmeric
black pepper to taste
3 cups buttermilk

1 tablespoon lemon juice
½ teaspoon salt
2 teaspoons cumin

Sprinkle the fillets with turmeric and black pepper. Pour the buttermilk into a heavy skillet and poach the fish for 5 minutes. Remove the fish.

Add the lemon juice and salt to the pan. Heat the buttermilk over high heat for 5 minutes. Stir in the cumin, reduce the heat, and return the fish to the pan. Cook for another 5 to 10 minutes until the fish is done. Spoon the sauce over the fish to serve.

To Poach Fish:

Simmer the fish gently on the stove in a covered pan with enough liquid to cover the fish. You can add white wine, herbs, lemon slices, or whole peppercorns to the water, if desired. Be careful that the water doesn't boil rather than simmer gently; the fish meat can become tough or break up. Watch carefully; it usually takes only 5 to 10 minutes for the fish to be done.

Skillet Fillet Dinner

Prep Time: 15 minutes   ⧗   Cook: 20 minutes

Serves: 4

5 tablespoons butter or olive oil
1 cup chopped red onion
1 1/2 cups diced small red potatoes with skins
1 cup corn
1 pound fish fillets (cod, bass, snapper, or halibut), cut
    into 1-inch chunks
salt and freshly ground pepper
1/3 cup chopped parsley

Heat 4 tablespoons of the butter or olive oil in a large skillet over medium-high heat, then add the onion and potatoes and cook slowly until tender. Stir in the corn and the remaining tablespoon of butter. Add the fish chunks and salt and pepper to taste. Continue cooking, stirring occasionally, until the fish is cooked through—about 5 minutes. Do not break up the fish chunks. Sprinkle with parsley and serve.

To Pan-Fry Fish:

Melt butter or place olive oil in a skillet and add the fish. Cook over medium heat and turn the fish when halfway through cooking. This is quick—it only takes perhaps 8 or 9 minutes, depending on the thickness of the fish.

Flounder Amandine

Prep Time: 12 minutes ⧖ Cook: 10 minutes

Serves: 4

5 tablespoons butter, divided
1 tablespoon olive oil
1 pound flounder fillets
flour for dredging
2 eggs, beaten
¼ cup slivered almonds
¼ cup white wine or vermouth
2 tablespoons fresh lemon juice

Melt 4 tablespoons of the butter with the oil in a large skillet. Dip the fillets in flour, then egg. Cook until golden (2 to 3 minutes per side). Remove from the skillet and keep warm.

Melt the remaining tablespoon of butter, scraping the pan. Add the almonds; cook 1 minute. Add the wine and lemon juice, and simmer until thick. Pour over the fish and serve.

Cooking Fish

In most cases, fish requires only a few minutes of cooking time on each side. A white-fleshed fish such as sole or halibut takes less time than a firm steaklike fish such as salmon or tuna. Generally, the fish is done when the flesh is opaque and can be flaked easily with a fork.

Lobster—Almost

Prep Time: 15 minutes ⧗ Boil: 10 minutes ⧗ Broil: 2 minutes

Serves: 6

3 quarts water
1 medium onion, quartered
3 stalks celery, cut into chunks
1/2 cup lemon juice
3 tablespoons salt
3 pounds pike fillets, skinned
1/4 cup melted butter
paprika
lemon wedges
melted butter

Preheat the broiler, setting the rack 6 inches below the element. Fill a large saucepan with 3 quarts of water. Add the onion, celery, lemon juice, and salt. Bring to a boil. Cut the pike fillets into 2-inch pieces. Drop the fish into the boiling water, and cook 3 minutes and no longer. Drain immediately, discarding the onion and celery.

Place the fish pieces on a foil-lined baking sheet. Brush with 1/4 cup melted butter and sprinkle with paprika. Broil 2 minutes, or just until fish starts to turn golden. Serve with lemon wedges and melted butter in small bowls for dipping.

Herb Linguine with Salmon, Cream, and Pistachios

Prep Time: 12 minutes 〖Ｘ〗 Cook: 10 minutes

Serves: 4

2 tablespoons chopped
  pistachio nuts
1/4 cup unsalted butter
1/4 red bell pepper, seeded and
  diced
1/2 teaspoon minced garlic
3/4 pound salmon fillet, diced
1 1/2 cups heavy cream

2 teaspoons grated lemon zest
salt and freshly ground white
  pepper to taste
1 tablespoon salt
12 ounces fresh herb linguine
1/4 cup freshly grated Parmesan
  cheese

Preheat the oven to 300°F. Toast the pistachios until lightly browned, about 5 minutes. Reserve.

In a large, deep skillet, melt the butter over medium-low heat. Add the bell pepper and garlic, raise the heat to medium, and sauté for 1 minute. Add the salmon and sauté for 1 minute. Add the cream, lemon zest, and salt and pepper to taste. Cook until reduced and thickened.

Meanwhile, in a large pot, bring at least 4 quarts water to a rolling boil. Add 1 tablespoon salt. Add the pasta, stir to separate, and cook until al dente. Drain.

Transfer the linguine to a large, warm bowl, add the sauce, and toss well. Sprinkle with the pistachios and Parmesan cheese.

One-Pot Salmon Dinner

Prep Time: 15 minutes | Cook: 15 minutes

Serves: 4

2 cups fusilli (pasta)
1 cup milk
1 cup ricotta cheese
1 cup frozen green peas
$^1/_4$ cup green onion, chopped
2 tablespoons Dijon mustard
2 tablespoons lemon juice
1 tablespoon chopped fresh dill
$^3/_4$ teaspoon salt
$^1/_4$ teaspoon freshly ground pepper
dash hot pepper sauce
1 7$^1/_2$-ounce can red salmon

Cook the fusilli in a pot of boiling salted water until firm. Drain well and set aside. Reserve $^1/_4$ cup of the pasta cooking water. In a blender, blend the milk with the ricotta until smooth, pour into a saucepan. Add the reserved cooking water, peas, green onion, mustard, lemon juice, dill, salt, pepper, and hot pepper sauce. Heat through over medium heat, stirring often.

Drain the salmon, keeping it in chunks. Stir the salmon into the saucepan along with the fusilli. Remove from heat, cover, and let stand for 3 to 4 minutes until the sauce has thickened slightly.

Salmon Cream Cheese Wrap

Prep Time: 12 minutes ⧖ Chill: 1 hour

Serves: 4

8 ounces, cream cheese, softened
1 tablespoon capers, drained and slightly chopped
1 teaspoon freshly ground black pepper
3 tablespoons fresh or 2 teaspoons dried chives
4 tortillas (plain or spinach)
10 ounces smoked salmon, cut into strips
1 small red onion, sliced or chopped
2 medium tomatoes, thinly sliced

In a small bowl, blend well the cream cheese, capers, pepper, and chives. Spread evenly on the tortillas. Layer with salmon, onion, and tomatoes. Roll the tortilla halfway from bottom to top, fold one side in about an inch so that no ingredient can slip out that side, and continue to roll the rest of the way. Repeat for the remaining tortillas. Chill before serving.

Selecting Fish

When purchasing fresh fish, check for clear and bright eyes, firm skin that bounces back when touched, and a fresh, clean smell. Try not to keep fresh fish more than a day in your refrigerator before cooking.

Salmon in Red Wine with Apricots

Prep Time: 15 minutes ⧗ Bake: 7 minutes

Serves: 4

1¼ pounds salmon fillets
¼ cup all-purpose flour
2 tablespoons olive oil
1 cup dry red wine
½ cup fish stock
1 cup dried apricots
salt and freshly ground pepper to taste
2 tablespoons unsalted butter

Preheat oven to 375°F. Pat the salmon dry on towels. Dust in the flour, shaking off the excess. Heat the oil in a 12-inch ovenproof skillet or roasting pan over medium heat on the stove. Add the salmon and brown on all sides. Remove to a plate and discard the oil. Add the wine and stock to the skillet and bring to a boil.

Replace the salmon in the skillet. Add the apricots and sprinkle with salt and pepper. Place, uncovered, in the oven. Cook 7 minutes. When done, transfer the skillet to the stovetop and remove the fish to a carving board.

Cook the liquid in the roasting pan over high heat, stirring, until it thickens slightly. Remove from the heat and whisk in the butter. Cut the salmon into ½-inch slices, arrange on a serving platter, and spoon the sauce over the top.

Salmon Sandwich with Herb Mayonnaise

Prep Time: 12 minutes   Bake: 20 minutes

Serves: 4

$1/4$ cup mayonnaise
1 teaspoon dried parsley
1 teaspoon dried tarragon
1 teaspoon marjoram
1 teaspoon red wine vinegar
2 teaspoons Dijon mustard
1 pound salmon fillets
1 tablespoon olive oil
4 large buns
4 large leaves of lettuce
4 slices red onion
8 slices tomato

Preheat oven to 350°F.

In a small bowl, mix the mayo, herbs, vinegar, and mustard until well blended. Brush both sides of the salmon fillets with olive oil and spread the fillets in a baking dish. With half of the mayo mixture, coat the top side of the fillets. Bake for 17 to 20 minutes, or until the fish flakes easily with a fork.

Place the cooked fillets on the buns and top with the lettuce, onion, and tomato. Spread an extra layer of mayo on the top bun. Can be served warm, or chill and serve cold.

Smoked Salmon and Dill in Cream Sauce with Angel Hair Pasta

Prep Time: 10 minutes 〰 Cook: 10 minutes

Serves: 4

2 cups heavy cream
1 cup milk
2 tablespoons chopped fresh dill
¹/₂ cup chopped scallions
2 teaspoons grated lemon zest
3 tablespoons capers, drained
salt and freshly ground pepper to taste
1 tablespoon salt
1 pound angel hair pasta
6 ounces thinly sliced smoked salmon, cut into thin
*   strips*

Combine the cream, milk, dill, scallions, and lemon zest in heavy-bottomed saucepan. Bring to a boil over medium-high heat. Reduce to a simmer and cook briefly until thickened. Stir in the capers. Season with salt and pepper.

Meanwhile, in a large pot, bring at least 4 quarts of water to a rolling boil. Add 1 tablespoon salt. Add the pasta, stir to separate, and cook until al dente. Drain. Transfer the pasta to a large, warm bowl. Pour the sauce over it and toss to coat. Add the smoked salmon and toss again to combine. Serve.

Grilled Snapper with Dill

Prep Time: 12 minutes ⧖ Grill: 25 minutes

Serves: 4

1 large snapper (about 2 pounds)
salt and black pepper
2 tablespoons extra virgin olive oil
1 lemon, sliced
3 to 4 sprigs fresh dill

Clean the fish and score several times on each side. Season inside and out with salt and pepper. Oil a large piece of aluminum foil and place the fish on the oiled part of the foil. Place the lemon slices and sprigs of dill inside the cavity and on top of the fish. Enclose the fish in the foil, folding the edges to seal tightly.

Place on the grill and cook, over medium heat, about 25 minutes. The fish is done when the flesh is tender and white.

Grilling Fish

When grilling fish, place fish steaks or fillets on a hot, well-oiled grill. Grill for about 10 minutes per inch of thickness of the fillet, measured at its thickest part. Turn once while on the grill. Thoroughly brush fish with vegetable oil or basting sauce several times during grilling. Grill until fish flakes when tested with a fork at its thickest part.

Red Snapper à la Ritz

Prep Time: 10 minutes 🕰 Bake: 20 minutes

Serves: 4

1 pound red snapper fillets
1 sleeve low-fat Ritz crackers
1 green pepper, cut into chunks
1 tablespoon honey

Preheat the oven to 350°F.

Place the fillets in a shallow baking dish or glass pie plate in one layer. In a blender, grind the crackers to crumbs and place in a bowl. Finely chop the green pepper in the blender. Add to the crumbs. Add the honey and mix well. Top the fillets with the crumb mixture to cover. Bake for 20 minutes or until fish flakes.

Quick Fix: Fish topper

Drizzling cooked fish with a little melted butter and then topping it with slivered, sliced, or coarsely chopped almonds, pecans, walnuts, or macadamia nuts is delicious! Using an oven-safe serving dish, you can lightly toast the nuts on the fish a few seconds under the broiler right before serving, if desired, but watch closely as it can burn easily.

Baked Creamy Sole

Prep Time: 15 minutes ⧖ Bake: 20 minutes

Serves: 4

2 pounds fresh or frozen sole fillets
butter
1 10³/₄-ounce can condensed cream of celery soup
2 tablespoons dry white wine
1 tablespoon lemon juice
¹/₂ teaspoon marjoram leaves or thyme leaves
¹/₄ teaspoon garlic powder
1 small onion, thinly sliced
³/₄ cup shredded carrot
¹/₄ cup grated Parmesan cheese
¹/₂ teaspoon ground nutmeg

Preheat oven to 450°F.

Arrange fish (overlap thin edges) in a buttered shallow 3-quart casserole or 9 × 13-inch baking dish. Mix separately the soup, wine, lemon juice, marjoram, and garlic powder. Top the fish with onion slices and sprinkle evenly with shredded carrot. Pour the soup mixture over the fish. Sprinkle with Parmesan cheese. Dust lightly with nutmeg.

Bake, uncovered, for 15 to 20 minutes, or until fish flakes readily when prodded in the thickest portion with a fork.

Fillets of Sole

Prep Time: 12 minutes ⧖ Cook: 5 minutes

Serves: 2

$^1/_3$ cup flour
$1^1/_4$ teaspoons salt
$^1/_4$ teaspoon freshly ground pepper
$1^1/_2$ pounds sole fillets
6 tablespoons butter
1 tablespoon olive oil
2 tablespoons lemon juice
$1^1/_2$ teaspoons minced fresh parsley

Preheat the oven to 225°F. Put an ovenproof platter in the oven. Combine the flour, salt, and pepper in a shallow dish. Coat each fish fillet with the flour mixture and shake off the extra. In a large skillet, heat 3 tablespoons of the butter with the oil. Without crowding the fillets, pan-fry each over medium heat, flipping once, until golden—about 1 to 2 minutes.

As each fillet is done, put it on the platter in the oven. Use the remaining butter for the remaining fillets. When all the fish fillets are cooked, turn the heat to high, stir in the lemon juice, and cook for a few seconds. Add the parsley, and drizzle over the fish fillets just before serving.

Lemon and Tarragon Sole

Prep Time: 10 minutes ⧗ Broil: 10 minutes

Serves: 4

$^1/_4$ cup plain yogurt
1 teaspoon all-purpose flour
1 teaspoon dried tarragon, crumbled
1 teaspoon minced lemon zest
1 pound sole fillets

Preheat the broiler. Spray a baking sheet with nonstick cooking spray.

In a small bowl, combine the yogurt, flour, tarragon, and lemon zest. Place the sole fillets on the prepared baking sheet. Spread the yogurt mixture on the fish. Place under the broiler until the fish tests done, 5 to 10 minutes. Serve immediately.

To Broil Fish:

This is best with thicker fillets or whole fish, but I often do it with thinner servings, too, by using generous amounts of butter or oil in the pan and on the fish and watching it very carefully. The fish should be placed with the skin side down, if there is a skin. Thicker pieces should be turned when half done; thinner pieces don't need turning. This only takes 10 or 15 minutes—or even less.

Quick Sole Florentine in the Microwave

Prep Time: 8 minutes   Microwave: 5 minutes

Serves: 4

1 pound sole fillets
salt and pepper to taste
$^1\!/_2$ teaspoon paprika
2 cups stemmed spinach leaves

On a large microwave-safe plate, arrange the fillets. Season the fillets with salt, pepper, and paprika. Cover the plate with plastic wrap. Cut a small slit in the plastic wrap. Microwave on high for 5 minutes. Remove the plastic wrap. Drain off the juices and sprinkle spinach leaves over fillets. Serve at once.

To Steam Fish:

Heat water to boiling but be sure it does not touch the steamer insert. Coat the fish with olive oil and place on the insert; cover and simmer until done. The fish will cook very quickly— perhaps taking only 5 to 10 minutes.

Grilled Japanese Swordfish

Prep Time: 12 minutes ⧗ Marinate: 5 hours ⧗ Grill: 10 minutes

Serves: 4

4 8-ounce swordfish steaks

Marinade:

1/2 cup tamari or good soy sauce
1/2 cup water
1 tablespoon sherry or Chinese rice wine
1 tablespoon grated ginger
1/2 cup minced scallions
2 cloves garlic, minced
2 teaspoons sesame oil
2 teaspoons cider vinegar
2 teaspoons sugar

Whisk all marinade ingredients together. Place the swordfish steaks in a zippered plastic bag, pour in the marinade, seal, and refrigerate for several hours.

Prepare the grill. Use a grilling rack or cover the grill with foil. Remove the swordfish from the marinade and grill until just cooked, a few minutes per side.

Grilled Swordfish Steaks
with Caper Sauce

Prep Time: 12 minutes ⧗ Grill: 8 minutes

Serves: 4

3 tablespoons drained capers
2 tablespoons lemon juice
¼ cup chopped fresh parsley
¾ teaspoon salt, divided
½ teaspoon freshly ground black pepper, divided
½ cup olive oil, divided
4 swordfish steaks

In a small glass bowl, mash the capers with a fork. Stir in the lemon juice, parsley, ½ teaspoon salt, ¼ teaspoon pepper, and ³⁄₈ cup of oil. Coat the swordfish with the remaining oil and season with the remaining salt and pepper.

Grill the swordfish for about 4 minutes. Turn and cook an additional 3 to 4 minutes or until done. Drizzle with the sauce before serving.

Did You Know?

• Frozen fish is available for your use anytime between shopping trips, so if you shop only every week or two, you might want to stock some in your freezer.
• Fresh fish should be used within one day of purchase.
• When buying fresh fish, check the smell—there should be no "fishy" odor. Also, the flesh should be firm, and the eyes should be clear.

Cajun Rainbow Trout

Prep Time: 10 minutes Broil: 5 minutes

Serves: 4

1 1/2 teaspoons paprika
3/4 teaspoon freshly ground pepper
salt
1/2 teaspoon dried oregano
1/2 teaspoon chili powder
1/2 teaspoon dry mustard
pinch cayenne pepper
1 pound rainbow trout fillets (1/2-inch thick)
2 teaspoons olive oil
2 teaspoons fresh parsley, chopped
1 green onion, chopped
lemon wedges

In a small bowl, combine paprika, pepper, salt, oregano, chili powder, mustard, and cayenne pepper; set aside. Pat the fillets dry and place skin side down on a broiler rack. Lightly brush both sides of the fillets with oil. Sprinkle both sides evenly with the paprika mixture. Broil 4 to 6 inches from the heat for 4 to 5 minutes or until the fish flakes easily when tested with a fork.

Arrange the fish on a warmed serving platter and sprinkle with parsley and chopped green onion. Squeeze one of the lemon wedges over the fish. Serve with the remaining wedges.

Grilled Trout with Herbs

Prep Time: 15 minutes   Grill: 4 minutes

Serves: 4

¼ cup olive oil
1 clove garlic, cut into thin slices
½ teaspoon crushed dried rosemary
½ teaspoon crushed dried basil
2 tablespoons red wine vinegar
½ teaspoon salt, divided
¼ teaspoon black pepper
6 trout fillets (about ¼-inch thick)

In a small saucepan, combine the oil, garlic, rosemary, and basil. Cook over low heat until the garlic begins to brown (approximately 2 minutes). Remove from the heat. Stir in the vinegar, ¼ teaspoon of the salt, and the pepper.

Put the trout fillets in a medium glass dish or stainless steel pan. Sprinkle with the remaining salt. Add half of the oil mixture and turn to coat evenly. Marinate for 1 to 2 minutes and then grill, skin side down, for 2 minutes. Turn and cook another 2 minutes longer. Pour the remaining oil mixture over the fish before serving.

Farm-Raised Fish

Until recently most farm-raised trout was almost tasteless compared to salmon. Now, several farm-raised fish like steelheads and orange-fleshed rainbow trout look and taste like salmon. These are best cooked like salmon and can be used in any salmon recipe.

Grilled Trout with Oregano

Prep Time: 10 minutes 🔲 Grill: 20 minutes

Serves: 4

3 cloves garlic, minced
2 tablespoons olive oil
2 tablespoons chopped fresh oregano
4 whole trout, cleaned
lemon wedges
salt and pepper

Combine the garlic, oil, and oregano, and rub the fish, inside and out, with the mixture. Put the fish in a grill basket or run a skewer lengthwise through each trout, from the mouth to the tail. Grill the trout on each side until done (time depends upon thickness of fish), approximately 20 minutes per pound. Serve with fresh lemon wedges, salt, and pepper.

To Grill Fish:

It's best to use a fish rack, which is a wire container with a handle, so the fish can be easily turned without breaking it up. Coat the fish with olive oil to prevent sticking; in addition you can lay lemon slices under and on top of the fish to add flavor, to prevent the fish from becoming embedded in the wire, and to make the fish easy to remove in one piece. Place on a grill preheated to medium; turn when it's half done. It is usually ready to serve in about 10 or 15 minutes.

Cheesy Tuna, Rice, and Peas

Prep Time: 10 minutes ⧗ Cook: 5 minutes

Serves: 4

1 ½ cups hot water
1 cube chicken bouillon
1 10-ounce package frozen baby peas
1 can condensed Cheddar cheese soup
1 6-ounce can tuna, drained and flaked
1 ½ cups instant rice

In a medium saucepan mix the water and bouillon until dissolved. Add the peas and bring to boil. Add the soup and stir until smooth. Add the tuna and bring to a boil again. Stir in the rice, cover, remove from heat, and let stand 5 minutes.

Fish You Can Grill

- Mahi-mahi
- Marlin fillets
- Whole baby coho salmon
- Chunk Norway salmon
- Shark fillets
- Whole gulf snapper
- Whole grey sole
- Swordfish fillets
- Pacific tuna

Tuna and Tomato "Pie"

Prep Time: 12 minutes   ⧗   Bake: 35 minutes

Serves: 6

butter
1 12-ounce can tuna, drained and flaked
1 tomato, seeded and chopped
⅓ cup shredded mozzarella cheese
1 cup milk
1 cup biscuit baking mix
2 eggs
1 teaspoon dried dillweed
salt and pepper to taste

Preheat the oven to 400°F. Butter a pie plate. Sprinkle the tuna, tomato, and cheese evenly in the pie plate. Blend all the remaining ingredients in a blender on high speed for 15 seconds, or with a hand beater or wire whisk for 1 minute, until smooth. Pour the mixture into the pie plate.

Bake for 30 to 35 minutes, or until a knife inserted in the center comes out clean. Allow to stand for 10 minutes before serving.

Tuna Melt

Prep Time: 10 minutes ⧖ Bake: 6 minutes

Serves: 3

1 6-ounce can tuna
²/₃ cup mayonnaise
salt and pepper to taste
3 slices bread, any type
1 thinly sliced tomato (optional)
3 thin bread-sized slices of Swiss or Cheddar cheese

Preheat the oven to 400°F.

Drain the tuna well and mix with the mayonnaise, salt, and pepper. Lightly toast the bread in the oven on the rack for 1 to 2 minutes, until light golden. Remove the bread and place on a baking sheet. Scoop the tuna mixture onto each slice of bread. If desired, place tomato slices on the tuna. Cover with cheese. Put the baking sheet in the oven on the top rack for 5 to 6 minutes, until cheese starts to bubble and is lightly browned. Serve immediately.

Quick Tip: Tuna

For a change of pace, use your favorite creamy salad dressing instead of mayonnaise in tuna fish.

Tuna Salad Sandwich

Prep Time: 10 minutes

Serves: 2 (generously)

1 6-ounce can tuna
2/3 cup mayonnaise
1 teaspoon regular or spicy mustard
1/3 cup chopped celery
salt and pepper to taste
lettuce
sliced tomato
4 slices bread, any kind

Drain tuna thoroughly. In a mixing bowl, combine all ingredients except lettuce, tomato, and bread. Spread mixture evenly on bread, and add lettuce and tomato.

Variations:
- Add 1/3 cup shredded carrots to the mixture.
- Reduce the mayo to 1/2 cup, and increase the mustard to 1 tablespoon. Add 1 tablespoon balsamic vinegar.
- Soak 1/3 cup sun-dried tomatoes in warm water. Drain and chop. Add to the mixture.

Tuna Teriyaki

Prep Time: 12 minutes   Grill: 4 minutes

Serves: 2 to 4

¼ cup soy sauce
2 tablespoons sugar
3 cloves garlic, minced
1 tablespoon rice vinegar
1-inch piece fresh ginger, peeled and chopped (about 4
    teaspoons)
1 pound fresh tuna

In a small bowl, stir together the soy sauce, sugar, garlic, vinegar, and ginger. Rinse the tuna under running water and pierce several times with a fork. Marinate for 15 minutes, turning once.

Remove the tuna from the marinade, and grill the tuna for about 4 minutes, depending on the thickness. Turn and brush with marinade halfway through cooking.

Cooking Fish by Texture

The way fish is cooked depends more on its texture than its size. Dense and sturdy fish like salmon can be prepared almost any way. Steaks and fresh fillets of Atlantic or pacific salmon are readily available. Salmon's high fat content (except for Coho) makes it suitable for grilling, roasting, or sautéing.

Seafood on English Muffins

Prep Time: 15 minutes ⧖ Cook: 10 minutes

Serves: 6

2 tablespoons butter
2 tablespoons all-purpose flour
$^1/_8$ teaspoon white pepper
1 cup 2% milk
1 egg, beaten
2 teaspoons lemon juice
2 cups seafood (crab, lobster, or firm whitefish), flaked
     into large pieces
8 English muffins, toasted
fresh parsley, chopped

In a heavy 1-quart saucepan, melt the butter over low heat. Blend in the flour and the pepper. Cook over low heat, stirring, until the mixture is smooth and bubbly. Remove from the heat and gradually stir in the milk.

Over medium heat, bring the white sauce to a boil, stirring constantly. Simmer for 1 minute, stirring constantly. Stir in the beaten egg. Heat for 1 to 2 minutes. Stir in the lemon juice and the seafood. Heat for 2 minutes. Serve over toasted English muffins and garnish with parsley.

Linguine with White Clam Sauce

Prep Time: 10 minutes   Cook: 10 minutes

Serves: 4

¹/₂ pound linguine
¹/₄ cup olive oil
4 cloves garlic, minced
2 tablespoons flour
2 tablespoons white vermouth
2 6¹/₂-ounce cans clams, juice reserved
¹/₄ cup chopped fresh parsley
salt and pepper to taste

Cook the linguine according to package directions, drain. In a large skillet, heat the oil and sauté the garlic until lightly golden, not burned. Add the flour, vermouth, and juice from the clams and stir, bringing to a boil. Add the clams and parsley and simmer a few minutes. Season with salt and pepper. Toss with the drained cooked pasta and serve immediately.

Crab-Stuffed Avocados

Prep Time: 15 minutes

Serves: 6

2 cups fresh crabmeat, drained and flaked
1 11-ounce can mandarin oranges, drained
¼ cup plus 1 tablespoon olive oil
½ cup sliced green onions with tops
2 tablespoons white wine vinegar
½ teaspoon garlic salt
3 small avocados, peeled
2 tablespoons lemon juice
lettuce leaves

Combine the crabmeat, oranges, oil, green onions, vinegar, and garlic salt, mixing well. Cut the avocados in half lengthwise and remove the seeds. Brush the avocado halves with lemon juice and fill with the crabmeat mixture. Arrange the avocado halves on lettuce leaves and serve.

French Country Mussels

Prep Time: 15 minutes ⧖ Cook: 12 minutes

Serves: 4

1 tablespoon olive oil
1 large onion, chopped
2 tablespoons minced garlic
1 16-ounce can peeled tomatoes, drained
½ cup fresh minced parsley
black pepper to taste
1 cup dry white wine
4 pounds fresh mussels, cleaned, with beards removed

In an 8-quart pot, heat the oil, and cook the onion and garlic until browned. Add the tomatoes, breaking them up with a wooden spoon. Add the parsley and pepper. Increase the heat, and cook for about 2 minutes. Add the wine and cook for another 2 minutes.

Add the mussels, tossing them well to coat. Cover, and cook the mussels for 3 minutes, stirring occasionally, until the mussels have opened. Discard any mussels that did not open up. Serve immediately.

Cleaning Mussels

When you first open a bag of mussels, throw away any with cracked shells or those that do not close to the touch. With the rest, scrape off the beards with a sharp knife, and scrub well with a stiff brush under running water. Place in a large pot and add cold water to cover. Let stand for 20 to 30 minutes. Drain them, and then rinse once more before cooking.

Coastal Oyster Stew

Prep Time: 12 minutes   Cook: 25 minutes

Serves: 4

1 pint shucked oysters, with their liquid
2 cups water
½ cup diced onions
½ cup diced celery
6 tablespoons sweet butter
1½ cups heavy cream
2 tablespoons chopped fresh parsley
1 tablespoon chopped fresh chervil
freshly ground pepper

Pick through the oysters, removing any bits of shell. Place in a small saucepan with their liquid and 2 cups of water. Heat slowly until the oysters begin to curl, about 5 minutes. Remove the oysters and set aside. Strain the liquid and set aside.

Slowly simmer the onion and celery in the butter in a soup pot until tender, about 6 minutes. Add the oyster liquid and heavy cream. Heat almost to the boiling point and simmer for 10 minutes. Add the oysters, parsley, and chervil. Season to taste with pepper. Simmer 1 minute more. Serve with crackers.

Barbara's Scallops

Prep Time: 12 minutes ⧗ Cook: 10 minutes

Serves: 2

2 cloves garlic, crushed
6 tablespoons butter
½ cup pale dry sherry
½ pound chopped mushrooms
3 scallions, chopped
½ cup chopped fresh parsley
½ pound baby scallops
2 tablespoons flour
½ cup half-and-half

Combine the garlic, butter, sherry, mushrooms, scallions, and parsley in a saucepan and sauté 2 minutes over medium heat. Add the scallops; stir and simmer for 1 minute. Add the flour and stir until scallops are lightly browned. Slowly add the half-and-half. Stir and cook until thickened and scallops are just done.

Coquilles St. Jacques Provençal

Prep Time: 15 minutes ⧖ Cook: 12 minutes

Serves: 6

2 pounds scallops
salt and pepper to taste
2 tablespoons minced onion
6 tablespoons butter, divided
½ pound sliced fresh or frozen mushrooms
2 large tomatoes, peeled and chopped
½ cup dry white wine
1 tablespoon minced chives
1 clove garlic, minced

Pat the scallops dry. If they are large, cut them into smaller pieces. Sprinkle the scallops lightly with salt and pepper.

Sauté the scallops along with the minced onion in 4 tablespoons of the butter until the onions look transparent, about 5 minutes, turning the scallops to brown all sides lightly. Remove the scallops and onions. Keep warm.

Add the remaining butter to the pan and sauté the mushrooms for 2 minutes. Add the tomatoes, wine, chives, and garlic, and simmer for 5 minutes. Pour over the scallops and serve.

Grilled Scallops with Bacon

Prep Time: 10 minutes ⧗ Grill: 8 minutes

Serves: 4

1 pound sea scallops
1 tablespoon olive oil
¾ teaspoon salt
½ teaspoon freshly ground black pepper
6 bacon slices, partially cooked and cut into 1-inch
  pieces
melted butter
fresh lemon wedges

Toss the scallops with oil, salt, and pepper. Thread on skewers, alternating with bacon pieces.

Preheat the grill. Grill the scallop and bacon skewers, turning once, until scallops are opaque in the center (approximately 3 to 4 minutes per side). Serve with melted butter and lemon wedges.

Scallop Preparation

The creamy and translucent scallop has the most complex flavor and enjoyable texture of any mollusk. Scallops are sold with their tendon, a white strip that attaches the muscle to the shell. To refine cleaning and preparation, strip this off before cooking.

Spiced Scallops

Prep Time: 12 minutes 　⧖　 Cook: 12 minutes

Serves: 4

1 ¹/₂ pounds sea scallops
¹/₂ teaspoon salt
¹/₄ teaspoon black pepper
1 tablespoon olive oil
¹/₃ cup sweet red wine
2 tablespoons fresh lemon juice
¹/₄ cup chopped fresh parsley
5 cloves garlic, minced
2 cups cooked long-grain rice

Sprinkle the scallops with salt and pepper. Heat 1 ¹/₂ teaspoons of the oil in a 10-inch cast-iron skillet or other heavy skillet until very hot—about 3 minutes. Add half the scallops; cook 2 minutes on each side or until browned. Remove the scallops from the pan and keep warm. Repeat the procedure with the remaining 1 ¹/₂ teaspoons oil and the remaining scallops. Remove the scallops from the pan.

Stir in the wine and lemon juice, scraping the pan to loosen bits. Add scallops, 3 tablespoons of the parsley, and garlic. Sauté 30 seconds over high heat. Serve the scallops over rice. Sprinkle with the remaining tablespoon of parsley.

Microwave Shrimp in Garlic and White Wine Sauce

Prep Time: 20 minutes ⧗ Microwave: 11 minutes

Serves: 4

1 pound large shrimp
3 tablespoons sweet butter, cut into small pieces
2 cloves garlic, minced
½ cup dry white wine
2 teaspoons finely chopped fresh parsley
1 teaspoon fresh lemon juice
salt and pepper to taste

Peel and devein the shrimp. Melt the butter in a 10-inch glass pie dish on high for 15 seconds. Stir in the garlic and microwave, uncovered, for 3 minutes, stirring once. Add the wine and microwave 5 minutes.

Stir in the shrimp and parsley. Cover with microwavable plastic wrap and vent one side. Microwave for 1 minute. Stir and carefully move the partially cooked shrimp toward the center and the uncooked shrimp toward the outside edges. Microwave, covered and vented, 1 minute longer. Allow to stand covered for 1 minute. Drizzle with lemon juice and season with salt and pepper. Serve immediately.

Spanish Grilled Shrimp

Prep Time: 10 minutes ⏳ Grill: 4 minutes

Serves: 2

½ pound jumbo shrimp in shells
sea salt
extra virgin olive oil
fresh lemon juice

Sprinkle both sides of the unshelled shrimp with salt and drizzle with oil. Let sit 15 minutes.

Preheat the grill. Place the shrimp on the grill and cook 1 to 2 minutes on each side, until shrimp meat is opaque. Sprinkle with lemon juice and serve.

Shrimp Basics

Avoid prepeeled and deveined shrimp, as cleaning before freezing may remove some of the flavor and texture from the shrimp. Shrimp should have no black spots on their shell; the spots indicate a breakdown of the meat has begun. Shrimp, like most fish, should smell of saltwater and nothing else.

Shrimp in Indian Sauce

Prep Time: 12 minutes ⧖ Cook: 10 minutes

Serves: 4

1 1/2 *pounds medium shrimp, shelled, cleaned, and*
   deveined
2 *tablespoons butter*
1/2 *cup finely chopped onion*
1/4 *teaspoon dried red pepper*
salt and pepper to taste
1/2 *teaspoon cardamom*
1/2 *teaspoon ground cumin*
juice of 1 lime
1 *cup sour cream*
1/2 *cup plain yogurt*
1/4 *cup chopped fresh cilantro*

Rinse the shrimp well and pat dry. Set aside. Heat the butter in a skillet and add the onion and red pepper. Cook briefly, then add the shrimp; salt and pepper to taste. Cook, stirring often, about 3 minutes. Add the cardamom and cumin and stir. Add the lime juice, sour cream, and yogurt. Stirring, bring gently to a boil. Sprinkle with cilantro and serve hot with saffron rice.

Stovetop Greek Rotelli

Prep Time: 12 minutes   Cook: 10 minutes

Serves: 4

2 1/2 cups marinara sauce
1 1/2 pounds large shrimp, peeled and deveined
8 ounces feta cheese, crumbled
1 pound rotelli pasta

Bring the marinara sauce to a simmer in a medium saucepan. Add the shrimp and simmer until cooked. Meanwhile, cook the pasta until al dente. Drain and place in a large serving bowl. Toss with the feta. Add the sauce and shrimp and toss again.

Quick Tip: Shrimp

To save time, buy pre-cleaned, frozen shrimp. Gently thaw frozen shrimp by rinsing them under lukewarm water.

Chapter 7

Vegetarian Entrees

E ven if your household is not vegetarian, you may wish to try some of these dishes. And you will want to include them on your quick menus when you are serving vegetarian guests.

Quick Tips

- Make an extra casserole and freeze it in an ovenproof dish. Later you can prepare it for serving without thawing it first by almost doubling the usual baking time.
- Remember that food placed in a deep casserole dish will take more time to cook than food placed in a shallow casserole dish. Try to match the size of the dish to the quantity of the food being placed in it.
- Foods bake faster in individual portions rather than in one large pan or dish. For example, use individual serving dishes for casseroles rather than one large casserole pan. These can be purchased inexpensively and often come with tight-fitting plastic lids to store unused and well-cooled portions in the refrigerator or freezer.
- To freeze a casserole, it's best to first cook or bake it, or perhaps just under-cook it. To conserve on the number of casserole dishes you use, first line the dish with heavy aluminum foil, then create the casserole in the dish, baking it if the recipe calls for it. Remove the casserole from the oven and allow it to cool, then cover it tightly and place the casserole in the freezer. When it is frozen solid, remove the casserole from the freezer, remove the solid block of food from the dish, and wrap it securely with plastic and freezer wraps, carefully pressing out any air. Be sure to label and date the package, and return it to the freezer.
- To reheat a frozen casserole, remove the plastic and foil wrapping and return the solid food to the original casserole dish. You can allow it to thaw in the refrigerator or return it directly to the oven, where it will take one and a half to two times the usual amount of time to heat.

Crustless Spinach Quiche

Prep Time: 15 minutes ⧖ Bake: 30 minutes

Serves: 6 to 8

1 *10-ounce package frozen chopped spinach*
3 *eggs*
1 *cup creamy cottage cheese*
2 *tablespoons minced onion*
$1/2$ *cup grated Parmesan cheese*
$1/8$ *teaspoon nutmeg*
1 *teaspoon seasoned salt*
pepper to taste
paprika

Preheat the oven to 350°F. Grease a 9-inch pie pan or an 8-inch square baking dish.

Thaw the spinach, drain in a colander, then squeeze in paper towels to remove excess moisture. In a blender, combine the eggs and cottage cheese on medium speed until well blended. Or, if you can beat the eggs well by hand with a wire whisk, then beat in the cottage cheese well. Stir in the Parmesan cheese, minced onion, nutmeg, salt, and pepper, then stir in the spinach until evenly distributed. Sprinkle with paprika. Bake 25 to 30 minutes, until the center is set.

Skillet (Crustless) Broccoli Quiche

Prep Time: 15 minutes Broil: 3 minutes

Serves: 6

6 slices bacon
3 cups chopped broccoli, fresh or frozen
1 1/2 tablespoons cooking oil
1/2 cup chopped onion
6 eggs
3/4 cup shredded Swiss cheese
3/4 cup shredded Cheddar cheese
salt and pepper to taste

Preheat the broiler.

Cook the bacon in a skillet until hard; drain well, crumble, and set aside. Bring a large saucepan about half full of water to a boil, then add the broccoli and cook 1 minute. (Broccoli can also be steamed or microwaved.) Drain well and set aside. In a 12-inch ovenproof skillet, heat the oil and sauté the onion for about 2 minutes.

Beat the eggs well. Stir in the cheeses, broccoli, salt and pepper, and bacon. When the onions have finished cooking, stir to distribute evenly (do not drain), and pour the egg mixture over them. Reduce the heat to medium and cook until set but still moist on top, about 8 minutes. Immediately put the skillet in the broiler, about 5 inches from the flame or element, and cook until the top is done but not browned.

Baba Ghanouj Sandwich Spread

Prep Time: 20 minutes ⧖ Refrigerate: 1 hour

Yield: about 3 cups

2 large eggplants
2 tablespoons sesame or vegetable oil
3 cloves garlic, divided
1 teaspoon salt
2 tablespoons extra-virgin olive oil
juice of 1 lemon
1 teaspoon cumin
1/4 cup tahini
ground black pepper to taste

Preheat the oven to 450°F.

Peel the eggplant and cut into 1-inch cubes. Toss with the sesame oil, 1 chopped clove of garlic, and salt. Spread in a single layer on a baking sheet, and roast until soft and lightly browned, about 15 minutes. Allow to cool slightly.

In a blender or food processor, blend the eggplant, olive oil, lemon juice, remaining 2 cloves garlic (peeled and quartered), cumin, tahini, and pepper. (It may be necessary to do more than one batch; if so, divide ingredients evenly, then combine all batches well.) Refrigerate for at least an hour, or up to 4 days.

After refrigeration, the spread can be brought to room temperature for serving. Stir if any separation has occurred.

Pitas with Baba Ghanouj

Prep Time: 12 minutes   Warm: 4 minutes

Serves: 4

4 whole-wheat pitas
³/₄ cup Baba Ghanouj (page 197)
1 cup fresh alfalfa sprouts
1 large vine-ripened tomato, thinly sliced
1 medium cucumber, peeled and thinly sliced

Preheat the oven to 300°F.

Warm the pitas in the oven for 3 to 4 minutes. Spread about 3 tablespoons Baba ghanouj in each warm pita and layer with sprouts, tomato, and cucumber.

Quick Tip: Cucumbers

If slippery cucumber seeds bother you, look for specifically grown seedless cucumbers in the grocery store. These longer, thin cucumbers taste just as good.

Basic Frittata

Prep Time: 15 minutes   ⧗   Cook: 20 minutes

Serves: 4

1 tablespoon olive oil
1 clove garlic, minced
¹/₄ cup chopped onion
³/₄ cup packaged broccoli slaw, or shredded broccoli,
*   or other shredded or diced vegetables*
4 eggs
salt and pepper to taste
¹/₂ cup shredded packaged Italian-blend cheeses or other
*   shredded cheese*
¹/₄ cup sliced black olives

In a 10-inch skillet heat the oil; sauté the garlic, onion, and broccoli or other vegetables until crisp-tender (no more than 5 minutes). Beat the eggs well and add salt and pepper to taste. When vegetables are done, distribute them evenly in the skillet with a spatula. Sprinkle the olives over top and pour the eggs over them. Sprinkle the cheese over the eggs. Reduce the heat to medium-low. As the eggs thicken, lift the edges with a spatula and allow the liquid on top to run underneath.

Traditionally, frittatas are placed under the broiler to finish cooking the top when the eggs are set. Or, you can cover the skillet after adding the cheese (do not cover tightly) and allow to cook until the eggs are completely done, up to 10 minutes.

Fettuccine Frittata à la Pesto

Prep Time: 10 minutes ⏳ Cook: 15 minutes

Serves: 4

water
1 3-ounce package dried tomato halves, halved or quartered
1 9-ounce package fresh spinach and/or egg fettuccine noodles or 8 ounces dried spinach or egg noodles
3 tablespoons prepared pesto
4 eggs, lightly beaten
¼ cup milk
fresh basil leaves for garnish (optional)
grated Parmesan cheese (optional)

Bring a large pot of water to boiling. Add the dried tomatoes and noodles and cook until al dente, about 8 to 10 minutes. Drain well. Return to the pot. Add the pesto. Toss until the noodles are evenly coated.

In a small bowl, beat together the eggs and milk until blended. Pour over the noodle mixture. Cook over medium heat, gently turning with a pancake turner, until the eggs are thickened and no visible liquid egg remains. Garnish with basil leaves, if desired. Serve immediately with cheese and additional pesto, if desired.

Black Beans, Tomatoes, and Rice

Prep Time: 10 minutes ⧖ Cook: 15 minutes

Serves: 4

2 cloves garlic
1 medium onion
1 14.5-ounce can stewed tomatoes
1 15-ounce can black beans, rinsed and drained
²⁄₃ cup water
¹⁄₂ teaspoon oregano
1¹⁄₂ cups instant brown rice

Sauté the garlic and onion in a bit of water or oil. Stir in the tomatoes, beans, water, and oregano. Bring to a boil. Add the rice. Bring to a boil again. Reduce the heat. Cover and simmer 5 minutes. Let stand for another 5 minutes.

Quick Tip: Sautéing

For a light taste, sauté onions and garlic in extra virgin olive oil, canola oil, or vegetable oil. For a richer flavor, use a darker olive oil or butter.

Caribbean Beans and Rice

Prep Time: 12 minutes ⧖ Cook: 10 minutes

Serves: 6

*1 large pimiento or roasted red pepper cut in short,
    thin strips*
$^1/_2$ green pepper cut in short, thin strips
2 cloves garlic, finely chopped
1 $^1/_2$ teaspoons olive oil
2 16-ounce cans black beans, drained and rinsed
2 tablespoons white vinegar
5 to 10 dashes hot pepper sauce
3 cups cooked white rice (1 cup raw)
3 tablespoons finely chopped fresh cilantro
salt and pepper to taste

Sauté the pimiento, green pepper, and garlic in the oil in a large
sauté pan for 2 minutes. Add the black beans, vinegar, and hot
pepper sauce. When hot, reduce the heat to low, cover, and simmer
5 minutes. Stir in the rice and cilantro. Taste and adjust the seasonings. Serve with additional hot pepper sauce.

Cashew Curry

Prep Time: 12 minutes ⧖ Cook: 15 minutes

Serves: 4

2 tablespoons olive oil
³/₄ cup cashews
2 medium onions, minced
1 tablespoon curry powder
2 cloves garlic, minced
1 teaspoon salt
1 teaspoon grated fresh ginger
¹/₄ cup water
1 block firm tofu, cubed
2 red peppers, cut into strips
1 10-ounce package frozen peas

Heat the oil in a skillet. Add the cashews and onions and sauté over medium heat. Cook for 5 minutes. Reduce the heat and add the curry, garlic, salt, ginger, water, tofu, and peppers. Cover and cook for 5 minutes. Add the peas. Cook for 5 more minutes.

Quick Tip

The microwave can greatly speed up meal preparation, but it doesn't evenly heat the food. If your microwave oven doesn't automatically rotate the food, you will need to periodically stop the oven and manually turn the dish a quarter turn, always rotating the dish in the same direction. Other tips: Stop the oven and stir watery foods like soups and stews because the edges heat up and leave the center cold. If you can't stir the food, try rearranging it.

Classic Swiss Fondue

Prep Time: 15 minutes ⧖ Cook: 15 minutes

Serves: 6

1 clove garlic, halved
2½ tablespoons flour
1 cup vegetable broth
⅔ cup evaporated milk
½ teaspoon brandy extract
2 ounces Swiss cheese, shredded
2 tablespoons grated Parmesan cheese
3 ounces cream cheese, cubed
⅛ teaspoon freshly ground pepper
⅛ teaspoon ground nutmeg
1 loaf crusty French bread, cubed

Rub the inside of a fondue pot or saucepan with cut sides of the garlic. Discard the garlic. Whisk the flour and ¼ cup of the broth in a measuring cup until blended. Add the remaining broth and milk to the pot, and heat over low heat until very hot but not boiling. Whisk in the extract and the flour mixture. Cook, stirring constantly, 2 to 6 minutes. Stir in the Swiss, Parmesan, and cream cheeses, pepper, and nutmeg. Cook, stirring constantly, until the cheeses melt and the mixture is very smooth.

If you don't have a fondue pot, transfer to a Crock-Pot or casserole with a warming unit. Serve with bread cubes.

Colorful Avocado Spirals

Prep Time: 12 minutes ⧖ Cook: 5 minutes

Serves: 4

2 tablespoons unsalted butter
¼ cup chopped scallions, white and green parts
1 teaspoon grated orange peel
1 teaspoon grated lemon peel
½ teaspoon coriander
¾ cup light cream
¼ cup plain yogurt
salt and freshly ground pepper to taste
2 to 3 avocados, cut into 1-inch cubes
1 tablespoon salt
1 pound of tricolor spirals

Melt butter in a large skillet over low heat. Add scallions and sauté 1 minute. Add orange and lemon peels and coriander. Stir and remove from heat.

In a bowl, combine the cream and yogurt, and salt and pepper to taste. Stir well.

Pour the cream mixture into the skillet, carefully add the cut-up avocado, and heat through on a low heat. Do not boil or the sauce will curdle and the avocado will become mushy.

Meanwhile, bring at least 4 quarts of water to a rolling boil. Add 1 tablespoon of salt. Add pasta and stir to separate. Cook until al dente. Drain. Transfer to a warm serving bowl. Pour sauce over pasta and toss carefully.

Crazy Ziti

Prep Time: 12 minutes   Cook: 20 minutes

Serves: 4

5 to 6 cloves garlic, minced
1 teaspoon red pepper flakes
3 tablespoons olive oil
3 tomatoes, chopped
¼ cup dry vermouth
¼ cup whole kalamata olives
1 7-ounce can Italian tuna, packed in olive oil
1 tablespoon capers
¼ cup chopped fresh parsley
1 tablespoon chopped fresh oregano
1 pound ziti pasta, cooked and rinsed

In a large heavy skillet sauté the garlic and red pepper flakes in the olive oil.

When the garlic is just about brown, add the tomatoes, vermouth, olives, tuna, capers, parsley, and oregano, and cook over a high flame until the sauce comes together, about 10 minutes.

Add the pasta to the tomato mixture and reheat over a low flame. Stir the sauce and pasta until well blended. Cook for a few minutes to let the pasta absorb the sauce and to make it piping hot.

Eggplant and Tomatoes with Gemelli

Prep Time: 12 minutes ⧗ Cook: 2 minutes

Serves: 4

2 tablespoons olive oil
3/4 cup onion, chopped
3 cloves garlic, minced
3/4 pound eggplant, cut in 1/2- to 1-inch cubes
2 tablespoons balsamic vinegar
1/2 cup chicken broth
1 16-ounce can Italian plum tomatoes with juice
1 tablespoon tomato paste
1/2 teaspoon dried oregano
2 tablespoons chopped fresh basil
dash hot red pepper flakes
salt to taste
12 ounces gemelli pasta, cooked

In a large, deep skillet, heat the oil over medium heat. Add the onion and cook until softened. Add the garlic and sauté briefly. Add the eggplant, vinegar, and chicken broth. Cover and cook until the eggplant is tender, about 10 minutes. Add the tomatoes, breaking them up with a wooden spoon, tomato paste, and oregano. Cook uncovered until the sauce becomes slightly thickened.

Stir in the basil and red pepper flakes. Add salt to taste. Combine the sauce with the hot pasta and toss thoroughly.

Fennel with Olive Oil and Smoked Mozzarella

Prep Time: 12 minutes   Grill: 20 minutes

Serves: 6

3 fennel bulbs, leaves trimmed off to about 6 inches
6 tablespoons extra virgin olive oil
sea salt
6 slices smoked mozzarella cheese

Preheat the grill.

Wash the fennel, trim any browned edges, and slice in half lengthwise. Place the fennel in a vegetable basket, wire fish basket, or on a sheet of foil. Brush with olive oil and sprinkle lightly with sea salt. Cook over medium-heat, turning once, about 20 minutes, or until a skewer piercing the bulb moves through easily.

In the last moments before removing from the grill, lay a slice of mozzarella cheese over the fennel and allow it to melt slightly before serving.

Fettuccine with Light Alfredo Sauce

Prep Time: 10 minutes ⧖ Cook: 5 minutes

Serves: 6

1 cup evaporated skim milk
$^1\!/_2$ cup grated Parmesan cheese
$^1\!/_2$ cup finely chopped fresh parsley
1 pound fettuccine, cooked
$^1\!/_4$ teaspoon white pepper
pinch of red pepper flakes (optional)

Heat the evaporated milk in a deep saucepan over medium heat. Simmer, but do not boil. Add the Parmesan cheese and parsley. As soon as the cheese has melted and the sauce is thick and creamy, remove from the heat and toss with the pasta. Season to taste with white pepper and red pepper flakes if desired. Serve immediately.

How to Cook Pasta

1. Fill a large pot with water—at least 4 quarts of water for 1 pound of pasta, 6 quarts if a large enough pot is available.
2. Bring the water to a boil and add 1 teaspoon of salt.
3. Add 1 tablespoon olive or vegetable oil if desired, which will help prevent the water from boiling over. It will also help prevent the pasta from sticking together.
4. Add the pasta when the water is at a roiling boil—not before.
5. Stir occasionally to prevent the pasta from sticking to the bottom of the pot.

Fusilli with Fresh Herbs and Ricotta

Prep Time: 15 minutes ⧖ Cook: 10 minutes

Serves: 4

1 15-ounce container part-skim ricotta cheese
²/₃ cup low-fat (1%) milk
¹/₄ grated Parmesan cheese
1 tablespoon olive oil
³/₄ cup chopped onion
3 cloves garlic, minced
¹/₂ cup chopped fresh basil
¹/₄ cup chopped scallions, including green parts
¹/₄ cup chopped fresh parley
salt and freshly ground pepper to taste
1 tablespoon salt
1 pound fusilli

In a food processor or blender, combine the ricotta cheese, milk, and Parmesan and process until smooth. Set aside.

In a large, deep skillet, heat the oil over medium heat. Add the onion and sauté until nearly browned. Add the garlic and cook until soft. Add the ricotta mixture and fold in the basil, scallions, and parsley. Cook until heated through. Season with salt and pepper.

Meanwhile, in a large pot, bring at least 4 quarts of water to a rolling boil. Add 1 tablespoon salt. Add the pasta, stir to separate, and cook until al dente. Drain.

Add the pasta to the skillet holding the ricotta mixture and toss well so that the pasta is coated. Transfer to a warm serving bowl.

Gazpacho Pasta with Cannellini Beans

Prep Time: 15 minutes ⧗ Cook: 10 minutes

Serves: 4

1 tablespoon salt
1 pound radiatori or ruffled pasta
3 large ripe tomatoes, finely diced
2 cucumbers, peeled, seeded, and finely diced
1 red onion, diced
2 cups vegetable juice
3 tablespoons red wine vinegar
1 16-ounce can cannellini beans, rinsed well and drained
¼ cup chopped fresh parsley
salt and freshly ground pepper to taste
1 tablespoon butter
½ cup fresh bread crumbs

In a large pot, bring at least 4 quarts water to a rolling boil. Add 1 tablespoon salt. Add the pasta, stir to separate, and cook until al dente. Drain. Rinse under cold water until cool and drain again.

In a large bowl, stir together the tomatoes, cucumbers, onion, vegetable juice, vinegar, beans, parsley, salt, and pepper. Add the pasta and toss to coat evenly.

In a small sauté pan, melt the butter over medium heat. Add the bread crumbs and toss to coat with butter; stir constantly until the bread crumbs are toasted.

Just before serving, sprinkle the toasted crumbs over the pasta.

Grilled Eggplant

Prep Time: 12 minutes ⧖ Strain: 1 hour ⧖ Grill: 10 minutes

Serves: 4

2 cloves garlic, minced
½ cup olive oil
salt
freshly ground pepper
2 medium eggplants
2 tablespoons red wine vinegar

In a mixing bowl, combine the garlic, olive oil, a pinch of salt, and pepper; set aside. Cut the eggplants into lengthwise slices about ¼-inch thick. Sprinkle with salt and set aside to drain on a sloping board or in a strainer for at least 1 hour so they will lose their bitter juices.

Preheat the grill. Rinse the eggplant slices to remove the salt, and dry with paper towels. Brush the slices with the oil and garlic mixture and grill for 3 to 5 minutes on each side. Transfer to a serving plate and let cool. Sprinkle with vinegar and serve.

Grilled Portobello Mushrooms

Prep Time: 10 minutes ⧗ Grill: 4 minutes

Serves: 4

4 large Portobello mushrooms
olive oil
salt and pepper to taste
10 fresh sage leaves
1 teaspoon chopped fresh parsley
¼ cup unsalted butter
lemon wedges

Preheat the grill. Brush the mushrooms with olive oil and sprinkle with salt and pepper. Put the sage leaves, parsley, and butter into a small pan and set over low heat (or on the grill) for 5 minutes or until the butter is aromatic. Grill the mushrooms about 2 minutes on each side or until tender.

Put the mushrooms on individual plates and spoon the sage-parsley seasoned butter (including sage leaves) over each mushroom. Squeeze fresh lemon juice over the mushrooms just before serving.

Linguine with Sun-Dried Tomatoes

Prep Time: 15 minutes ⧗ Cook: 5 minutes

Serves: 6

1 tablespoon salt
1 pound linguine
3 tablespoons unsalted butter, divided
1/3 cup olive oil
1 cup thinly sliced mushrooms
1/2 cup minced scallions
3/4 cup sun-dried tomatoes, coarsely chopped
1 tablespoon fresh lemon juice
1/2 teaspoon dried thyme
salt and freshly ground pepper to taste
2 cups chopped spinach leaves
1/2 cup freshly grated Parmesan cheese

In a large pot, bring at least 4 quarts of water to a rolling boil. Add 1 tablespoon salt. Add the linguine, stir to separate, and cook until not quite al dente. Reserve 1 cup of the pasta cooking water. Drain. Transfer the pasta to a warm bowl and toss with 1 tablespoon of the butter while making the sauce.

In a large, deep skillet, heat the oil over medium heat. Sauté the mushrooms and scallions for 4 minutes. Add the sun-dried tomatoes, pasta water, lemon juice, and thyme, and season with salt and pepper to taste. Simmer briefly. Swirl in the remaining butter. Add the spinach and toss just to coat. Add the linguine, toss again, and transfer to a warm bowl. Sprinkle with Parmesan cheese and serve.

Meatless Burritos

Prep Time: 15 minutes ⧗ Cook: 30 minutes

Serves: 4

1 16-ounce can kidney beans, drained
1 10-ounce can enchilada sauce, mild or hot
1 cup water
1 16-ounce can whole tomatoes, diced, liquid reserved
1 cup corn (fresh or frozen)
$1/2$ cup peas (fresh or frozen)
1 cup shredded carrot
$1 1/2$ cups cooked brown rice
10 to 12 flour tortillas
$1 1/2$ cups shredded Monterey Jack or Cheddar cheese
sour cream

In a large, deep skillet with a lid, combine the beans, enchilada sauce, water, tomatoes, and vegetables. Mix well and bring to a boil over medium heat. Stir in the cooked rice. Cover and reduce heat. Simmer until the liquid is absorbed, about 20 minutes, stirring occasionally.

Warm the tortillas in the microwave or conventional oven. Place $1/2$ cup of the mixture in the middle of each tortilla and top with cheese. Fold and serve with sour cream.

Meatless Chili

Prep Time: 12 minutes   ⧗   Cook: 25 minutes

Serves: 4

1 tablespoon olive oil
2 Spanish onions, chopped
1 teaspoon cumin
½ teaspoon cinnamon
4 cloves garlic, minced
1 35-ounce can whole tomatoes
    with purée, drained, with
    liquid reserved

⅓ cup water
1 tablespoon Tabasco sauce
   salt to taste
1 cup bulgur wheat
1 19-ounce can kidney beans,
    drained (or two 8-ounce
    cans)

Heat the oil in a skillet over medium heat for 20 seconds. Add the onions and cook until translucent. Add the cumin, cinnamon, and garlic. Stir, then add the reserved tomato liquid along with the water, Tabasco, and salt. Cook for 5 minutes.

Add the bulgur; stir and cook for 5 more minutes. Chop the canned tomatoes and add to the skillet with the kidney beans. Reduce the heat; cover and cook for 10 more minutes.

Bulgur

Bulgur is a crunchy, nutty wheat grain that adds texture to dishes. Similar to cracked wheat, it can be substituted for rice or tiny pasta in many menus. It is also easy to prepare, for all you need to do is pour boiling water over it and then let it sit until the liquid is absorbed. You can create your own recipes by adding onion and garlic, vegetables, chicken, or anything else you'd like.

Hummus

Prep Time: 12 minutes ⧗ Cook: 2 hours

Yield: about 3 cups

2 cups dried garbanzo beans (chickpeas)*
6 cups water
4 cloves garlic, peeled and chopped
1 cup tahini
1 teaspoon dried cumin
1 teaspoon salt
3 tablespoons olive oil
¹/₂ cup lemon juice, divided

Soak garbanzo beans in cold water in a large kettle for 24 hours (or, alternatively, bring to a boil, boil for 1 minute, remove from heat, and allow to stand for 1 hour).

When beans have been soaked by one of these methods, bring them to a boil. Turn down the heat and simmer for 2 hours. Drain and pick out any shells. Rinse to clear off any thick juice.

In a food processor or blender, blend the garbanzos until almost smooth. Add the chopped garlic, tahini, cumin, salt, olive oil, and half of the lemon juice. Blend until smooth. Taste, and add more lemon juice, salt, or cumin to taste. Hummus can be served at room temperature or cooler; refrigerate for up to 4 days.

*Canned garbanzo beans can also be used. Use 2 16-ounce cans, well drained.

Meatless Tacos

Prep Time: 15 minutes ⧖ Cook: 6 minutes

Serves: 4

1 tablespoon olive oil
1 small yellow onion, chopped
1 stalk celery, chopped
¹/₃ cup chopped sweet red or green
pepper
1 teaspoon finely chopped jalapeño
pepper
1 clove garlic, minced
1 19-ounce can chickpeas, drained
2 tablespoons picante sauce or salsa

¹/₂ teaspoon ground cumin
salt and pepper
8 taco shells, warmed

Toppings:

1¹/₂ cups shredded Cheddar cheese
1 cup shredded iceberg lettuce
1 cup salsa
1 teaspoon chopped fresh cilantro

In a large, heavy skillet, heat the oil over medium-high heat; cook the onion, celery, sweet pepper, jalapeño pepper, and garlic in the oil, stirring often, for 3 minutes or until softened. Add the chickpeas, picante sauce, and cumin. Cook, stirring, for 2 minutes or until heated through. Season with salt and pepper to taste.

Spoon into taco shells. Top each taco with cheese, lettuce, salsa, and cilantro.

Iceberg Lettuce

To put the crunch back into iceberg lettuce (the only kind to serve in tacos), plunge leaves into cold water and let stand for 5 minutes. Drain, dry well, and store, wrapped in cotton towels, in the crisper of the refrigerator.

Original Egg Salad Sandwich

Prep Time: 12 minutes 〰 Chill: 1 hour

Serves: 3 (generously)

6 hard-boiled eggs, peeled
1/3 cup chopped celery
1 tablespoon pickle relish
1 teaspoon spicy mustard (such as Dijon)
2/3 cup mayonnaise
salt and pepper to taste
6 slices wheat or white bread
lettuce and sliced tomato (optional)

Run peeled eggs under water to make sure all shell is removed. Coarsely chop the eggs. In a mixing bowl, combine the eggs, celery, relish, mustard, mayonnaise, and salt and pepper. Chill thoroughly.

Spread on bread, and add lettuce and tomato, if desired.

Add-a-kick suggestions:
• Add 1 teaspoon curry powder.
• Replace mayo with cottage cheese.
• Add 2 teaspoons garlic powder.

Pasta with Garlic and Olive Oil

Prep Time: 10 minutes ⧖ Cook: 10 minutes

Serves: 4 to 6

Aglio e olio, Italian for garlic and oil, could not be simpler or better. This sauce sometimes includes red pepper flakes, an essential ingredient by some counts. If desired, add ¼ teaspoon pepper flakes and see for yourself.

½ cup virgin olive oil
1 tablespoon finely minced garlic
2 tablespoons finely chopped flat-leaf parsley
salt to taste
16 ounces pasta

In a large saucepan gently cook the garlic and optional red pepper flakes in the olive oil until the garlic is soft and barely golden. Add the parsley and salt to taste, and remove the pan from the heat.

Cook the pasta in the meantime and when al dente, toss in the pan with the sauce.

Preventing Boil-Over

A lump of butter or a few teaspoons of cooking oil added to water when boiling rice, noodles, macaroni, or spaghetti will prevent the liquid from boiling over.

Pasta with Jalapeño Butter Sauce

Prep Time: 10 minutes   Cook: 10 minutes

Serves: 4 to 6

6 tablespoons unsalted butter
¼ cup diced jalapeño peppers
½ teaspoon minced garlic
1 ½ cups peeled and diced tomatillos (available in the
*   fresh produce sections of most supermarkets)*
2 tablespoons chopped fresh cilantro
½ cup dry white wine
3 tablespoons fresh lime juice
salt and freshly ground black pepper to taste
16 ounces pasta

In a large skillet, melt the butter over medium heat. Add the jalapeños, garlic, and tomatillos and sauté briefly. Add the cilantro, wine, lime juice, and salt and pepper to taste; simmer, stirring, for 3 minutes.

Serve hot over drained cooked pasta.

Pasta with Zucchini Sauce

Prep Time: 15 minutes ⧖ **Cook: 15 minutes**

Serves: 4 to 6

2 tablespoons olive oil
1 clove garlic, crushed
3 to 4 small zucchinis, cut into 2-inch-long strips
1 cup coarsely chopped walnuts
1 cup ricotta cheese
$1/2$ teaspoon dried hot red pepper flakes
1 large tomato, seeded and cut into cubes
16 ounces pasta

Heat a large skillet. Add the olive oil and in it sauté the garlic until just golden. Add the zucchini and sauté until crisp-tender. Add the walnuts, ricotta, and pepper flakes. Stir in the tomato and continue to cook until just heated.

Serve hot over drained cooked pasta.

Pasta for Sauced Dishes

When cooking pasta to be used in sauced pastas rather than baked dishes follow the timing directions on the package. Fresh pasta cooks in a much shorter time than dried pasta. Test the pasta when the end of the cooking time nears to determine when it is done "al dente" or "to the tooth." Al dente describes pasta that is firm to the bite. It will be chewy rather than soft or mushy. Al dente is the preferred level of doneness for most pasta recipes.

Pasta with Salsa Verde (Green Sauce)

Prep Time: 10 minutes ⧗ Cook: 10 minutes

Serves: 4 to 6

*1 cup lightly packed flat-leaf
    Italian parsley, leaves only*
2 anchovy fillets
2 cloves garlic
½ teaspoon salt
freshly ground black pepper

2 tablespoons lemon juice
½ cup olive oil
*1 tablespoon softened green
    peppercorns*
16 ounces pasta

In a blender or food processor with a metal blade, blend the parsley leaves, anchovies, garlic, salt, pepper, and lemon juice. When puréed, gradually add the olive oil. Remove the sauce to a bowl and stir in the whole green peppercorns.

Serve hot over drained cooked pasta.

Fresh or Dried Pasta?

Most of us grew up eating dried spaghetti out of a box. If you've ever eaten fresh pasta, it may actually seem mushy to you. Fresh pasta can be heavenly in taste and texture, but since it is fresh, it needs only a minute or two of cooking, just to heat through. Nowadays, you can buy freshly made pasta in the supermarket, and although it's more expensive than the boxed variety, you can look at it as a special treat. Read the label, however; many fresh pastas contain more egg than dried pastas do.

Pitas with Hummus

Prep Time: 15 minutes   Warm: 4 minutes

Serves: 4

4 whole-wheat pitas
³/₄ cup hummus (page 217)
1 large vine-ripened tomato, thinly sliced
1 cup shredded carrots
1 avocado, peeled and thinly sliced

Preheat oven to 300°F.

Warm the opened pitas in the oven for 3 to 4 minutes. Spread about 3 tablespoons hummus in each warm pita and layer with tomato, carrots, and avocado.

Quick Tip: Avocado Swap

If the fat content of the avocado worries you, substitute cucumber slices for this rich vegetable in sandwiches.

Quick Lasagna

Prep Time: 15 minutes 　 Bake: 45 minutes

Serves: 8

$1/4$ cup grated Parmesan cheese
1 cup ricotta cheese
1 cup shredded mozzarella cheese
1 28-ounce jar spaghetti sauce
1 12-ounce package no-cook lasagna noodles

Preheat oven to 350°F.

In a medium bowl, stir together the Parmesan cheese, ricotta cheese, and mozzarella. Spray a 9 × 13-inch baking dish with nonstick spray. Spread some of the sauce in the dish. Layer a third of the noodles atop the sauce. Spread a third of the cheese mixture over the noodles. Repeat the layers until the ingredients are used up, ending with sauce. Cover with foil.

Bake until heated through, about 45 minutes. Remove from the oven and let cool for 10 minutes before serving.

Quick Pasta with Basil and Tomatoes

Prep Time: 15 minutes ⧖ Cook: 5 minutes

Serves: 4

1 8- to 10-ounce package refrigerated angel hair pasta, or
   8 ounces dried pasta
4 tablespoons olive oil, divided
12 medium Roma tomatoes (use fewer if tomatoes are
   large)
2 or more cloves garlic, crushed
$^1/_4$ cup chopped fresh basil
$^1/_2$ cup shredded fresh Parmesan cheese

Break or cut the pasta into smaller pieces, and cook according to package directions, adding 1 tablespoon olive oil to the cooking water. Seed and coarsely chop the tomatoes (do not peel). In a large skillet, heat 3 tablespoons olive oil. Cook the garlic in the oil about 1 minute, then add the tomatoes and basil and cook just until warmed—do not allow the tomatoes to become mushy. In a large bowl, toss together the hot pasta, tomato mixture, and Parmesan cheese.

Rice with Black Beans and Ginger

Prep Time: 10 minutes 🕱 Cook: 25 minutes

Serves: 4

1 tablespoon olive oil
2 cloves garlic, minced
2 tablespoons chopped onion
1 tablespoon peeled and minced fresh ginger
1 cup white rice
2 cups chicken broth
1 cup cooked black beans
salt and pepper to taste

In a skillet, heat the oil over medium heat. Add the garlic, onion, and ginger and cook, stirring, for 1 minute. Add the rice and chicken broth. Lower the heat, cover, and cook until the rice is tender and the liquid has been absorbed, about 20 minutes.

Add the black beans, salt, and pepper, and stir to heat through, then serve.

Spinach and Pasta Frittata

Prep Time: 20 minutes ⧗ Cook: 10 minutes

Serves: 4

$^1/_2$ pound spaghetti, cooked and drained
$^1/_2$ cup finely diced fontina cheese
$^1/_2$ cup freshly grated Parmesan cheese
1 10-ounce package frozen chopped spinach, thawed and
    squeezed of all moisture
2 tablespoons chopped parsley
3 eggs, lightly beaten
salt and freshly ground pepper to taste
1 tablespoon unsalted butter

Mix together all the ingredients except the butter. In a large nonstick skillet melt the butter. Add the pasta mixture, and spread evenly over the pan. Cook until the bottom is set. Invert the omelet onto a large plate, then slip it back into the skillet and cook until completely set. Cut into wedges to serve.

Pasta for Baking

When cooking pasta to be used in baked dishes undercook by 1 or 2 minutes. Cook 1 or 2 minutes less than the shortest cooking time given in the package directions. The pasta will be a better consistency when the dish has been baked.

Summer Vegetable Paella

Prep Time: 8 minutes ⧗ Cook: 10 minutes

Serves: 6

1 teaspoon olive oil
3 cups broccoli florets
2 zucchini, sliced on the diagonal
1 tomato, diced
2 nectarines, pitted and sliced

In a large nonstick skillet, heat the oil over high heat. Add the broccoli and zucchini and cook, stirring often, for 5 minutes. Add the tomato and nectarines, cover, lower the heat to medium, and cook until the vegetables are crisp-tender, 2 to 3 minutes longer.

Quick Tip: Broccoli

To save time, buy pre-cut broccoli florets in the prepared salad section of the grocery store.

Summer Vegetable Spaghetti

Prep Time: 20 minutes   ⊠   Cook: 25 minutes

Serves: 8

2 cups small yellow onions, cut in eighths
2 cups chopped, peeled fresh ripe tomatoes
1 cup thinly sliced yellow squash
1 cup thinly sliced zucchini
1 1/2 cups fresh green beans
2/3 cup water
2 tablespoons minced fresh parsley
1 clove garlic, minced
1/2 teaspoon chili powder
1/4 teaspoon salt
1/8 teaspoon freshly ground black pepper
6 ounces tomato paste
1 pound uncooked spaghetti
1/2 cup grated Parmesan cheese

Combine the onions, tomatoes, yellow squash, zucchini, beans, water, parsley, garlic, chili powder, salt, and pepper in a large saucepan; cook for 10 minutes, then stir in the tomato paste. Cover and cook gently for 15 minutes, stirring occasionally, until the vegetables are tender.

Cook the spaghetti in unsalted water according to package directions.

Spoon the sauce over the drained hot spaghetti and sprinkle Parmesan cheese over the top.

Sweet and Sour Tofu

Prep Time: 15 minutes ⧖ Marinate: 5 hours ⧖ Stir-fry: 10 minutes

Serves: 6

1 pound tofu
¼ cup lemon juice
¼ cup tamari sauce
6 tablespoons water
¼ cup tomato paste
2 tablespoons honey
1 teaspoon ginger
4 cloves garlic, minced
8 scallions, minced

1 green bell pepper, sliced in
   strips
1 red bell pepper, sliced in
   strips
1 pound mushrooms
2 teaspoons oil
1 cup toasted cashews
3 cups hot cooked white rice

    Cut the tofu into small cubes; set aside. Combine the lemon juice, tamari, water, tomato paste, honey, ginger, and garlic; mix until well blended. Add the tofu to this marinade, stir gently, and let marinate for several hours (or overnight).

    Stir-fry the scallions, bell peppers, and mushrooms in the oil. After several minutes, add the tofu with all the marinade. Reduce heat, and continue to stir-fry until everything is hot and bubbly. Remove from the heat and stir in the cashews. Serve over rice.

Szechuan Tofu Stir-Fry

Prep Time: 20 minutes   Stir-fry: 10 minutes

Serves: 6

⅓ cup teriyaki sauce
3 tablespoons Szechuan spicy stir-fry sauce
2 teaspoons cornstarch
1 red bell pepper
½ pound snow peas
1 14-ounce can baby corn
1 onion, chopped
3 cups chopped bok choy
2 to 3 tablespoons oil, divided
1 cup broccoli florets
1 pound tofu, cubed
1 7-ounce can straw mushrooms
3 cups cooked white rice

Combine teriyaki sauce, stir-fry sauce, and cornstarch; set aside. Cut bell pepper into strips. Cut snow peas and baby corn in half. In the wok, stir-fry the onion and bok choy in 1 tablespoon of oil for 2 minutes. Add the broccoli and bell pepper; stir-fry 2 minutes. Remove from the wok.

Stir-fry the cubed tofu in 1 tablespoon of oil for 2 minutes; add more oil if necessary. Stir the sauce mixture and add it to the tofu; cook until bubbly. Add all the vegetables; heat through. Serve over hot rice.

Tomato-Basil Pasta

Prep Time: 10 minutes ⧗ Cook: 10 minutes

Serves: 3

¹/₄ cup extra virgin olive oil
2 cloves garlic, minced
2¹/₂ cups diced tomatoes
¹/₃ cup chopped fresh basil
salt and freshly ground pepper to taste
³/₄ cup chicken stock
1 tablespoon salt
12 ounces tomato fettuccine
¹/₄ cup freshly grated Parmesan cheese

In a large, deep skillet, heat the oil over medium heat. Add the garlic and sauté until soft. Add the tomatoes and basil and season with salt and pepper. Sauté for about 5 minutes. Add the chicken stock and bring to a simmer.

In a large pot, bring at least 4 quarts water to a rolling boil. Add 1 tablespoon salt. Add the pasta, stir to separate, and cook until al dente. Drain.

Combine the pasta with the sauce in the skillet. Stir to combine well. Top with Parmesan and serve.

Quick Tip: Plum Tomatoes

For a slightly different taste, substitute plum tomatoes for the regular variety.

Vegetable Basket Medley

Prep Time: 20 minutes Grill: 15 minutes

Serves: 6

8 ounces whole button mushrooms
12 cherry tomatoes
1 each: red, yellow, and green pepper, cut into strips
3 zucchini, thickly sliced
1 small onion, chunked
½ cup extra virgin olive oil
¼ cup freshly squeezed lemon juice
½ teaspoon crushed thyme
¼ teaspoon crushed mustard seed
¼ teaspoon ground black pepper

Preheat the grill. Wash and prepare all vegetables; slice off the ends of the mushrooms; remove the stems from the tomatoes. Set aside. Combine the oil, lemon juice, and seasonings in a large bowl and whisk together. Stir in the vegetables and toss until coated.

Spoon the vegetables into a grill basket, reserving any excess liquid for basting while grilling. Grill about 15 minutes or until desired texture is reached. Baste at least once.

Vegetable Wrap with Dill Sauce

Prep Time: 15 minutes

Serves: 4

Sauce:

1/2 cup plain (regular or low-fat) yogurt
1 medium cucumber, finely chopped
3 tablespoons chopped fresh dill or 1/2 tablespoon dried dill
1 teaspoon wine vinegar
1/2 teaspoon salt
freshly ground black pepper to taste

Other Ingredients:

4 tortillas (spinach or whole-wheat recommended)
about 8 leaves romaine lettuce
1/2 pound sliced provolone or other mild cheese
2 tomatoes, thinly sliced
1 small red onion, sliced thin or chopped
1 medium avocado, peeled and sliced
1 cup alfalfa sprouts

In a small bowl or in a food processor, mix the yogurt, cucumber, dill, vinegar, salt, and pepper. If mixing by hand, be sure to chop the cucumber very finely.

Spread a large spoonful of the sauce in the middle of a tortilla. Layer with the rest of the ingredients. Roll the tortilla halfway from the bottom, fold one side in about an inch so that no ingredients can slip out that side, and continue to roll the rest of the way. Repeat with the remaining tortillas. Serve immediately at room temperature, or chill before serving.

Wash Those Veggies!

• Vegetables should be washed carefully to remove dust and dirt.

• To retain the peel of root vegetables, wash with a stiff brush. Do not use a woven plastic or metal pad to wash vegetables as bits of each can loosen and fall unseen into the food.

• Leave the peel/skin on vegetables whenever possible unless you know or suspect the vegetable has been sprayed or waxed.

• The easiest and most efficient tool for peeling vegetables is a carbon-steel swivel bladed peeler which can be purchased at most supermarkets.

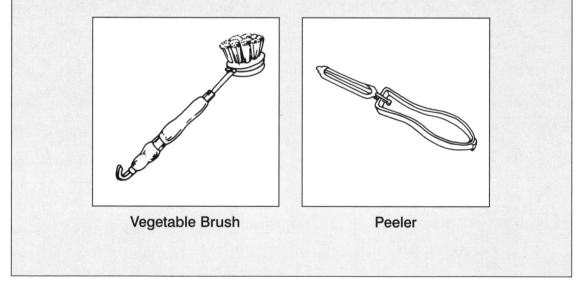

Vegetable Brush   Peeler

Chapter 8

Vegetables and Side Dishes

This is my favorite part of the meal, not only because vegetables look and taste great, but also because of their important nutritional contribution. Even if you aren't a gardener, marvelous fresh vegetables and herbs are now available nearly year-round, or you can stock the frozen or canned forms.

Steaming or simmering fresh vegetables until they are tender-crisp is all that is needed for a quick and colorful addition to your meal. Or you can enjoy one of the recipes or quick fixes that follow. Don't hesitate to experiment on your own!

Quick Fix: Vegetable combos

Instead of having a single vegetable, jazz up the colors and textures by cooking two together. Here are some ideas:

- Cauliflower and green peas
- Green peas and pearl onions
- Green peas and mushrooms
- Pea pods and mushrooms
- Carrot slices with lima beans
- Carrot slices with broccoli
- Diced carrots with French-style green beans
- Tomatoes and zucchini
- Carrots and celery
- Tomatoes and okra slices
- Cauliflower and red sweet peppers
- Brussels sprouts and celery slices
- Corn and green peas
- Diced carrots and peas

Quick Tip: Avoid the prep

You can purchase precut and cleaned fresh vegetables to save yourself some time, although these will cost more money.

Amazing Garlic Bread

Prep Time: 12 minutes 　⧖　 Grill: 12 minutes

Serves: 3

1 loaf French bread
½ cup virgin olive oil
4 cloves garlic, minced
freshly ground pepper to taste
¼ teaspoon onion salt
3 tablespoons butter, melted
1 teaspoon chopped fresh or dried parsley

Preheat the grill. Slice the bread into 1-inch slices without cutting all the way to the bottom of each slice.

Combine the remaining ingredients in a mixing bowl and stir well. Using a basting brush, apply to both sides of the bread slices without separating the slices too far. Wrap the entire loaf in aluminum foil and set on the grill. Flip over after 4 to 6 minutes and heat for another 4 to 6 minutes.

Quick Fix: Tomatoes

Halve fresh tomatoes horizontally and place the halves close together in an ovenproof pan, cut sides up. Sprinkle with Italian spice blend (available in the spice section of the store) or garlic salt. Place under the broiler about 2 minutes. Top with shredded or grated cheese, like Parmesan or mozzarella, and return to the broiler a few more seconds until the cheese is lightly browned. Prep time is only six minutes!

Apple Accompaniment

Prep Time: 15 minutes ⧗ Cook: 6 minutes

Yield: about 2 cups

3 tablespoons butter
2 cups sliced, chunked, or coarsely chopped apple
2 tablespoons packed brown sugar
1/2 teaspoon cinnamon
1/4 cup water

In a medium skillet, melt the butter over medium-high heat (do not allow to brown) and sauté the apples 2 to 3 minutes. In a small bowl, mix the brown sugar, cinnamon, and water. Add to the apples, reduce the heat to low, and continue cooking an additional 2 or 3 minutes. Apples should be tender but remain firm. Use as a topping for pancakes or an accompaniment to eggs or ham. It's also a great ice cream topping!

Seasoning variation: Add 1/4 teaspoon pumpkin pie spice to the cinnamon.

Quick Fix: Minted peas or carrots

Heat canned, fresh, or frozen peas or carrots or a combination of both. Drain and add 2 pats of butter plus 1/4 teaspoon crushed dried mint or 1 teaspoon finely snipped fresh mint.

Basic Drop Biscuits

Prep Time: 12 minutes   ⧖   Bake: 15 minutes

Yield: 12 biscuits

2 cups flour
1 tablespoon baking powder
½ teaspoon salt
1 tablespoon sugar
⅓ cup butter or shortening
¾ to 1 cup milk

Preheat the oven to 425°F. Sift together the flour, baking powder, and salt. Stir in the sugar. Cut the butter or shortening into the dry ingredients until the mixture resembles coarse crumbs. Add the milk all at once and mix quickly with a fork just until a dough forms.

Combine ingredients well but do not knead. Drop by tablespoons onto a greased cookie sheet. Bake 12 to 15 minutes, or until golden brown.

Buttermilk Biscuits: Add ¼ teaspoon baking soda and omit sugar. Substitute buttermilk for whole milk.

Quick Fix: Green beans with almonds or sesame seeds

Heat up canned or frozen French-cut green beans in a little liquid. Drain, then add a pat of butter plus some toasted sliced almonds or sesame seeds and perhaps a few drops of soy sauce.

California Rarebit*

Prep Time: 12 minutes ⧖ Cook: 10 minutes

Serves: 4

3 tablespoons butter, divided
1/2 cup dry white wine
2 1/2 cups cubed Jack cheese, divided
1 large egg, lightly beaten
1 teaspoon Worcestershire sauce
1/2 teaspoon crushed basil
2 cups sliced mushrooms
1/2 teaspoon garlic powder
toast points or triangles

Melt 1 tablespoon of the butter in the top of a double boiler. Add the wine and heat, then stir in 2 cups of the cheese. Heat until melted. Add a little of the cheese mixture to the beaten egg and then add the egg mixture back into the cheese. Cook and stir about 1 minute. Add the Worcestershire sauce and basil; set aside, keeping the sauce warm.

Sauté the mushrooms in the remaining butter until just tender, then sprinkle with the garlic powder. Remove from the heat.

Arrange toast points or triangles on individual heatproof plates. Spoon the sauce over the toast, then top with the sautéed mushrooms. Sprinkle with the remaining cheese and broil until bubbly.

*Rarebit is pronounced "rabbit" and is an open-faced sandwich with a tangy cheese sauce.

Chickpeas and Red Onions

Prep Time: 10 minutes

Serves: 4

$\frac{1}{2}$ cup slivered red onion
1 19-ounce can chickpeas, drained and rinsed
$\frac{1}{2}$ cup fresh parsley, chopped
2 tablespoons lemon juice
1 tablespoon olive oil
1 tablespoon capers, drained, rinsed, and coarsely
   chopped
$\frac{1}{2}$ cup crumbled feta cheese
red lettuce leaves

In a medium-sized bowl, cover the onions with cold water and let soak for 10 minutes. Drain well and return the onions to the bowl. Add the chickpeas, parsley, lemon juice, oil, capers, and feta cheese. Stir to combine. Season with salt and pepper. Serve on lettuce leaves.

Quick Tip: Prep ahead

Chop several days worth of vegetables at one time. Do this in your food processor for really quick preparation. Store the vegetables in plastic bags in the refrigerator, with the exception of onions, which should be stored in a tightly lidded glass jar to prevent the onion smell from contaminating other foods.

Chinese Coleslaw

Prep Time: 15 minutes   Chill: 1 hour

Serves: 6

4 cups shredded Chinese cabbage
1 8$\frac{1}{4}$-ounce can crushed pineapple, drained
1 8-ounce can sliced water chestnuts
1 cup snipped fresh parsley
$\frac{1}{4}$ cup sliced green onions
$\frac{1}{4}$ cup mayonnaise
1 tablespoon mustard
1 teaspoon grated gingerroot

Combine the cabbage, pineapple, water chestnuts, parsley, and onion. Cover and chill.

For the dressing, combine the mayonnaise, mustard, and ginger-root. Cover and chill.

Spoon the dressing over the cabbage mixture; toss to coat.

Quick Fix: Stir-fried vegetables

Toss together your choice of celery, carrots, green or yellow or red sweet peppers, onions, broccoli, cauliflower, and water chestnuts (or buy vegetable blends already cleaned and chopped) and stir-fry in olive oil until just tender. The many bright colors make a striking dish and the combination of flavors is delicious. Add a few kumquat slices to the stir-fry for a citrus zip that will make your vegetable stir-fry absolutely wonderful!

Couscous with Yogurt and Fruit

Prep Time: 5 minutes ⧖ Cook: 6 minutes

Serves: 4

1 cup milk
1 tablespoon butter
¼ teaspoon salt
⅔ cup quick cooking couscous
½ cup vanilla yogurt
2 tablespoons sugar
½ cup diced fresh fruit or berries
sugar

In a medium saucepan, combine the milk, butter, and salt and bring to a boil. Stir in the couscous. Cover. Remove from the heat and let stand 5 minutes. Fluff the couscous with a fork to separate. Stir in the yogurt and sugar, and fold in the fruit. Sprinkle with sugar.

Pita Bread

Although pita bread has long been a Middle Eastern staple, Americans have only recently become familiar with this pocket bread.

It's not surprising that it has caught on so quickly. You can stuff a pita with everything from vegetables to peanut butter and, unlike a conventional sandwich, the filling won't fall out of the sides. That makes a pita sandwich a genuinely portable meal. In addition, pita bread is virtually fat free. Try some of the new flavors, from onion to sourdough.

Easy No-Cook Pasta Sauce

Prep Time: 12 minutes ⧗ Chill: 3 hours

Yield: Enough sauce for 1 pound of cooked pasta

2 1/2 cups fresh, ripe tomatoes, chopped
1/2 cup virgin olive oil
1 green bell pepper, seeded and chopped
1 1/2 cups cubed white cheese (Gouda, provolone, or
  Monterey Jack)
4 cloves garlic, minced
1 tablespoon lemon juice
1/4 cup fresh basil
1/2 teaspoon dried oregano
salt and pepper to taste

In a large mixing bowl, stir together all ingredients. Chill up to 3 hours before serving.

Pasta Is Low-Fat

One cup of cooked spaghetti or elbow macaroni, without salt or oil has 0.1 grams of saturated fat, 0 mgs cholesterol and only 4 calories from fat with a total number of 197 calorie. That's something to think about when choosing a quick, low-fat meal. Spice up the pasta sprinkling garlic powder and fresh or dried basil on the hot pasta. Or for a really zesty pasta dish, add chopped hot peppers. Remember—a little hot pepper goes a long way.

Eggs in Tomato Broth

Prep Time: 8 minutes ⧗ Cook: 20 minutes

Serves: 2

1 tablespoon olive oil
1 clove garlic
1 16-ounce can crushed tomatoes
1/2 cup water
1 1/2 teaspoons chopped thyme
1 1/2 teaspoons basil
1/4 teaspoon salt
1/4 teaspoon sugar
4 large eggs

Heat the oil in a large skillet over medium heat. Add the garlic and stir 3 to 4 minutes, until the garlic is tender and golden. Discard the garlic. Stir in the remaining ingredients except for eggs. Bring slowly to a boil. Reduce the heat and simmer uncovered for 7 minutes. Stir occasionally.

Break eggs one at a time into a cup and gently slide them into the sauce. Cover and simmer for 5 to 6 minutes or until the eggs are set.

Quick Fix: Wilted spinach

Fresh spinach can be stir-fried in a little butter or olive oil till wilted. For variety, try it with a sprinkle of allspice or onion powder or a splash of lemon juice, or stir in a little crumbled bacon or chopped hard-boiled egg.

Gorgonzola and Fresh Thyme Sauce for Pasta

Prep Time: 12 minutes 🖾 Cook: 15 minutes

Serves: 4

1½ cups heavy cream
6 ounces aged Gorgonzola cheese, crumbled
1 teaspoon fresh thyme or ½ teaspoon dried thyme
*3 generous grates nutmeg or ⅛ teaspoon ground
    nutmeg*
salt and white pepper
1 pound hot cooked pasta

Stir together the cream, cheese, thyme, and nutmeg in a large skillet. Cook gently over medium heat until the mixture reduces by one-fourth. Add salt and pepper to taste. Toss with the pasta to coat well. Serve with extra nutmeg, if desired.

Quick Fix: Mixed vegetables with herbs

After heating and draining mixed vegetables, top them with a pat or two of butter, sprinkle with dried thyme and ground sage, and toss together.

Guacamole

Prep Time: 8 minutes

Serves: 6

2 ripe avocados, peeled and lightly mashed
1 medium-small ripe or canned tomato, diced
1 small onion, chopped (2 full tablespoons)
$\frac{1}{4}$ to $\frac{1}{2}$ teaspoon finely cut jalapeño or several dashes
*   Tabasco sauce*
2 tablespoons lemon or lime juice
$\frac{1}{4}$ to 1 teaspoon cilantro
dash salt
$\frac{1}{4}$ cup salsa

In a medium bowl, combine all the ingredients. Mix well, keeping the guacamole lumpy.

Quick Fix: Corn on the cob

Sweet corn purchased still in the husks fresh from the garden is not to be missed when it's in season. Remove the husks and the silks (rub the ear with a dampened washcloth) and break off the tips of undeveloped kernels (this makes the ears fit better into a pan). Arrange the ears in a roasting pan with a lid. Add water to cover the ears; place the pan on the largest burner on the stove. Cover, bring to a boil, and cook a few minutes until the corn is tender. Serve with salt and plenty of butter!

Herbed Rice Pilaf

Prep Time: 15 minutes ⧗ Cook: 25 minutes

Serves: 4

1 yellow onion, chopped
2 ribs celery, chopped
1 clove garlic, minced
1 teaspoon dried thyme
1 tablespoon olive oil
1 bay leaf
2 ½ cups water
1 cup uncooked long-grain rice
thyme sprig for garnish

In a medium saucepan, sauté the onion, celery, garlic, and thyme in oil for 5 minutes or until the onions are translucent. Add the bay leaf and water. Bring to a boil; add the rice. Cover and simmer for 20 minutes or until all the water is absorbed and the rice is tender. Remove the bay leaf. Spoon into a serving bowl. Garnish with a sprig of thyme.

Lemony Asparagus and Carrots

Prep Time: 6 minutes ⧗ Chill: 1 hour

Serves: 6

½ pound bag baby carrots
1 8-ounce package frozen asparagus spears
2 tablespoons lemon juice
1 teaspoon lemon pepper

Place the carrots in a steamer basket above boiling water. Cover
and steam about 15 minutes or till crisp-tender. Rinse the carrots in
cold water; drain. Meanwhile, cook the frozen asparagus spears
according to package directions. Rinse the asparagus in cold water;
drain. Cover and chill the drained carrots and asparagus.

To serve, arrange the carrots and asparagus on a platter. Sprinkle
with a little lemon juice and lemon pepper.

Quick Fix: Vegetable toppers

- A pat of butter
- Finely chopped green onion plus the tops
- Chopped chives, scallions, or parsley
- Slivered or sliced almonds (can be lightly toasted)
- Curry powder, onion powder, or garlic powder
- Lemon juice
- Sliced black olives
- Sesame seeds (can be lightly toasted)
- Grated Parmesan cheese

Marinara Sauce

Prep Time: 10 minutes ⧖ Cook: 15 minutes

Yield: About 1 quart

1 28-ounce can plum tomatoes, drained
4 large cloves garlic, minced
1 6-ounce can tomato paste
2 teaspoons dried oregano
black pepper to taste
¹/₄ cup minced fresh basil

Place the tomatoes in a food processor and blend until smooth. Spray a pan with nonstick cooking spray and place over low heat; add the garlic and sauté briefly. Add the puréed tomatoes, tomato paste, oregano, and pepper. Bring to a boil, then reduce the heat to low and simmer, uncovered, to blend the flavors and thicken slightly, about 10 minutes. Remove from the heat and stir in the basil. Toss with pasta to serve.

Quick Tip: Frozen vegetables

Frozen vegetables separate quickly if you place them in a colander and run hot water over them.

Mixed Bean Salad

Prep Time: 12 minutes ⧗ Cook: 10 minutes

Serves: 12

2 pounds fresh green beans
1 pound fresh wax beans
1 16-ounce can kidney beans, drained
1 cup chopped or thinly sliced onions
$1/2$ cup olive oil
$1/2$ cup cider vinegar
$1/2$ cup sugar
$1/2$ teaspoon salt
$1/4$ teaspoon ground black pepper

Wash the fresh beans. Snap or cut, then cook the fresh beans together in about 2 cups of boiling water for 8 to 10 minutes. Drain. Mix with the drained kidney beans and onions. Combine the oil, vinegar, sugar, salt, and pepper in a jar or bottle and shake until well blended. Pour the dressing over the beans and toss. Refrigerate at least 2 hours before serving.

Hard-Boiled Eggs

Hard-boiled eggs make a great garnish to add extra oomph to the tops of many dishes. To make a perfect hard-boiled egg, poke a hole with a needle in the round part of the egg. Boil water then remove the pot from the flame. Add eggs and boil gently 9 to 10 minutes. Pour water out of the pan, and shake eggs in the pan to crack them. Drop eggs into a bowl of water and ice. Peel under water for easier peeling. This will prevent green-tinged egg yolks and a sulfur smell.

Onion-Cilantro Relish

Prep Time: 12 minutes

Yield: About 2 cups

1 small white onion, minced
2 fresh serrano chili peppers, seeded
*   and minced*
1 bunch fresh cilantro, coarsely
*   chopped*

1 teaspoon salt
juice of 1 lime
1 tablespoon olive oil

Combine all ingredients and mix well. Serve with grilled beef.

Quick Fixes

Spinach
Heat spinach (fresh, canned, or frozen) in a little water. Drain and toss with butter and chopped hard-boiled eggs.

Lima Beans
Heat canned lima beans, drain, and add a pat of butter and a small jar of diced pimientos.

Onions
Onions are delicious sautéed in butter or olive oil until lightly golden. They go well with many meat dishes, and are especially good with grilled beef.

Mushrooms
Fresh mushrooms are great sautéed in olive oil or butter and make a wonderful accompaniment to many main dishes. For a different flavor, you can cook them with minced garlic, a splash of lemon juice, chopped onions, or green or red peppers.

Radishes
Fresh radishes are great sautéed whole in butter or olive oil and served with a garnish of parsley.

Corn
Heat frozen corn in a little water. Drain, then add diced red sweet pepper and a pat of butter.

Oven Wedges

Prep Time: 10 minutes   Bake: 15 minutes

Serves: 4

4 large potatoes (about 2 pounds)
2 tablespoons butter, melted
seasoned salt

Preheat oven to 400°F.

Do not peel potatoes; scrub well. Cut them into quarters, then cut each quarter into two or more wedges about 1-inch wide on the skin side.

Coat a jellyroll pan well with cooking oil spray. Place the potato wedges in the pan, standing upright with the skin side down. Drizzle with the butter and sprinkle with seasoned salt. Bake 12 to 15 minutes, or until fork tender and nicely browned.

Eyes on the Potato

Whenever you cook potatoes, try not to peel them if there is a choice. Potato skins can add a nice crunch to the overall texture of a dish, plus they carry valuable dietary fiber and vitamins. If you're in a hurry and need precooked potato chunks for a recipe, cut them into thin slices. They'll cook faster than larger pieces.

Pear Brown Rice

Prep Time: 15 minutes 🗓 Chill: 1 hour

Serves: 8

3 tablespoons lemon juice
2 teaspoons finely chopped garlic
¼ teaspoon ground ginger
¼ teaspoon freshly ground black pepper
3½ cups cooked brown rice
½ cup sliced green onions
½ cup grated carrots
½ cup thinly sliced celery
3 tablespoons olive oil
2 fresh Bartlett pears, diced

In a medium bowl, combine the lemon juice, garlic, ginger, and black pepper. Mix in the rice, onions, carrots, celery, and olive oil. Gently fold in the pears. Chill.

A Grain of Rice

If you like your cooked rice to have every grain separate from the rest, add a few drops of lemon juice to the pot of simmering rice. The acid in the juice will help keep the grains separate as they cook.

Polenta

Prep Time: 10 minutes ⧗ Cook: 10 minutes

Serve: 6

¹/₄ cup olive oil
3 teaspoons kosher salt
2 cups finely ground cornmeal
4 tablespoons (¹/₂ stick) unsalted butter at room temper-
ature
¹/₂ cup grated Parmesan cheese*

Bring 8¹/₂ cups of water to a boil in a large, heavy pot. Add the olive oil and salt. Slowly add the cornmeal in a steady stream and stir continuously. After all the cornmeal has been added, cook and stir over low heat until the polenta pulls away from the sides of the pot. Water is absorbed quickly and it is done almost immediately. The polenta should be thick, smooth, and creamy.

Stir in the butter and the cheese. Either serve immediately or allow to cool in a 9 × 11-inch pan.

Note: A nonstick saucepan is best for making polenta as it takes the pressure off the "continuous stirring" direction, although it still cannot be left unattended for more than a minute or two.

*Other cheeses can be used, depending on the dish you are preparing. Good choices are provolone, Cheddar, and smoked cheeses of all kinds.

Quick Fix Biscuits

Prep Time: 10 minutes ⧗ Bake: 12 minutes

Serves: 6

16-ounce package refrigerator biscuits
¹/₄ cup butter
¹/₂ teaspoon dried onion flakes or minced fresh onion
¹/₂ teaspoon dill, rosemary, or Italian seasoning

Preheat the oven to 425°F. Separate the biscuits and cut each into 4 pieces. In an 8- or 9-inch round pie or cake pan or a ring mold, melt the butter. Into the butter stir the onion and herbs. Roll the biscuit pieces quickly in the mixture and arrange them, touching, in the pan. Bake for about 12 minutes, or until browned.

Quick Fix: Cheese topper

Steam or cook fresh broccoli, cauliflower, or zucchini slices in a little water till crisp-tender. Drain, then top with a shredded cheese like mozzarella, Cheddar, or a three- or four-cheese blend. You can pop the vegetables under the broiler for a few seconds to melt and lightly brown the cheese, if desired, or serve it as is because the heat of the vegetables will partially melt the cheese.

Quickie Pasta Bake

Prep Time: 15 minutes ⧖ Bake: 20 minutes

Serves: 6

1 tablespoon olive oil
1 onion, chopped
2 cloves garlic, minced
1 28-ounce can tomatoes, crushed
1 teaspoon oregano
salt and pepper to taste
1 pound ziti or rotini, cooked and drained
2 cups grated cheese, any type

Preheat the oven to 350°F. Heat the oil in a heavy, large ovenproof skillet. Add the onion and garlic; sauté till soft (about 5 minutes). Add the tomatoes, oregano, salt, and pepper. Cook till heated through, about 5 minutes. Add the cooked pasta and ¹/₂ cup grated cheese to the mixture. Sprinkle the remaining cheese on top.

Bake 15 to 20 minutes or until cheese on top is bubbly.

Quick Tip: Frozen cheese

Packages of frozen shredded cheese can be pounded with the smooth side of a meat mallet to break up the clumps.

Salsa Black Beans and Rice

Prep Time: 12 minutes ⧗ Cook: 15 minutes

Serves: 6

½ cup diced onion
1 strip bacon
2 cloves garlic, minced
2 16-ounce cans black beans
¼ cup or more prepared picante sauce

4 heaping tablespoons prepared picante sauce
salt and pepper to taste
4 cups cooked white rice

Sauté the onions in oil or nonstick spray until slightly translucent. Cut the bacon strip into 1-inch pieces. Add the garlic and bacon to the onions and sauté until the bacon is somewhat cooked but still limp. Stir in the beans. Stir in the picante sauce. Simmer for about 10 minutes. Keep covered and stir occasionally. You may want to try to mash up some of the beans with a spoon.

Add salt and pepper to taste. This mixture should be slightly soupy. Serve over rice in a bowl.

Rice Tips

- Do not stir rice during cooking.
- Do not rinse rice before or after cooking, unless it is imported or the package instructs otherwise.
- For firmer rice, reduce the cooking liquid by ¼ cup and reduce the cooking time by 5 or more minutes.
- For softer rice, allow rice to sit in the covered pan for up to 10 minutes after cooking.
- Use a pan with a tight-fitting lid and keep it tightly covered during cooking to prevent steam from escaping.
- Fluff cooked rice with a fork before serving to separate the grains.

Sautéed Swiss Chard

Prep Time: 8 minutes ⧗ Cook: 8 minutes

Serves: 4

2 bunches young Swiss chard
2 tablespoons olive oil
2 tablespoons butter
1 clove garlic, chopped
salt and pepper to taste

Leave the chard whole or slice it. In a sauté pan, heat the oil and butter over medium heat until the butter is just melted. Stir in the chopped garlic and the raw chard. Toss until coated with butter and oil.

Cover the pan, reduce the heat, and cook for 3 to 4 minutes, stirring occasionally. Uncover the pan and raise the heat to evaporate the moisture. Shake the pan so the chard doesn't stick. Add more butter if necessary, and season to taste.

Use Chard for Spinach

Substitute chard leaves in most spinach recipes to get a heartier texture and taste. Unwashed chard can be kept in a perforated plastic bag in the refrigerator for 3 to 5 days.

Southwestern Apricot Salsa

Prep Time: 12 minutes ⧖ Refrigerate: 2 hours

Makes: 1 pint salsa

1 16-ounce can apricots in light syrup, drained, rinsed,
    and cut into chunks
2 tablespoons chopped red onions
$1/2$ tablespoon olive oil
1 tablespoon fresh cilantro
$1/2$ tablespoon lime juice
$1/2$ teaspoon white vinegar
$1/2$ teaspoon minced jalapeño peppers
$1/4$ teaspoon grated lime peel
$1/4$ teaspoon ground cumin
salt to taste
white pepper to taste

Combine all ingredients in a medium bowl; stir gently. Cover and
refrigerate for 2 hours before serving.

Quick Fix: Green beans with pizzazz

After heating and draining green beans, top them with a pat or
two of butter, and sprinkle with some minced dried onion and
a few drops of Worcestershire sauce. Stir together.

Special Occasion Tomato Sauce

Prep Time: 8 minutes ⧗ Heat: 10 minutes

Yield: 2 cups

1 cup plain yogurt
1 cup tomato sauce
¹⁄₄ cup grated Parmesan cheese
handful of fresh basil leaves, torn

Combine all the ingredients in a saucepan, stir well, and place over low heat. Heat until hot and well blended; do not allow to boil. Toss with hot pasta to serve.

Quick Fixes

Oregano Carrots
Heat baby carrots (fresh, frozen or canned) or carrot slices in a little water. Drain, then top with a pat or two of butter and a sprinkle of dried oregano.

Broccoli with Almonds
Steam or cook fresh broccoli, drain, then top with a pat or two of butter or olive oil, sprinkle with toasted almond slices, and toss.

Cinnamon Carrots
Heat baby carrots (fresh, frozen, or canned) or carrot slices in a little water.

Drain, then drizzle a little cinnamon schnapps over the carrots and top with a pat of butter.

Carrot-orange Curry
Cook and drain carrots, then add a pat of butter, a splash of orange juice, and a sprinkle of curry powder. Mix together and serve.

Beets
Heat canned or frozen beets, drain, toss with a pat or two of butter, and add a sprinkle of nutmeg or allspice or a splash of lemon or orange zest.

Steamed Cabbage

Prep Time: 10 minutes ⧗ Cook: 7 minutes

Serves: 4

1 tablespoon olive oil
3 cups shredded green cabbage
1 cup thinly sliced celery
1 green pepper, chopped
½ cup chopped yellow onion
salt and pepper to taste

In a large deep skillet with a lid, heat the oil over medium heat. Add the vegetables, stirring and cooking for 1 minute. Cover the pan tightly, and allow to steam for approximately 5 minutes, stirring occasionally. Remove from the heat, season with salt and pepper, and serve immediately.

Quick Fix: Cabbage

Slice cabbage into a little olive oil in a skillet and sauté until crisp-tender for a colorful yet quick vegetable. (Do not cover or it will cook too much and lose its bright color.)

Summertime Potato Salad

Prep Time: 15 minutes ⧗ Chill: 30 minutes

Serves: 8

Dressing:

1 cup plain yogurt
1 teaspoon ground cumin
1 teaspoon ground coriander

Salad:

2 pounds medium potatoes, peeled, boiled until tender,
*   and cut into chunks*
1 large onion, thinly sliced into rings
2 tablespoons minced fresh basil
dash of paprika

Whisk together all the dressing ingredients in a serving bowl. Add the potatoes and toss them gently to coat thoroughly. Place the onion rings on top, and sprinkle the salad with basil and paprika. Cover and refrigerate for at least 30 minutes.

Quick Fix: Coating for vegetables

Stir some cream cheese into a saucepan of cooked and drained vegetables, and mix until the vegetables are coated. Do not return the coated vegetables to the burner, but you can cover them with a lid to keep them warm.

Texas Caviar

Prep Time: 20 minutes

Yield: About 5 cups

2 ripe, firm avocados
2 tablespoons vegetable oil
3 tablespoons Tabasco sauce
2 tablespoons red wine vinegar
1 teaspoon coarse ground black pepper
1 clove fresh garlic, minced
1 15-ounce can whole kernel corn, drained and rinsed
1 15-ounce can black-eyed peas, drained and rinsed
1 15-ounce can black beans, drained and rinsed
1 bunch fresh cilantro, chopped
2 medium-size tomatoes, cubed
1 small red onion, chopped

Cut the avocados into half-inch cubes. In a small bowl, mix together the vegetable oil, Tabasco sauce, vinegar, pepper, and garlic. Pour the mixture over the avocados and stir gently to coat. In a large bowl, mix the corn, peas, beans, cilantro, tomatoes, and onion. Add the avocado mixture and gently mix with the other ingredients. Serve with tortilla chips or crackers.

Quick Fix: Green beans and pimiento

Heat canned, fresh, or frozen green beans, drain, and add a pat of butter and a small jar of diced pimientos.

Welsh Rarebit with Vegetables

Prep Time: 15 minutes ⧗ Broil: 5 minutes

Serves: 2

$^1/_4$ *cup finely chopped cabbage*
$^1/_4$ *cup finely chopped carrot*
2 tablespoons finely chopped green bell pepper
2 tablespoons finely chopped celery
2 tablespoons finely chopped onion
2 tablespoons finely chopped radishes
2 slices whole-wheat bread, toasted
$^1/_2$ *cup shredded Cheddar cheese*
dash of red pepper flakes
2 tablespoons water
$^1/_4$ *cup alfalfa sprouts*

Preheat the broiler.

In a bowl, combine the cabbage, carrot, bell pepper, celery, onion, and radishes. Top each slice of toast with an equal amount of the vegetable mixture. Place the slices on a baking sheet. In a small saucepan, combine the cheese, red pepper flakes, and water. Place over low heat and stir until the cheese melts. Spoon over the sandwiches, dividing evenly.

Slip the baking sheet under the broiler about 4 inches from the heat source and broil until the cheese is bubbly, about 5 minutes. Transfer to serving plates. Top with the sprouts.

Steaming Tips

- Steaming (or blanching) vegetables or fruits preserves more of their nutritional value.

- If vegetables or fruits are simmered or boiled in water to cover them, much of their vitamin content will go down the drain when the water is drained.

- Raisins, dried cherries or cranberries, and dry (rather than oil-packed) sun-dried tomatoes can be plumped by steaming briefly.

- Folding "steamer inserts" can be used in standard saucepans; specially designed two-part steamer saucepans are also available.

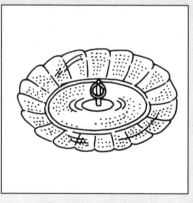

Steamer Insert

Two-Part Steamer Pot

Chapter 9

Crock-Pot Recipes

Chicken Cacciatore

Prep Time: 25 minutes   ⧖   Cook: 7–9 hours on low or 3–4 hours on high

Serves: 6

1 large onion, thinly sliced
3 pounds chicken, cut up
2 6-ounce cans tomato paste
4 ounces sliced mushrooms
1 teaspoon salt
2 cloves garlic, minced
1 teaspoon oregano
¹/₂ teaspoon celery seed
1 bay leaf
¹/₂ cup water
hot cooked spaghetti

Place the onions in the Crock-Pot. Add the chicken pieces. Stir together the remaining ingredients except the spaghetti. Pour over the chicken. Cook on low 7 to 9 hours or high 3 to 4 hours.

Remove the bay leaf before serving. Serve over spaghetti.

Crock-Pot Chicken Broth

Prep Time: 15 minutes ⧗ Cook: 8–9 hours

Yield: About 6 cups chicken and
3+ cups double-strength chicken stock

1 onion, sliced
1 carrot, sliced
1 celery rib, sliced

1 large whole chicken
  (3½ pounds)
½ cup chicken broth or water

Place the sliced vegetables in a Crock-Pot. Set the whole chicken on top, neck up. If you wish you may season with herbs, pepper, etc., but this is not necessary. Pour the broth over the chicken, cover, and cook on low 8 or 9 hours.

Remove the chicken from the pot and let cool until easy to handle. Meanwhile, strain the stock and skim the fat. This stock is double strength, so mix with equal parts water for use. Remove the chicken from the bones and cut into pieces sized appropriately for your recipe.

Doubling and Tripling Recipes

If you find a recipe that you really like, you may want to prepare two or three times the original recipe in order to freeze the dish in individual containers to cook for a busy dinner. Most of the recipes in *The Everything® Quick Meals Cookbook* can be doubled or tripled without affecting the quality of the dish. However, before you try a new dish on company, make it in its original quantity so you can see how the dish is supposed to look and taste. And be sure to allow extra time for preparation and cooking when you increase the quantity of a recipe.

Gone-All-Day Stew

Prep Time: 25 minutes ⧗ Cook: 8 hours

Serves: 6

1 10³/₄-ounce can tomato soup
1 cup water
¹/₄ cup flour
2 pounds beef chuck, cut into 1-inch cubes
3 medium carrots, cut diagonally in 1-inch pieces
6 medium yellow onions, quartered
4 medium potatoes, peeled and cut into 1¹/₂-inch cubes
¹/₂ cup celery chunks
2 beef bouillon cubes
1 tablespoon Italian herb seasoning
1 bay leaf
pepper to taste

Mix the soup, water, and flour together until smooth. Combine with the remaining ingredients in a covered Crock-Pot. Cook on low for 8 hours. When ready to serve adjust the seasonings to taste and discard the bay leaf.

Reducing Saltiness

Is your dish tasting too salty? Add a teaspoon each of cider vinegar and sugar to the dish to help cut down on the salty flavor in the recipe.

Crock-Pot French Onion Soup

Prep Time: 12 minutes   ⧗   Cook: 6–8 hours

Serves: 6

4 large yellow onions, thinly sliced
¹/₄ cup butter
3 cups rich beef stock
1 cup dry white wine
¹/₄ cup medium dry sherry
1 teaspoon Worcestershire sauce
1 clove garlic, minced
6 slices French bread, buttered
¹/₄ cup grated Romano or Parmesan cheese

In a large frying pan, slowly sauté the onions in butter until limp and glazed. Transfer to the Crock-Pot. Add the beef stock, white wine, sherry, Worcestershire, and garlic. Cover. Cook on low 6 to 8 hours.

Preheat the broiler. Place the buttered French bread on a baking sheet. Sprinkle with the cheese. Place under the broiler until lightly toasted. To serve, ladle the soup into 6 bowls. Float a slice of toasted French bread on top of each serving.

Hearty Smoked Sausage Stew

Prep Time: 20 minutes ⌛ Soak: overnight ⌛ Cook: 8 hours

Serves: 8

1 pound dried red kidney beans
1 46-ounce can chicken broth
2 cups water
1 pound smoked sausage, sliced
1 cup barley
2 bay leaves
½ teaspoon garlic powder
1 teaspoon thyme

The night before, rinse the beans, place in a large bowl with plenty of water to cover, and soak overnight.

Drain and rinse the beans. Put all ingredients in a large Crock-Pot, stir, cover, and cook on low for 8 hours. Remove the bay leaves before serving.

Crock-Pot Recipes on the Move

You'll probably want to take many of the dishes in this chapter to potluck dinners and other community or social events. Most travel well; just be sure to keep the casserole level during the trip. A cardboard box lined with a dish towel or newspaper is useful to set the casserole dish in.

Simple Cassoulet

Prep Time: 20 minutes ⧖ Cook: 7–8 hours on low or 3 ½–4 hours on high

Serves: 6

8 ounces skinless, boneless chicken thighs

2 medium carrots, sliced into ½-inch pieces

1 medium green or red sweet pepper, cut into ½-inch pieces

1 large onion, chopped

3 cloves garlic, minced

2 15-ounce cans cannellini beans, rinsed and drained

1 14½-ounce can Italian-style stewed tomatoes

8 ounces fully cooked smoked turkey sausage, halved lengthwise and cut into ½-inch slices

1½ cups chicken broth

⅓ cup dry white wine or chicken broth

1 tablespoon snipped parsley

1 teaspoon dried thyme, crushed

¼ teaspoon ground red pepper

1 bay leaf

Rinse the chicken and pat dry with paper towels. Cut into 1-inch pieces. Layer the carrots, sweet pepper, onion, garlic, beans, undrained tomatoes, chicken, and sausage in a 3½ to 5-quart Crock-Pot.

Combine the broth, wine, parsley, thyme, red pepper, and bay leaf in a bowl. Add the mixture to the cooker. Cover; cook on low for 7 to 8 hours or cook on high for 3½ to 4 hours. Discard the bay leaf.

Slow-Cook Texas Barbecued Beef Sandwiches

Prep Time: 15 minutes   Cook: 9 hours

Serves: 8

1 4-pound boneless chuck roast, trimmed
$\frac{1}{2}$ cup water
1 14-ounce bottle ketchup
10 ounces cola
$\frac{1}{4}$ cup Worcestershire sauce
2 tablespoons prepared mustard
2 tablespoons liquid smoke
$\frac{1}{4}$ teaspoon hot sauce
8 hamburger buns

Cook the roast with $\frac{1}{2}$ cup water in a 5-quart slow cooker on high 8 hours or until tender.

Drain the roast, reserving 1 cup of drippings in the slow cooker. Shred the meat, removing and discarding the fat, and return to the slow cooker. Stir in the ketchup and the next 5 ingredients, and cook on high 1 hour. Serve on buns.

Chapter 10

Breakfasts and Brunches

Basic Pancakes

Prep Time: 10 minutes ⧖ Cook: 6 minutes

Yield: 8 to 10 4-inch pancakes

1 cup flour
1 tablespoon sugar (granulated or brown)
2 1/2 teaspoons baking powder

1/4 teaspoon salt
1 egg
1 cup milk
2 tablespoons cooking oil

Combine the flour, sugar, baking powder, and salt in a bowl by stirring, then make a well in the middle of the flour mixture. In a different bowl, beat the egg well and thoroughly combine with the milk and oil. Add the liquid to the flour mixture and stir quickly until moistened; the batter will have some lumps.

Preheat a greased or buttered griddle or skillet over medium-high heat. Cook pancakes on the hot griddle, using about 1/4 cup batter per cake. Cook about 2 or 3 minutes on each side; pancakes are ready to turn when the tops have broken bubbles on the surface and the edges appear dry.

Pancake Variations

Whole-Wheat Pancakes: Use brown sugar and substitute whole-wheat for all-purpose flour.

Buckwheat Pancakes: Use brown sugar and replace ½ cup of the all-purpose flour with buckwheat flour.

Blueberry Pancakes: Add ½ cup fresh or frozen (thawed and drained) berries to the batter.

Apple Blender Pancakes: Peel and slice one medium apple. Place the apples, egg, milk, and oil in a blender and blend on low until liquids are combined and apples are chopped. Proceed as directed.

Buttermilk Pancakes

Prep Time: 12 minutes ⧗ Cook: 6 minutes

Yield: 8 to 10 4-inch pancakes

1 cup flour
1 tablespoon sugar
1 teaspoon baking powder
¹/₂ teaspoon baking soda
¹/₄ teaspoon salt
1 egg
1 cup buttermilk or sour milk
2 tablespoons cooking oil

Combine the flour, sugar, baking powder, baking soda, and salt in a bowl by stirring, then make a well in the middle of the flour mixture. In a different bowl, beat the eggs well and thoroughly combine with the milk and oil. Add the liquid to the flour mixture and stir quickly until moistened; the batter will have some lumps.

Preheat a greased or buttered griddle or skillet over medium-high heat. Cook the pancakes on the hot griddle, using about ¹/₄ cup batter per cake. Cook about 2 or 3 minutes on each side; pancakes are ready to turn when the tops have broken bubbles on the surface and the edges appear dry.

How to Cook Pancakes

- Most pancakes will need to cook about 2 or 3 minutes on each side.
- Pancakes are ready to turn when the tops have broken bubbles on the surface and the edges appear dry.

Cornmeal Pancakes

Prep Time: 10 minutes ⧖ Cook: 6 minutes

Yield: about 6 pancakes

$^3/_4$ cup flour

$^1/_2$ cup cornmeal

1 tablespoon baking powder

$^1/_2$ teaspoon salt

1 egg

$1^1/_4$ cups milk

2 tablespoons vegetable oil

Combine the flour, cornmeal, baking powder, and salt in a bowl by stirring, then make a well in the middle of the flour mixture. In a different bowl, beat the egg well and thoroughly combine with the milk and oil. Add the liquid to the flour mixture and stir quickly but thoroughly; the batter will have some lumps.

Preheat a greased or buttered griddle or skillet over medium-high heat. Cook on the hot griddle, using about $^1/_4$ cup batter per cake. Cook about 2 or 3 minutes on each side; pancakes are ready to turn when the tops have broken bubbles on the surface and the edges appear dry.

When is the Griddle or Skillet Ready?

- When using a greased griddle or skillet, it is hot enough for cooking when a drop of water "skitters" across it.
- When using a small amount of oil or butter in the skillet, it is ready just before it begins to sizzle. Do not allow it to brown!

High-Protein Pancakes

Prep Time: 10 minutes ⏳ Cook: 10 minutes

Yield: about 9 4-inch pancakes

3 eggs, separated
³/₄ cup cottage cheese, small curd preferable
¹/₂ teaspoon salt
¹/₂ cup flour
1 tablespoon sugar

Combine the eggs, cottage cheese, and salt in a blender and blend well until smoother. Add the flour and sugar and blend again. Pour onto a hot, well-greased griddle, keeping cakes no larger than 4 inches in diameter. Cook until golden brown, turning once. These cakes will take longer to cook through than ordinary pancakes.

Egg Facts

The *yolk* contains protein and all of the vitamins and minerals in an egg. Unfortunately, it also contains all of the fat and cholesterol. The white *contains* protein and water, but no other nutrients or fat or cholesterol.

Usually, 2 egg whites can be substituted for 1 whole egg. However, in a recipe calling for many eggs, this substitution will not be satisfactory.

Eggs of different grades (AA or A) do not differ in nutritive value.

Brown and white eggs do not differ in nutritive value, although some people believe they differ in taste.

Basic Omelet

Prep Time: 8 minutes ⧖ Cook: 10 minutes

Serves: 1

2 eggs per omelet if using 8-inch omelet pan or skillet

3 eggs per omelet if using 10-inch omelet pan or skillet

cooking spray if using nonstick skillet

1 teaspoon butter for each egg if using traditional noncoated omelet pan or skillet

Beat the eggs well in a bowl, but do not allow them to become frothy.

If using an uncoated omelet pan or skillet: Melt the butter over medium to medium-high heat, tilting the skillet to coat the bottom, until the butter just begins to turn brown. Pour in the eggs; stir gently with a fork while they thicken to distribute the eggs from top to bottom. Stop stirring when the eggs begin to set.

If using a nonstick pan or skillet: Coat well with cooking spray. Preheat the skillet for a minute or so but do not allow the spray to begin to brown. Add the eggs. As they thicken, lift the edges of the omelet and allow the uncooked eggs to flow underneath.

Allow to cook until the bottom is golden and the top is set but shiny. With a long turner, gently loosen the edge of the omelet and fold the omelet in half toward you. With the help of the turner, slide it out of the pan and onto the plate.

If making multiple omelets, cover them with foil to keep warm.

To add additional ingredients like cheese, meat, or vegetables, distribute them down the center of the omelet when the top is set but still shiny, and before folding the omelet. Use ⅓ to ½ cup if adding one ingredient; reduce amounts accordingly if multiple ingredients are used.

Cheesy Golden Apple Omelet

Prep Time: 15 minutes ⧖ Cook: 15 minutes

Serves: 2

1 Golden Delicious apple,
    pared, cored, and sliced
2 tablespoons butter, divided
4 eggs
1 tablespoon water
¹/₄ teaspoon salt

dash pepper
2 tablespoons crumbled blue
    cheese
2 tablespoons grated Parmesan
    cheese

Sauté the apple in 1 tablespoon butter until barely tender; remove from the pan. Combine eggs, water, salt, and pepper until blended. Heat the remaining butter in an omelet pan; add the egg mixture. Cook slowly, lifting the edges to allow the uncooked portion to flow under. Arrange the apple slices on half of the omelet. Sprinkle with the cheeses; fold in half.

Egg Safety

- When bringing an egg or egg white to room temperature, do not allow it to stand for more than a half-hour.
- To separate whites and yolks, use an inexpensive kitchen tool called an egg separator, available at any variety or cooking store. **Do not** use the traditional method of pouring the egg from one half of the egg shell to the other, which increases the chances that the egg might come in contact with a contaminated outer shell.
- When finished working with eggs, wash the work surface, dishes, and utensils with hot soapy water. Wash your hands before and after.

Basic French Toast

Prep Time: 8 minutes   Cook: 6 minutes

Serves: 3 or 4

2 eggs
¹/₂ cup milk
2 teaspoons sugar
¹/₄ teaspoon vanilla
¹/₂ teaspoon cinnamon
¹/₄ teaspoon salt
5 or 6 slices day-old French or other bread*
cooking oil

Beat the eggs lightly, then combine with the milk, sugar, vanilla, cinnamon, and salt. Pour into a flat-bottomed dish somewhat larger than the slices of bread. Dip the bread into the mixture on both sides, one slice at a time, restirring the mixture after each. Do not soak. Place bread on a plate and allow to stand for a few minutes.

In a medium skillet, heat about 1 tablespoon of oil over medium-high heat. Cook bread for 2 to 3 minutes on each side. Add more oil if needed for the second batch. Serve with syrup.

*French bread should be sliced about 1 inch thick. If bread is fresh, it can be dried slightly in an oven set at 300°F; watch carefully.

Basic Muffins

Prep Time: 12 minutes ⧖ Bake: 20 minutes

Yield: 12 muffins

2 cups all-purpose flour
¼ cup sugar
1 tablespoon baking powder
½ teaspoon salt
1 large egg
1 cup milk
⅓ cup vegetable oil

Preheat the oven to 400°F. Grease well a 12-cup muffin tin, or line with paper cups.

Sift together the flour, sugar, baking powder, and salt. Place the sifted dry ingredients into a bowl and make a well in the center.

In a second bowl, beat the egg lightly. Add the milk and oil and combine.

Pour the egg mixture into the well in the dry ingredients and combine quickly, until dry ingredients are just moistened. Some lumps will remain in the batter.

Fill the muffin cups about ⅔ full. Bake about 20 minutes, or until the center tests done.

Basic Waffles

Prep Time: 12 minutes ⧖ Cook: 5 minutes

Yield: about 6 waffles

2 cups flour
4 teaspoons baking powder
¹/₄ teaspoon salt
2 eggs
1³/₄ cups milk
¹/₂ cup vegetable oil

Preheat waffle iron following manufacturer's instructions.

Stir together the flour, baking powder, and salt, and make a well in the middle of the mixture. Beat the eggs lightly, then beat in the milk and oil until well combined. Add all at once to the dry ingredients and combine until just moistened. Batter will have a few lumps.

Use the manufacturer's directions to determine how much batter to use per waffle; use about 1 cup for a standard 7-inch circular waffle. Do not open the iron while the waffle is cooking! Remove with a fork.

Break an Egg!

Always break eggs one at a time into a small bowl, then add them one at a time to the skillet or pan. If you break them directly into the pan, and you accidentally break the yolk of the sixth egg, the first five will be spoiled as well! The same holds true for any recipe calling for eggs.

Cold Swiss Oatmeal (Muesli)

Prep Time: 10 minutes ⧖ Refrigerate: 8 hours

Serves: 6

2 cups quick-cooking rolled oats
½ cup orange or apple juice
¾ cup chopped prunes, raisins,
  or currants

⅓ cup chopped nuts or wheat germ
¼ teaspoon salt
¼ cup honey
1¼ cups milk

Place the oats in a bowl and pour the juice over them; toss till it is evenly absorbed. Stir in the fruit, nuts, and salt. Pour the honey over the mixture and toss until evenly combined. Stir in the milk. Cover and refrigerate at least 8 hours.

Do not cook; serve cold with brown sugar and additional milk or cream if desired.

Low-Fat Substitutions

To reduce the fat and cholesterol in breakfast and brunch recipes:

• Use liquid egg substitute. Made from egg whites, it has no cholesterol. Substitute ¼ cup for each whole egg.

• Use reduced or low-fat shredded cheeses, cream cheese, or sour cream. Substitute with no change in measurements. These products contain more moisture, and some dishes will be more moist.

• *Do not* substitute fat-free cheeses or sour cream in recipes. The resulting dish will be unsatisfactory. Use *fat-free products* only in recipes designed for them.

Eggs and Lox

Prep Time: 15 minutes ⧖ Cook: 10 minutes

Serves: 4 to 5

3 ounces lox or smoked salmon
1 3-ounce package cream cheese
6 eggs
1/2 cup milk or water
1/2 teaspoon dill
salt and pepper to taste
1 tablespoon butter

Chop the lox. Soften the cream cheese well. With a whisk, beat the eggs and milk lightly. Add the cream cheese and combine thoroughly. Stir in the dill, salt and pepper, and lox.

Melt the butter in a 10- or 12-inch skillet. Scramble the egg mixture until thickened but still moist.

Size of Your Eggs

Recipes are based on *large* eggs unless otherwise specified. However:

For 1 large egg, you can substitute 1 extra large, medium, or small.

For 2 large eggs, substitute 2 extra-large or medium, but 3 small.

For 3 large eggs, substitute 3 extra-large or medium, but 4 small.

For 4 large eggs, substitute 4 extra-large, but 5 medium or small.

Scrambled Eggs

Prep Time: 10 minutes ⧖ Cook: 8 minutes

Serves: 2 or 3

6 eggs
$1/3$ cup milk or cream
salt and pepper to taste
1 tablespoon butter

Beat the eggs, milk, and seasonings together lightly (with white and yellow streaks still visible) or well (until a uniform color) as preferred, using a fork or whisk. Heat the butter in a skillet and pour the egg mixture in. After the eggs begin to thicken, stir *gently* with a wooden spoon until eggs are thick but still moist. **OR, instead of stirring,** after the eggs begin to thicken, lift portions to allow the uncooked egg to flow to the bottom until the eggs are uniformly thickened. Total cooking time after the eggs begin to thicken will be 2 to 4 minutes.

Denver Eggs: Before adding the eggs to the skillet, cook $1/3$ cup chopped onion, $1/3$ cup diced green pepper, and $1/3$ cup diced ham in the melted butter.

Cheesy Eggs: Add $1/2$ cup shredded American or other process cheese to the eggs after they have begun to thicken.

Sausage Eggs: Cook $1/2$ pound of bulk sausage until no longer pink; drain well. Add to the eggs after they begin to thicken.

Skillet (Crustless) Quiche Lorraine

Prep Time: 15 minutes ⏳ Cook: 25 minutes

Serves: 4 to 6

6 slices bacon
1 medium onion
1 1/2 tablespoons cooking oil
6 eggs
1 1/2 cups shredded Swiss cheese or a mixture of Swiss
*   and Gruyère cheese*
dash nutmeg
salt and pepper to taste

Preheat the broiler. Cook the bacon in a skillet until hard. Drain well, crumble, and reserve. Slice the onion very thinly. In a 10-inch ovenproof skillet, heat the oil and sauté the onion for about 2 minutes.

Beat the eggs well. Stir in the cheese, nutmeg, salt and pepper, and bacon. When the onions have finished cooking, stir to distribute evenly (do not drain), and pour the egg mixture over them. Reduce the heat to medium-low and cook until set but still moist on top, about 8 minutes. Immediately put the skillet in the broiler, about 5 inches from the flame or element, and cook until the top is done but not browned.

Vegetable Egg Scramble

Prep Time: 12 minutes   ⧖   Cook: 10 minutes

Serves: 6

1 teaspoon olive oil	1 green bell pepper, chopped
3 scallions, minced	1 8-ounce can corn, drained
2 cloves garlic, minced	6 eggs
½ pound fresh mushrooms, sliced	salt and pepper to taste

In a large skillet, heat the oil over medium heat. Add the scallions, garlic, mushrooms, bell pepper, and corn. Sauté, stirring occasionally, until the vegetables are tender, about 5 minutes.

Meanwhile, beat the eggs lightly in a bowl. Add the eggs to the vegetables, season with salt and pepper, and scramble until thoroughly cooked. Serve at once.

Egg Safety

- Raw eggs can be harmful to some people. Pregnant women, infants and young children, the elderly, and those who are already ill (especially with immune disorders) should not eat them unless on a doctor's advice.
- Raw eggs are an ingredient in *homemade* mayonnaise, ice cream, eggnog, and some salad dressing. Commercially prepared varieties of these foods are pasteurized and do not pose a risk.
- If preparing a recipe that uses raw eggs as an ingredient, use pasteurized eggs, available at most groceries.

Raspberry Cream Cheese Breakfast Biscuits

Prep Time: 15 minutes ⧗ Bake: 10 minutes

Yield: 15 biscuits

3 cups flour
2 tablespoons baking powder
³/₄ teaspoon salt
3 tablespoons shortening
³/₄ cup orange juice or milk

1 3-ounce package cream
* cheese*
2 tablespoons raspberry all-fruit
* spread or jam*
sugar

Preheat the oven to 450°F. Sift together the flour, baking powder, and salt. Cut in the shortening until the mixture resembles coarse crumbs. Add the orange juice and beat to form a soft dough. Turn the dough onto a surface well dusted with flour and knead 10 times. Roll or pat the dough till it's ¹/₂ inch thick. Cut rounds with a biscuit cutter or a 2¹/₂-inch round cutter (a drinking glass can be used). Place the rounds on an ungreased cookie sheet.

Soften the cream cheese. Add the jam and mix until marbled but not thoroughly combined. Spoon about 1 teaspoon onto the center of each round. Sprinkle with sugar. Bake 8 to 10 minutes, or until golden brown.

Note: You can replace the flour, baking powder, salt, and shortening by substituting 3 cups of prepared biscuit mix, such as Bisquick.

Scones

Prep Time: 12 minutes 🕐 Bake: 15 minutes

Yield: 12 scones

2¼ cups cake flour*
1 tablespoon baking powder
½ teaspoon salt
2 tablespoons sugar
5 tablespoons butter
1 egg
½ cup light or heavy cream**
extra cream and sugar

Preheat the oven to 425°F. Sift the flour, baking powder, salt, and sugar together. Cut in the butter until the mixture is the size of small peas. Make a well in the mixture. Beat the egg lightly and combine with the cream. Pour the liquids into the dry ingredient well and combine quickly but thoroughly.

Turn onto a lightly floured work surface. Pat or roll the dough to a thickness of about ¾ inch. With a sharp knife, cut into diamond shapes. Brush the tops with cream and sprinkle with sugar. Bake 12 to 15 minutes on an ungreased cookie sheet.

Variation: Add ½ cup raisins or currants when adding the egg-cream mixture to the dry ingredients. Or use ⅓ cup dried cherries or dried mixed fruits that have been steamed briefly to plump.

*If substituting all-purpose flour for the cake flour, reduce the amount to 2 cups and knead 10 times before shaping and cutting.

**Cream gives scones their characteristic richness; do not substitute milk.

How to Cook It

| Bake | Boil | Simmer | Stir-Fry |

Bake—to cook food with the indirect dry heat of an oven. Covering food while baking it preserves moistness; leaving food uncovered results in a drier or crisp surface.

Barbecue—to cook with barbecue sauce or spices, or to cook slowly on a grill or spit, usually outdoors.

Blanch—to cook fruits, vegetables, or nuts very briefly in boiling water or steam, usually to preserve the color or nutritional value or to remove the skin. Also called *parboiling.*

Boil—to cook a liquid at a temperature at which bubbles rise and break on the surface. *Bring to a boil:* Heat just until bubbling begins. In a full or rolling boil, the bubbles are larger and form quickly and continuously.

Braise—to cook food slowly in a tightly covered pan in a small amount of liquid. Usually, food is first browned in a small amount of fat. Braising tenderizes food and can be done on either the stovetop or in the oven.

Broil—to cook food directly under a direct source of intense heat or flame, producing a browned or crisp exterior and a less well done interior.

Deep-Fry—to cook food in hot, liquefied fat (usually kept at 350 to 375 degrees) deep enough to cover and surround the food completely.

Fry—to cook in hot fat or oil, producing a crisp exterior.

Grill—to cook foods directly above a source of intense heat or flame. Foods can be *pan-grilled* on a stovetop by using a specially designed pan with raised grill ridges.

Oven-Fry—to cook food, usually breaded, in a hot oven with a small amount of fat, usually dotted or drizzled on top of the food.

Pan-Fry—to fry with little or no added fat, using only the fat that accumulates during cooking.

Parboil—see *Blanch.*

Poach—to cook in a simmering (not boiling) liquid.

Roast—to cook meat or poultry in the indirect heat of the oven, uncovered. Roasted foods are not cooked in added liquid (compare *braise*), but are often basted with liquids for flavor and moisture.

Sauté—to cook in a small amount of fat over high heat.

Scald—to heat a liquid to just below the boiling point, when small bubbles begin to appear around the edges of the pan. When milk is scalded, a film will form on the surface.

Sear—to brown on all sides over high heat to preserve juiciness.

Simmer—to keep a liquid just below the boiling point; a few bubbles will rise and break on the surface.

Steam—to cook food above (not in) boiling or simmering water.

Stew—to cook food, covered, very slowly in liquid.

Stir-fry—to cook small pieces of food in a hot wok or skillet, using a small amount of fat and a contant stirring motion.

Chapter 11

Quick Desserts

That delightful ending to a delicious meal, dessert can be served elegantly at the table, as a separate course with coffee or tea. Or it can be served more casually while relaxing in the family room or on the patio. When entertaining a crowd, an entire dessert bar can be served buffet-style.

At our house, prepared desserts are reserved for entertaining. For ordinary meals, fresh fruit is our preferred ending to meals. Wedges of fresh cantaloupe, watermelon, slices of kiwi or pineapple, grapes, apples, strawberries, apricots, nectarines, oranges, mangoes, tangerines, tangelos, peaches, pears, pomegranates—what could be easier—or faster?

Do you need a quick dessert that looks like it took hours? Keep a pound cake or two in the freezer. Take one out to thaw as you make the coffee to go with it, or let it thaw as you prepare the rest of the quick meal. Then slice the cake in half horizontally; spread soft-style cream cheese on the bottom layer and top this with some kind of fruit preserves from the pantry (apricot is delicious). All of this is easier if the cake is still partially frozen. Replace the top and repeat the cream cheese and preserves. Slice and serve with the coffee.

Tips for Better Microwave Desserts
- Defrosting pies in the microwave is quick and easy. A frozen fruit pie will

Whipped cream

To make whipped cream, chill the mixer bowl and beater or wire whip in the freezer for a few minutes. Pour in the heavy whipping cream that is also very cold, a little powdered sugar (maybe 1 or 2 tablespoons sugar per cup of cream), and a little vanilla extract (perhaps ½ to 1 teaspoon). Whip to the desired stiffness, until soft or stiff peaks form. The cream will double in volume when it's whipped if the cream, bowl, and beater are well chilled.

To keep the whipping cream from losing volume while it's stored in the refrigerator, add 1 tablespoon of powdered milk per 1 cup of cream before beating—it will last two or three days without losing volume.

take 4 to 5 minutes on defrost, with an additional 5 minutes standing time. A frozen cream pie will take about 1 1/2 minutes on defrost, with an additional 5 minutes standing time. Always remove the pie from its metal pan and place it in a glass or paper pan before putting it into the microwave. Using metal of any kind in a microwave is dangerous and may ruin your oven.

- A frozen layer cake will take about 2 minutes on defrost, with an additional 5 minutes standing time. Leave the cake in its package for defrosting unless there is metal in the package, in which case remove the metal and then defrost the cake.
- Defrost packages (boxes) of frozen fruit for 5 minutes on defrost, with an additional 1 minute standing time. Pouches of frozen fruit will defrost in about 3 minutes on defrost, with about 1 minute standing time. These times are variable as is the power of your microwave.

- Always use round dishes instead of square dishes if possible in your microwave. Using round dishes will eliminate burned or dry corners.
- Sauces are easily prepared in the microwave. Use the microwave setting that seems best for each kind of sauce. Stir the sauce every few seconds and heat to a temperature of 140°F to 150°F. Use the microwave to heat up premade sauces just before serving, and don't worry about overcooking or scorching. Hot chocolate sauce poured over a dish of ice cream and sprinkled with chopped nuts is easy and delicious.
- You can easily toast coconut in the microwave. Spread the coconut thinly on a paper plate or towel and use the high setting for 2 or 3 minutes. Watch it closely because it will brown quickly when it heats up.
- Microwave ovens vary in power output. Some recipes may have to be adjusted to come out right in your microwave.

Amaretto Cake

Prep Time: 15 minutes ⧖ Bake: 30 to 45 minutes ⧖ Cook: 15 minutes

Serves: 10

1 package (regular) yellow cake mix

Pudding Mixture:

$\frac{1}{2}$ cup cornstarch
$\frac{1}{2}$ cup sugar
2 cups milk
2 eggs, well beaten
1 teaspoon vanilla extract

1 teaspoon rum extract
$\frac{3}{4}$ cup amaretto liqueur
1 10-ounce jar apricot preserves

Frosting:

2 cups whipping cream
$\frac{1}{4}$ cup amaretto liqueur
fresh strawberries

Bake the yellow cake in two layers according to the package directions and let cool completely (can be done a day ahead).

To make the pudding, combine all the ingredients except the preserves in a saucepan over low heat and cook, stirring constantly, for 15 minutes, or until a skin begins to form. Remove from the heat and let cool.

Using a serrated knife, cut each cake layer in half horizontally, to yield 4 layers. Place a layer on a serving plate. Spread with a third of the preserves and top with a third of the pudding. Repeat with the remaining layers.

Make the frosting: Whip together the cream and amaretto until soft peaks form. Frost the top and sides of the cake with the cream. Arrange the strawberries on top.

Angelic Strawberry Cake

Prep Time: 12 minutes 〼 Freeze: 15 minutes

Serves: 8

1 purchased angel food cake
2 cups strawberry frozen yogurt, thawed slightly
1 pint strawberries, stemmed and sliced

Cut the cake in half horizontally. Spread the strawberry yogurt on the bottom half of the cake. Place half of the strawberry slices on top of the yogurt. Replace the top half of the cake. Place more strawberry slices on top of the cake. Freeze for 15 minutes before serving.

Quick Fix: Chocolate-covered strawberries

Melt ½ cup semisweet chocolate morsels with 1½ teaspoons shortening in the microwave. Stir. Dip fresh strawberries that have been cleaned and are completely dry into the chocolate, leaving half the strawberry and the entire green stem and cap uncovered. Place on waxed paper until the chocolate is set. You can repeat the process using white chocolate for a contrasting dessert tray that is simple and elegant. Or you can insert wooden skewers into the cooled chocolate-covered strawberries and stick them into pots filled with floral foam; the strawberries will look like flowers and can be used as a centerpiece until it's time to "pick" them!

Baked Pears

Prep Time: 15 minutes ⧗ Bake: 35 minutes

Serves: 6

2 tablespoons lemon juice
6 pears, peeled and cored
2 to 4 tablespoons sugar
whipped cream (optional)

Preheat the oven to 375°F.

In a 2-quart baking dish, combine the lemon juice with enough water to cover the bottom. Add the pears, cover, and bake for 20 to 25 minutes, or until tender.

Remove from the oven. Uncover and sprinkle each pear with 1 to 2 teaspoons sugar. Bake, uncovered, for 10 minutes longer to glaze. Serve warm or chilled. Top with whipped cream, if desired.

Quick Fix: Fresh pears

Fresh pears are wonderful served with a tray of cheese slices.

Buttermilk Fruit Sherbet

Prep Time: 12 minutes

Serves: 4

2 cups frozen unsweetened blueberries
¹/₂ cup nonfat buttermilk, divided
2 or 3 drops of honey (optional)

In a food processor, combine the frozen berries with ¹/₄ cup of the buttermilk. Process until the berries are coarsely chopped. Process again, adding the remaining ¹/₄ cup buttermilk a little at a time through the cover opening. Uncover and redistribute the berries. Cover and process again until the mixture is smooth and has the texture of frozen custard or soft-serve ice cream. Don't overprocess. If desired, sweeten to taste with a few drops of honey.

Serve immediately.

Quick Fix: Crème fraîche

A favorite topping for any fresh fruit, especially berries, crème fraîche can be made simply by placing 1 tablespoon of buttermilk into 1 cup of heavy whipping cream. Cover tightly and allow to stand at room temperature until it's about twice as thick as the original cream, usually 12 to 24 hours. Refrigerate until ready to use.

Buttermilk Pops

Prep Time: 10 minutes ⧖ Freeze: 3 hours

Serves: 10 pops

*1 6-ounce can frozen orange juice concentrate, thawed
    and undiluted
1 cup buttermilk
1 cup evaporated skim milk*

In a large bowl, combine all the ingredients. Using an electric mixer, beat until blended. Pour into 4-ounce paper cups or popsicle molds and freeze until hardened. If you are using cups, freeze for about 15 minutes until thick and then insert the stick and continue to freeze until solid. Then, when ready to serve, just tear off the paper cup.

Quick Fix: Pudding

Mix some coconut into vanilla pudding for a quick dessert with a twist. You can even top it with some sliced strawberries or bananas, if desired.

Cake Mix Cookies

Prep Time: 8 minutes ⧗ Bake: 10 to 12 minutes

Yield: 36 to 40 cookies

1 package yellow cake mix	*1 cup semisweet chocolate*
¼ cup vegetable oil	*morsels*
2 teaspoons water	*1 cup nuts, chopped*
2 eggs	

Preheat an oven to 375°F.

In a large bowl, mix together all the ingredients to form a soft dough. Using your hands, form the dough into small balls the size of walnuts. Place on ungreased baking sheets, spacing the balls about 2 inches apart.

Bake for 10 to 12 minutes, or until delicately browned. Let cool on the baking sheets for a few minutes before removing to racks to cool completely.

Quick Tip: Freezing cookies

Most cookies freeze well. When you have the time, bake different varieties. If possible, go on a baking marathon, making several batches of the same cookies, because you can use the same preparation pans without washing them between uses—a great time-saver. Allow the cookies to cool completely, then wrap well and freeze. You can conveniently pull them out of the freezer any time they're needed. When placed on a serving plate, they will thaw in a few minutes on the counter, perhaps while you're making the coffee, or you can thaw them, or even heat them up a bit, in the microwave.

Candy Bar Cookies

Prep Time: 15 minutes ⧖ Bake: 15 minutes

Yield: 24 cookies

1 1/4 cups flour
3/4 teaspoon baking powder
1/4 teaspoon salt
1/2 cup unsalted butter, softened
1/2 cup sugar
1 egg
1 teaspoon vanilla extract
1 cup chopped chocolate-covered candy bars (about 5
    to 6 ounces, 1/2-inch pieces)

Preheat an oven to 325°F.

In a bowl, sift together the flour, baking powder, and salt. In a large bowl, using an electric mixer set on medium speed, beat together the butter and sugar until fluffy and smooth, about 30 seconds. Mix in the egg and vanilla and beat for 1 minute, stopping the mixer once at the midway point to scrape down the sides with a rubber spatula. Reduce the speed to low and add the flour mixture, mixing just until incorporated. Gently mix in the candy bar pieces.

Drop the batter by large tablespoons onto ungreased baking sheets.

Bake for 15 minutes, or until lightly browned. Remove while warm to prevent sticking. Cool on wire racks.

Chocolate Yummies

Prep Time: 8 minutes 　⧖　 Bake: 30 minutes

Yield: 12 squares

1 1/2 cups (18 squares) graham cracker crumbs
1 12-ounce can sweetened condensed milk
1 6-ounce package semisweet chocolate morsels

Preheat an oven to 350°F. Butter an 8-inch square cake pan.

Place the crumbs in the prepared pan and add the milk. Mix until the crumbs are moist. Add the chocolate morsels. Spread evenly in the pan. Bake for 30 minutes, or until firm. Remove from the oven; let cool.

Variation: If you want, add 1/2 cup chopped nuts with the chocolate chips.

Chocolate Tips

Nestlé and other companies that make chocolate chips and other add-ins for baking are coming out with a wide variety of deliciously different products to add zip to recipes that would normally use chocolate chips. Of course, peanut butter chips have been around for a while, but what about chocolate-covered raisins, toffee bits, or white chocolate chips? Combine two different "chips" for even more fun.

The easiest way to melt chocolate morsels is to use the microwave. Place the chocolate in a microwave-safe container, but don't cover the container, because this could cause moisture condensation and even a tiny drop of water will ruin the chocolate. Stop the microwave and stir the chocolate every few seconds, because chocolate will be melted without looking melted. Do not microwave the chocolate any longer than barely necessary to melt it.

Classic Pecan Pie

Prep Time: 15 minutes ⧗ Bake: 50 minutes

Serves: 10

3 eggs
²/₃ cup sugar
pinch of salt
1 cup dark corn syrup
¹/₃ cup butter or margarine, melted
1 cup pecan halves
1 unbaked 9-inch pastry shell

Preheat an oven to 350°F.

In a bowl, combine the eggs, sugar, salt, corn syrup, and melted butter. Beat thoroughly. Stir in the pecans. Pour into the pastry shell.

Bake for 50 minutes, or until a knife inserted halfway between the edge and the center of the filling comes out clean. Let cool completely on a rack before serving.

Quick Tip: Freezing pies

Generally, pies freeze well, and you will probably want to have several on hand for quick entertaining. Fruit pies can be frozen in their baked or unbaked state—or freeze them after baking them three fourths of the usual time, and finish the baking later. They'll seem like they're freshly baked. You can freeze pumpkin pies, but only after they've been baked; or else freeze the unbaked filling and the crust separately and bake after thawing. Do not freeze cream or custard-type pies or pies with meringue topping.

Coffee Almond Float

Prep Time: 8 minutes

Serves: 1

1 teaspoon brown sugar
¹/₄ cup brewed cold coffee
splash of orgeat (almond) syrup
ice cubes
¹/₂ cup 1% milk
¹/₂ cup coffee or chocolate low-fat frozen yogurt

In a parfait glass, dissolve the sugar in the coffee. Add the syrup, stirring to mix well. Add the ice and milk and stir well. Top with the frozen yogurt.

Quick Fix: Fruit parfait

For a beautiful instant dessert, use parfait glasses and alternate layers of:

• Fresh, frozen, or drained canned fruit or canned pie-filling and
• Vanilla or fruit-flavored yogurt, plain yogurt flavored with a little honey, pudding, or whipped cream

Top with your choice of ground nuts, shredded coconut, granola, and/or a piece of reserved fruit. If desired, garnish with a mint leaf. Chill until serving time.

For a variation, add layers of torn-up sponge cake pieces to the parfait.

Coffee Royale

Prep Time: 8 minutes

Serves: 1

1 teaspoon sugar
½ cup hot freshly brewed coffee
2 tablespoons brandy
2 tablespoons whipping cream

In a mug or Irish coffee glass, dissolve the sugar in the coffee. Add the brandy and stir well. Add the cream by pouring it over the back of a spoon so that it floats on top.

Quick Fix: Fresh berries

We love blackberries, blueberries, boysenberries, gooseberries, raspberries, and strawberries plain, the way nature grew them. Just rinse, hull, and serve! To dress them up a bit, top the berries with whipped cream. Or serve the fresh berries as a topping for ice cream.

Irish Coffee

Prep Time: 4 minutes

Serves: 1

1 jigger Irish whiskey
1 teaspoon sugar
1 cup very hot after-dinner coffee*
2 tablespoons whipped cream

Pour the whiskey into a glass or mug. Stir in the sugar and add the hot coffee. Top with whipped cream and serve immediately.

*After-dinner coffee made with a liqueur (also called a "cordial") or other alcoholic addition if often served after a special meal.

Quick Fix:
Fresh cantaloupe or muskmelon

For food safety reasons, always wash the rind before cutting the cantaloupe or muskmelon. Cut the fruit in half, following the segment lines, and then cut it into quarters. Scoop out the seeds. Top with whipped cream or vanilla ice cream or yogurt, and perhaps sprinkle with fresh berries. Lovely and delicious!

Marshmallow Refrigerator Squares

Prep Time: 12 minutes ⧗ Chill: 1 hour

Yield: 30 squares

30 marshmallows, quartered
8 maraschino cherries, cut up
½ cup walnuts, chopped
2 cups graham cracker crumbs
1 14-ounce can condensed milk
½ cup flaked dried coconut, divided

In a bowl, mix together the marshmallows, cherries, walnuts, and cracker crumbs. Add the milk and mix well. Butter a 9 × 13-inch pan. Sprinkle the bottom of the prepared pan with ¼ cup of the coconut. Add the mixture and press down. Sprinkle with the remaining ¼ cup coconut. Cover and chill. Cut into squares.

Cherries Jubilee

Prep Time: 10 minutes ⧖ Cook: 6 minutes

Serves: 6

1 16-ounce can pitted sweet cherries
¹/₃ cup sugar
2 tablespoons cornstarch
water
1 tablespoon fresh lemon juice
¹/₃ cup brandy (optional)
ice cream or cake à la mode

Drain the cherries, reserving the juice. Add water to make 1 cup liquid. In a small saucepan, mix together the sugar and cornstarch. Gradually stir in the cherry juice until smooth. Bring to a boil over medium heat, stirring constantly. Boil for 1 minute. Add the cherries and lemon juice; keep warm.

Just before serving, add brandy, if desired, and ignite. After the flame dies down, spoon the cherries over ice cream or cake à la mode.

Quick Fix: Broiled grapefruit

Cut the grapefruit in half and loosen the sections with a knife. Sprinkle a little brown sugar on the halves and top with a pat of butter. Broil a few minutes until heated through.

Easy Chocolate Mousse

Prep Time: 10 minutes ⧗ Chill: 2 hours

Serves: 6

1 6-ounce package chocolate pudding mix
³/₄ cup milk
1 teaspoon instant coffee powder
1 8-ounce package cream cheese, cubed

In a saucepan, combine the pudding mix, milk, and instant coffee and stir well. Place over medium heat and cook, stirring constantly, until the mixture comes to a boil. Add the cream cheese and beat until blended. Pour into a 1-quart mold. Place wax paper directly on the surface. Chill before serving.

Mousse

Some people feel that mousse is just another name for pudding. Not true. Mousse is a lighter form of pudding that is usually whipped at some point in the recipe. To ensure a light, fluffy mousse, be extra gentle when folding the whipped cream into the cooked mousse base.

Eggnog Mold

Prep Time: 10 minutes ⧗ Chill: 3 hours

Serves: 6

2 envelopes unflavored gelatin
½ cup water
1 quart eggnog
1 cup blanched almonds, ground
1 12-ounce can mandarin oranges, drained

Oil a 5-cup mold.

In a saucepan, sprinkle the gelatin over the water and let stand for 5 minutes to soften. Place over low heat and cook, stirring constantly, for 2 to 3 minutes, or until the gelatin granules dissolve completely and the mixture is clear. Add the eggnog, stirring until blended. Add the almonds. Pour into the prepared mold.

Cover and refrigerate until set, about 3 hours. To serve, unmold and garnish with the mandarin oranges.

Canned Versus Fresh Fruit

Fruit and cake-type desserts are one of the few kinds of desserts where canned fruits can be easily substituted for fresh fruits, which can create wonderful surprise desserts during cold weather. Just be sure to drain the fruit thoroughly—if specified—before using it in the recipe, or else you could end up with a mushy mess. You can even mix two different types of fruit in the same recipe with ease.

Estelle's Cream Cheese Pound Cake

Prep Time: 15 minutes ⧗ Bake: 1 ½ hours

Yield: large bundt cake

1 ½ cups butter
3 cups sugar
1 8-ounce package cream cheese
6 eggs
1 teaspoon vanilla
3 cups cake flour
powdered sugar

Preheat oven to 300°F. Grease a bundt pan well.

Cream together the butter, sugar, and cream cheese until light and fluffy. Add the eggs one at a time, beating well after each, then add the vanilla. Add the flour slowly. Bake in the bundt pan for 1 ½ hours.

Dust with sifted powdered sugar before serving. Cake may be served when cool, but is even better the second day.

Is It Done?

To test a cake, insert a toothpick or cake tester (an inexpensive kitchen gadget) in the center of the cake. If it comes out clean, the cake is done. If crumbs or batter stick to it, it needs to bake longer.

Some cooks prefer the "touch" method. Touch the cake lightly in its center. If it springs back, the cake is done. If the indentation from your finger remains, it needs to bake longer.

When done, the cake will also begin to shrink slightly away from the sides of the pan.

Fresh Strawberries Devonshire

Prep Time: 12 minutes

Serves: 6

¹/₂ cup whipping cream
¹/₂ cup sour cream
2 to 3 tablespoons orange-flavored liqueur
2 pints strawberries, hulled
brown sugar
mint sprigs

In a bowl, beat the cream until stiff peaks form. Fold in the sour cream and the liqueur. Place the strawberries in individual bowls and spoon the cream mixture over the top. Sprinkle with brown sugar to taste. Garnish with mint sprigs.

Quick Fix: Rhubarb sauce

Cut off the green leaves from the fresh rhubarb ribs as well as the whitish portion of the root end. Rinse, but do not soak the stalks in water. Cut the ribs into ¹/₂-inch chunks or run them through the thickest food processor slicing blade. Place the rhubarb in a saucepan with a little water. Simmer, covered, until the rhubarb is tender. Add sugar to taste (perhaps ¹/₃ cup per pound of rhubarb) and simmer a few minutes longer until the sugar is dissolved. Serve the sauce in bowls as is, hot or cold, or spoon over shortcake or ice cream. Strawberries are great sliced into the sauce.

Frozen Yogurt with Berry Sauce

Prep Time: 8 minutes

Serves: 4

1 10-ounce package frozen strawberries, thawed
¹/₂ teaspoon pure vanilla extract
1 pint low-fat vanilla frozen yogurt

Place the strawberries and vanilla extract in a food processor. Purée until smooth. Spoon the yogurt into individual dishes and drizzle the strawberry sauce over the top. Serve immediately.

Quick Fix: Papaya

Cut the fruit in half lengthwise and scoop out the seeds. Fill the seed cavity with a scoop of ice cream or sherbet, or a dollop of whipped cream.

Mardi Gras Cake

Prep Time: 25 minutes ⧗ Bake: 45 to 50 minutes

Serves: 8

1 30-ounce can fruit cocktail
½ cup margarine or butter
1 cup packed light brown sugar

1 18½-ounce package lemon cake mix
1 cup water
ice cream (optional)

Preheat an oven to 350°F.

Drain the fruit cocktail, reserving
⅓ cup of the syrup. Melt the margarine in a 9 × 13-inch cake pan or a 12-inch ovenproof skillet. Add the brown sugar, spreading it evenly over the bottom of the pan. Arrange the fruit in the sugar mixture. Prepare the cake mix according to package directions, using 1 cup water and ⅓ cup reserved syrup for the liquid specified in the directions. Spread the batter over the fruit.

Bake for 45 to 50 minutes, or until a knife comes out clean. Let cool for 5 minutes in the pan, then invert onto a large serving dish. Serve warm or at room temperature with ice cream, if desired.

Pan Placement

Place a cake pan or cookie sheet in the middle of an oven rack that has been centered in the oven. It's best to bake only one large pan or cookie sheet at a time, but if you must bake more than one:

- Arrange the pans so there is at least 1 inch of space between the pans and between the pans and the oven walls if they are on the same rack.
- If the pans are on different racks, do not place them directly under each other; stagger them.

Minted Middle Eastern
Buttermilk Shake

Prep Time: 5 minutes

Serves: 1

handful of ice cubes
1 cup nonfat buttermilk
pinch of salt
small handful of fresh mint leaves

Combine all of the ingredients in a blender. Cover and blend until the ice becomes blended. Pour into a tall mug and garnish with more mint leaves.

Chilled Cups

For a delightful presentation, chill the shake glasses before serving. These cold treats are perfect for a summer afternoon!

Old-Fashioned Pound Cake

Prep Time: 20 minutes ⧖ Bake: 1 ½ to 1 ¾ hours

Yield: large tube cake

1 cup butter
5 eggs
2 cups sugar
2 cups flour
1 teaspoon vanilla, almond, or citrus extract

Preheat oven to 300°F. Butter a large tube pan well.

Cream the butter well. Add the eggs, one at a time, beating 1 minute after each. While beating continuously, gradually add the sugar, then the flour, then the flavoring.

Pour into the tube pan, and bake for 1½ to 1¾ hours, or until a toothpick or knife inserted in the middle comes out clean. Serve with strawberries or other berries if desired.

Quick Fix: Fresh berries shortcake

Use one of the pound cake recipes in this chapter that you've made ahead and frozen, or use any white or yellow cake or even plain cheesecake as the base. Cut the cake into individual servings. Place fresh cleaned and hulled berries in a bowl and gently crush them with a potato masher. Add a little honey, if desired. Spoon the berries over each cake slice. Top with a dollop of whipped cream and serve. (Incidentally, you can substitute peaches for the berries.)

One-Minute Rice Pudding

Prep Time: 10 minutes ⧖ Cook: 7 minutes

Serves: 2

$^1/_2$ cup cooked rice
$^1/_2$ cup milk
1 tablespoon wheat germ
2 tablespoons raisins
2 tablespoons sunflower seeds
1 teaspoon honey

Mix together all the ingredients in a saucepan and cook over medium heat until it just begins to boil. Reduce heat, cover, and cook for 5 minutes.

Rice Pudding Memories

For me and for many other people, a cold dish of rice pudding conjures up all kinds of good feelings about childhood: it's sweet, it's not much work to eat it, and if your grandmother prepared it in a slightly different way than your mother, you probably liked hers better. Today, you can create new memories for you and your family by giving it your own personal touch. Grated chocolate on top is always nice, but a nip of amaretto stirred into the pudding after cooking, or using citron instead of raisins, are new ways to add spice.

Peach Crumble

Prep Time: 10 minutes ⧗ Bake: 45 minutes

Serves: 4

1 20-ounce can sliced peaches,
   drained
1 teaspoon grated lemon rind
   (optional)
$^1/_4$ cup dry pie crust mix

$^3/_4$ cup packed brown sugar
2 tablespoons butter or
   margarine, cut into bits
whipped dessert topping or
   light cream

Preheat an oven to 325°F.

Place the peaches in a medium-sized baking dish. Add the lemon rind, if using. Crumble the pie crust mix into a bowl; add the brown sugar and mix well. Dust the peaches with the pie crust mixture and dot liberally with the butter or margarine. Bake for 45 minutes, or until the top is crusty. Serve warm with dessert topping or cream.

Quick Fix: Peaches

Fresh Peaches

Peel and slice some peaches into a bowl and sprinkle with a little lemon juice to keep them from turning dark. Then drizzle the peach slices with honey; toss well and serve. For an extra punch, you can add a splash of dark rum.

Frozen peaches

It's so easy to buy peaches, allow them to ripen on your counter, and then freeze them whole in large plastic bags. When you want to use them, take out the desired number of peaches and immerse them in a large bowl of cold water for a few minutes until the skins readily slide off in your hands. Remove the peaches from the water and slice while they are still partially frozen. Do not leave the frozen peaches in the water too long or they will become soggy. Then follow the preceding tip for fresh peaches.

Pears à la Compote

Prep Time: 15 minutes ⧖ Cook: 25 minutes

Serves: 4

1 cup sugar
3 cups water
1/3 cup lemon or lime juice
pinch of salt
4 pears
2 cups grapes

In a saucepan, combine the sugar, water, lemon juice, and salt. Bring to a boil. Meanwhile, halve the pears lengthwise, leaving the stems intact, and core but do not peel. Add the pears to the syrup. Cover and cook over low heat for 20 minutes, or until tender.

Arrange the grapes and pears in a serving dish. Pour the hot syrup over the fruit. Chill before serving.

Quick Fix: Poached pears

Peel the pears, cut them in half lengthwise, and core each half. Place the halves in a covered saucepan with a little water and simmer on low for a few minutes until tender. Transfer the pear halves to a serving dish with a slotted spoon and serve them warm as is, or place a dollop of almond paste in each seed cavity.

Pineapple Milk Sherbet

Prep Time: 15 minutes ⧗ Freeze: 1 to 2 hours

Serves: 4

1 ³/₄ cups milk
¹/₂ cup sugar
1 8-ounce can crushed pineapple
2 tablespoons lemon juice
¹/₄ cup orange juice

Combine the milk and sugar. Add the remaining ingredients and stir until the sugar is dissolved. Pour into a loaf pan and freeze 1 to 2 hours. Stir twice during freezing to break up the sugar crystals.
Scoop into individual serving dishes.

Quick Fix: Pineapple

Fresh Pineapple
Peel and core a pineapple and cut it into bite-size chunks. Place the pineapple in a bowl and sprinkle with kirsch and lemon zest. Toss and serve.

Grilled pineapple
Fresh pineapple wedges are terrific on the grill; place the pineapple on skewers or in a wire basket and heat till lightly browned.

Broiled pineapple
Peel and core a fresh pineapple and cut it into rings. Drizzle a little honey and melted butter over the rings and broil them a few seconds in an ovenproof pan until tender and lightly browned. You can serve it with a dollop of whipped cream, if desired.

Pineapple Stuffing

Prep Time: 10 minutes   Bake: 1 hour

Serves: 6

¹/₂ cup butter
1 cup sugar
4 eggs

1 28-ounce can crushed pineapple, drained
6 slices bread, cubed or torn
1 teaspoon vanilla

Preheat the oven to 350°F.

In a large mixing bowl, cream the butter and sugar; add the eggs and vanilla and beat well. Add the pineapple and stir in the bread cubes. Bake in a greased 1¹/₂-quart casserole for 1 hour.

Quick Fix: Pineapple glaze

Place unsweetened pineapple juice (it can be canned or frozen) into a saucepan with a sprinkle of cinnamon. Bring just to a boil and add a pat or two of butter. Remove the pan from the heat.

Pineapple glaze on fruit
Cool the glaze somewhat and pour it over your choice of fresh fruit pieces and shredded coconut, and toss together. (The coconut can be omitted if desired.) This can easily be made in advance and stored in the refrigerator a few hours; the pineapple juice will keep fresh fruit from turning brown.

Pineapple glaze on cake
Pour the glaze over individual slices of pound cake or other white or yellow cake. Or, prick the entire top of an uncut cake with a drinking straw or a meat fork and pour the warm glaze over the whole cake; slice and serve with whipping cream, if desired. (Don't drench the cake with glaze; too much liquid will make it a soggy mess.) You can accent each serving with a maraschino cherry for added color. This can easily be made in advance. The cake will keep nicely a day or two in the refrigerator; the glaze prevents it from drying out.

Quick and Easy Cranberry Apple Pie

Prep Time: 15 minutes ⧗ Bake: 40 minutes

Serves: 10

1 package frozen pie-crust shells (2 shells)
1 can (1 pound 5 ounces) apple pie filling
1 cup whole berry cranberry sauce
¹/₂ cup walnuts, chopped
1 egg, beaten

Preheat the oven to 400°F.

Separate the 2 pie shells in the package; let thaw at room temperature for about 30 minutes, or until the dough becomes soft. In a bowl, combine the pie filling, cranberry sauce, and nuts, and mix well. Pour into one pie shell. Brush the edge of the pie shell with water. Carefully remove the second pie shell from its pan and turn it upside down on top of the apple filling. Press the edges of the two pastry layers together with the tines of a fork. Trim the edges with a sharp knife and cut vents in the top crust. Brush with the egg.

Bake for 35 to 40 minutes, or until the pie is brown and bubbly. Let cool completely on a rack before serving.

Quick Fix: Fresh apples

Slice apples into bite-sized chunks, then stir in some mayonnaise, plain yogurt with a little honey added, or whipped cream. Serve in a pretty bowl or individual dessert dishes and top with toasted pecans, walnuts, slivered almonds, or shredded coconut. Don't make this more than a few hours in advance.

Spicy Cold Pears

Prep Time: 10 minutes ⧗ Cook: 20 minutes

Serves: 4

4 pears, peeled, cored, and halved lengthwise
2 cups cranberry juice
2 tablespoons sugar
¹/₂ teaspoon ground cinnamon
¹/₂ teaspoon ground cloves
1 teaspoon grated orange zest
1 teaspoon grated lemon zest

In a saucepan, combine all the ingredients. Bring to a boil, cover, reduce the heat to low, and simmer until tender, about 15 minutes. Serve the pears warm or chilled.

Quick Tip: How to make zest

Zest is the very outer layer of the peel from citrus fruits, like lemons, but it should not include any of the white pith underneath the skin, as this can be bitter. Make zest by rubbing the unpeeled fruit on a grater; or better yet, invest in a zester, a hand tool that you drag over the rind. Never throw away the skins of oranges or lemons without taking the zest; you can freeze it in small plastic containers for later use.

Strawberry Whip

Prep Time: 12 minutes ⧗ Chill: 1 hour

Serves: 2

1 egg white
1¼ cups sliced strawberries
¼ cup sugar
a few drops of lemon juice

In a bowl, using an electric mixer, whip together the egg white and strawberries. When the mixture begins to thicken, gradually add the sugar. Continue to beat until the mixture holds soft peaks. Stir in a few drops of lemon juice. Chill before serving.

Did you know?

For the sweetest flavor, fruits need to be ripe. Some, like strawberries, should be picked ripe, when the entire flesh is red. Others, like peaches, nectarines, bananas, and mangoes, will ripen on your counter in a paper bag. Check daily. Overripe fruit should be eaten promptly as it will easily spoil.

Sweet Banana Risotto

Prep Time: 10 minutes ⧗ Bake: 1 hour

Serves: 4

1 cup Arborio rice, uncooked
3 ripe bananas, peeled and sliced
¼ cup brown sugar
3 cups milk
¼ cup crème de cacao liqueur
½ teaspoon cinnamon

Preheat oven to 375°F.

Spread about a third of the rice in a 2-quart casserole dish. Then sprinkle a third of the bananas and a third of the brown sugar on top of them. Repeat the layers in thirds until you're done. Pour on the milk and crème de cacao and sprinkle with cinnamon.

Cover and bake until the liquid has been absorbed and the rice is tender, about 1 hour. Serve warm.

Quick Fix: Baked bananas

Peel and slice bananas and toss the slices in melted butter. Bake a few minutes in a conventional oven or a few seconds in the microwave, until fork-tender. Sprinkle with cinnamon, if desired, and drizzle with a little honey, if desired.

Sweet Cocoa Sauce

Prep Time: 10 minutes   Cook: 2 minutes

Yield: 1 cup

¹/₂ cup cocoa powder
¹/₂ cup sugar
¹/₄ cup water
1 teaspoon pure vanilla extract

In a saucepan, stir together the cocoa powder and sugar. Stir in the water and place over high heat. Bring to a boil, stirring constantly. Remove from the heat and stir in the vanilla. Refrigerate.

Sweet Vanilla Sauce

Prep Time: 8 minutes

Yield: 1¹/₄ cups

¹/₄ cup nonfat buttermilk
2 teaspoons sugar
1 cup vanilla low-fat yogurt

In a small bowl, mix together buttermilk and sugar. Add the yogurt and mix well. Serve over fruit.

Cake Pan Tips

- The best pans for cake baking are shiny metal. If using dark coated (nonstick) or glass pans, follow the manufacturer's directions; if the directions are not available, reduce the oven temperature by 25 degrees. Glass and dark pans absorb the heat instead of reflecting it.

- To prevent sticking, grease both the bottom and sides of the pan generously. Dust the bottom with flour; shake the pan to coat the bottom, then turn over and discard the excess flour.

- For chocolate cakes, dust the baking pan with cocoa powder instead of flour.

- Even if using a cooking spray, dust the pan with flour if the recipe instructs you to do so. Sprays containing flour are also available specifically for baking.

- The bottom of the pan can also be lined with waxed paper to help cakes release without sticking.

- Solid shortening is the best choice for greasing pans. Butter browns or burns at a lower temperature, and will sometimes result in a browner "crust" on the bottom and sides of the cake.

Several cake pans

Bundt pan

Greasing the pan

Flouring the pan

Index

Index

A

Al dente, defined, 222
Almonds
  with broccoli, 263
  flounder amandine, 156
  with green beans, 241
Amaretto cake, 298
Appetizers, 14–31
  bruschetta, tomato, 27
  cashews, tamari, 26
  celery, stuffed, 14, 23
  cucumbers, sweet summer, 24
  dips
    apple, 29
    black bean, 29
    garlic-red pepper, creamy, 30
    mustard, easy, 30
    sour cream, 21
    spinach, 31
    yogurt, 31
  Dungeness crab, hot, 17
  eggplant caviar, 15
  fruit as, 14
  guacamole, 249
  parmesan crisps, 19
  presentation, 15
  quick fixes, 14
  relish trays, 14, 15
  roll-ups
    ham, 16
    seafood, 20
    veggie, 28
  spinach balls, 22
  taco scoop, 25
  Texas caviar, 266
  tortilla chips, low-fat, 18
  vegetables as, 28
Apple(s)
  accompaniment, 240
  and cranberry pie, quick and easy, 325
  dip for, 29
  omelet, with cheese, 283
  pancakes, blender, 278
  quick fixes, 325
  and red cabbage salad, hot, 62
  in salads, 57
  and sweet potato salad, warm, 81
  yields, 82
Apricot(s)
  with salmon, in red wine, 161
  salsa, Southwestern, 262
Asparagus and carrots, lemony, 251
Avgolemono, with orzo, 37
Avocado(s)
  crab-stuffed, 182
  cucumbers substituted for, 224
  guacamole, 249
  spirals, colorful, 205
  Texas caviar, 266

B

Baba ghanouj
  pitas with, 198
  sandwich spread, 197
Bacon
  in cappelletti carbonara, 107
  with scallops, grilled, 187
Bake, defined, 294
Banana(s)
  baked, 328
  risotto, sweet, 328
  yields, 82
Barbecue, defined, 294
Basil
  fettuccini frittata á la pesto, 200
  pasta with basil and tomatoes, quick, 226
  pepper pesto pasta, 98
  tomato pasta, 233
Beans, dried
  black beans
    dip, 29
    with rice and ginger, 227
    and rice, Caribbean, 202
    and rice, salsa, 260
    salad, California, 54
    with tomatoes and rice, 201
  in burritos, 215
  cannellini, with gazpacho pasta, 211
  chili, easy stovetop, 91
  cool bean salad, 58
  garbanzos (chickpeas)
    and black-eyed pea salad, 52
    in hummus, 217
    and red onions, 243
  mixed bean salads, 77, 253
  pinto bean soup, 48

Beans, dried—*continued*
  soup, hearty, 42
  in tacos, 218
  in Texas caviar, 266
  yields, 82
Beans, fresh
  mixed bean salads, 77, 253
  quick fixes, 241, 254, 262, 266
Beef. *See also* Veal
  barbecued beef sandwiches,
    crock-pot, 276
  burgers, with variations, 99
  butter toppings for, 86
  in chili, easy stovetop, 91
  in chili mac, 87
  corned, classic Reuben
    sandwich, 88
  filet Southwestern, 92
  hash, Texas, 106
  internal temperatures when
    roasting, 122
  London broil
    garlicky, 93
    with mushrooms, 95
  meatloaf, Mom's, 96
  sirloin
    pepper pesto pasta, 98
    sassy, 101
  spicy Chinese, 103
  steak
    and cheese wraps, 104
    chicken fried, 86
    easy pepper, 90
    rib-eye, grilled with onions,
      94
  stew
    gone-all-day, crock-pot, 272
    quick microwave, 100
    sloppy Joe, 102
  stroganoff
    easy, 89

  open-face sandwiches, 97
  steak, 105
  tri-tip, California, 85
Beer soup, 38
Beets, quick fix, 263
Berries
  blueberry pancakes, 278
  as dessert, 308
  raspberry and cream cheese
    breakfast biscuits, 292
  sauce, for yogurt, 316
  with shortcake, 319
  strawberries
    cake, angelic, 299
    and chicken salad, 73
    chocolate-covered, 299
    Devonshire, 315
    as garnish, 128
    whip, 327
    yields, 82
Beverages
  coffee almond float, 307
  coffee, Irish, 309
  coffee royale, 308
  freezing glasses, 318
  minted Middle Eastern
    buttermilk shake, 318
Biscuits
  basic drop, 241
  quick fixes, 258
  raspberry cream cheese,
    breakfast, 292
  scones, 293
Blanch, defined, 294
Blenders, 7
Blueberry pancakes, 278
Boil, defined, 294
Boil-over, preventing, 220
Borscht, 49
Bouillon cubes, 51
Braise, defined, 294

Bread(s)
  crumbs, yields, 82
  French toast, basic, 284
  garlic, amazing, 239
  parmesan crisps, 19
  pita, 198, 224, 245
  with spinach dip, 31
  tomato bruschetta, 27
Breads. *See also* Sandwiches
Broccoli
  with almonds, 263
  buying, 229
  and chicken with lemon,
    simmered, 138
  quiche, skillet, 196
  soup, 39
Broil, defined, 294
Bulgur, about, 216
Burritos, meatless, 215
Butter (margarine)
  as fat, 82
  herb, 86, 113
  jalapeño sauce, 221
  to prevent boil-over, 220
  sauces for poultry, 134
  yields, 82
Buttermilk
  and fruit sherbet, 301
  pancakes, 279
  popsicles, 302
  sauce, spicy, 154
  shake, minted Middle Eastern,
    318

C
Cabbage
  and apple salad, hot, 62
  coleslaw, Chinese, 56, 244
  sautéed, 264
  steamed, 264

Cake(s)
    amaretto, 298
    frozen, thawing, 297
    Mardi Gras, 317
    pineapple glaze for, 324
    pound, 296
        Estelle's cream cheese, 314
        old-fashioned, 319
    shortcake, with fresh berries,
        319
    strawberry, angelic, 299
    testing doneness, 314
Cannellini, with gazpacho pasta,
    211
Caper sauce, 171
Cappelletti carbonara, 107
Carrots
    and asparagus, lemony, 251
    with cinnamon, 263
    minted, 240
    orange-curry, 263
    with oregano, 263
Cashews
    curry, 203
    tamari, 26
Casseroles
    dishes for, 7
    freezing and reheating, 194
Cassoulet, crock-pot, 275
"Caviar"
    eggplant, 15
    Texas, 266
Celery
    stuffed, 14, 23
    yields, 82
Chard, Swiss
    sautéed, 261
    as substitute for spinach, 261
Cheese
    as appetizer, 14
    fondue, classic Swiss, 204

freezing, 16
gorgonzola and fresh thyme
    sauce, 248
low-fat substitutes, 287
mozzarella (smoked), with
    fennel and olive oil, 208
omelet, with apples, 283
parmesan crisps, 19
with pears, 300
rarebit
    California, 242
    Welsh, with vegetables, 267
ricotta, with fusilli and fresh
    herbs, 210
and steak wraps, 104
in strachiatella à la Romana,
    49
thawing, 259
as topping for vegetables, 258
with tuna, peas, and rice, 175
Cherries
    jubilee, 311
    yields, 82
Chicken
    boneless, 139
    broccoli lemon, simmered, 138
    broth, crock-pot, 271
    butter sauces for, 134
    cacciatore, crock-pot, 270
    cooking temperatures, 125
    and corn soup, Chinese, 41
    easy Sunday afternoon, 130
    grilled, 129
        ginger, marinated, 134
        Japanese, 132
        kebobs, marinated, 133
    kung pao chili, authentic, 125
    with penne, garlic, and sun-
        dried tomatoes, 131
    piccata, quick, 136
    with potato chips, baked, 129

reduced-fat cooking methods,
    137, 138
and rice skillet, Guadalajara,
    127
safety precautions, 130
salads, 127
    fruity, 61
    with pasta, 55
    with strawberries, 73
    with wild rice, California,
        128
    with wild rice, Minnesota,
        63
souper, 139
stir-fry, stellar, 140
substituting turkey for, 144
types of, 132
vinaigrette, simple, 137
with yogurt and spices,
    broiled, 126
Chickpeas. *See* Garbanzos
Chili
    easy stovetop, 91
    and macaroni, 87
    meatless, 216
Chocolate
    cocoa sauce, sweet, 329
    -covered strawberries, 299
    mousse, easy, 312
    tips on, 305
    yields, 82
    yummies, 305
Chop, how to, 32
Cilantro
    dressing, 72
    and onion relish, 254
Citrus
    glaze, 143
    how to section, 32
    zest, 326
Clam sauce, with linguine, 181

Coconut, toasting in microwave, 297
Cod, with spicy buttermilk sauce, poached, 154
Coffee
  almond float, 307
  Irish, 309
  royale, 308
Coleslaw, Chinese, 56, 244
Cookies and bars
  cake mix cookies, 303
  candy bar cookies, 304
  chocolate yummies, 305
  freezing, 303
  marshmallow refrigerator squares, 310
Cooking equipment and tools, 6–8
Cooking pans
  arranging in oven, 317
  for microwaving, 297
  tips on, 7, 330
Cooking terms, defined, 32, 294
Coquilles St. Jacques Provençal, 186
Corn
  and chicken soup, Chinese, 41
  chowder, hearty, 42
  on the cob, 249
  with sweet pepper, 254
Cornish hens, about, 132
Cottage cheese salad, 53
Couscous, with yogurt and fruit, 245
Crab
  appetizer, hot, 17
  avocados stuffed with, 182
  seafood on English muffins, 180
  seafood roll-ups, 20
Cranberry(ies)

and apple pie, quick and easy, 325
  yields, 82
Cream cheese
  as coating for vegetables, 265
  pound cake, Estelle's, 314
  and raspberry breakfast biscuits, 292
  and salmon wrap, 160
Crème fraîche, 301
Crock-pots
  barbecued beef sandwiches, Texas, 276
  cassoulet, 275
  chicken broth, 271
  chicken cacciatore, 270
  onion soup, French, 273
  selecting, 7
  stew, gone-all-day, 272
  stew, hearty smoked sausage, 274
  transporting food in, 274
Crumbs, yields, 82
Cube, how to, 32
Cucumbers
  about, 198
  as substitute for avocados, 224
  sweet summer, 24
Cumin, with lime, 151
Curry powder
  about, 81
  with carrots, 263
  cashew curry, 203
Cutting techniques, 32

D

Deep-fry, defined, 294
Desserts, 296–330
  fresh fruit as, 296
  microwaving tips, 296–297

Dice, how to, 32
Dill
  and parsley dressing, 58
  sauce, for vegetable wrap, 235
  snapper grilled with, 164
Dips
  apple, 29
  black bean, 29
  garlic-red pepper, creamy, 30
  mustard, easy, 30
  sour cream, 21
  spinach, 31
  yogurt, 31
Dishwashers, 8
Dressings. *See* Salad dressings

E

Eggnog mold, 313
Eggplant
  baba ghanouj
    in pitas, 198
    sandwich spread, 197
  caviar, 15
  grilled, 212
  and tomatoes, with gemelli, 207
Egg(s)
  about, 82, 281, 286, 288
  frittatas
    basic, 199
    fettuccine, á la pesto, 200
    spinach and pasta, 228
  hard-cooked, 37, 253
  low-fat substitutes, 287
  and lox, 288
  as main course, 55
  omelets
    basic, 282
    cheesy golden apple, 283
  safety precautions, 283, 291

salad sandwich, 219
scrambled, 289
in strachiatella à la Romana,
    49
in tomato broth, 247
and vegetables, scramble,
    291
Entertaining
    asking guests to help, 17
    buffets, 47
    ham for, 109
    tips for, 9–10

F

Farfalle, with turkey and sausage,
    142
Farmer's supper, 108
Fats
    about, 24
    in eggs, 281
    low-fat poultry tips, 137, 138
    low-fat substitutions, 287
    in pasta, 246
Fennel, with olive oil and
    smoked mozzarella, 208
Fettuccine
    frittata á la pesto, 200
    with light Alfredo sauce, 209
Fish and seafood, 150–191
    baking, 152
    broiling, 168
    buying, 171
    cod, with spicy buttermilk
        sauce, 154
    cooking, 156
    farm-raised, 173
    fillets
        baked, 152
        grilled, with herbed mustard
            sauce, 153

with lime and cumin, 151
    skillet dinner, 155
flounder amandine, 155
freezing, 150
garnishes, 150
grilling, 164, 174, 175
lobster-almost, 157
lox and eggs, 288
mussels, French country, 183
oyster stew, coastal, 184
pan-frying, 155
pasta salad, 70
poaching, 154
roll-ups, 20
safety precautions, 150
salad, with cilantro dressing,
    72
salmon
    with cream and pistachios,
        158
    and dill in cream sauce,
        163
    one-pot dinner, 159
    in red wine with apricots,
        161
    sandwich, with herb
        mayonnaise, 161
    and tortellini salad, 69
    trout as substitute for, 173
seafood on English muffins,
    180
selecting, 160
shrimp
    about, 190, 192
    in garlic and white wine
        sauce (microwave), 189
    grilled Spanish, 190
    in Indian sauce, 191
    seafood pasta salad, 70
    seafood roll-ups, 20
    stovetop Greek rotelli, 192

snapper
    with dill, grilled, 164
    red, á la Ritz, 165
sole
    creamy baked, 166
    fillets, baked, 167
    Florentine, quick
        (microwave), 169
    with lemon and tarragon,
        168
    steaming, 169
    testing doneness, 150, 179
    thawing, 150
    toppings for, 165
trout
    Cajun rainbow, 172
    farm-raised, 173
    grilled with herbs, 173
    grilled with oregano, 174
    as substitute for salmon,
        173
tuna
    cheesy, with rice and peas,
        175
    chowder, 50
    in crazy ziti, 206
    melt, 177
    and rice salad, 78
    salad, 50, 177
    salad sandwich, 178
    teriyaki, 179
    and tomato "pie", 176
Flounder amandine, 155
Fondue, classic Swiss, 204
Food processors, 7
Freezing
    casseroles, 194
    cheese, 16
    cookies, 303
    fish, 150
    ham, 118

Freezing—*continued*
  meats, 89, 114
  pies, 306
  serving glasses, 318
  soups, 34–35
  stocking freezer, 4, 11
French toast, basic, 284
Frittatas
  basic, 199
  fettuccine, á la pesto, 200
  spinach and pasta, 228
Fruit. *See also specific fruits*
  as appetizers, 14
  and buttermilk sherbet, 301
  canned, 66
  and chicken salad, 61
  citrus, how to section, 32
  as dessert, 296
  dried, 14, 268
  fresh vs. canned, 313
  frozen, thawing, 297
  parfait, 307
  preventing from browning, 26
  ripeness, 327
  salads
    apple, 57
    five-cup, 59
    peach-spinach, 66
    red cabbage and apple, hot, 62
    sweet potato and apple, warm, 81
    Waldorf, classic, 57
    Waldorf-style, 79
  serving portions, 62
  steaming, 268
  yields, 82
  and yogurt, with couscous, 245
Fry, defined, 294
Fusilli, with fresh herbs and ricotta, 210

G
Garbanzos (chickpeas)
  and black-eyed pea salad, 52
  in hummus, 217
  and red onions, 243
Garlic
  bread, amazing, 239
  in a jar, 80
  London broil with, 93
  and olive oil, with pasta, 220
  penne and chicken, with sun-dried tomatoes, 131
  red pepper dip, 30
  sautéing, 201
  shrimp, and white wine sauce (microwave), 189
  yields, 82
Garnishes
  for fish and seafood, 150
  for meats, 84
  for poultry, 128
  for soups, 34
  for vegetables, 251, 258
Gemelli, with eggplant and tomatoes, 207
Ginger
  with black beans and rice, 227
  marinade, 134
Glazes
  citrus, 143
  honey mustard, 143
  pineapple, 324
Grapefruit, broiled, 311
Grilling
  chicken, 129
    ginger marinated, 134
    Japanese, 132
    kebobs, marinated, 133
  defined, 294
  eggplant, 212
  fish, 153, 164, 175

  ham steaks, with pineapple, 109
  portobello mushrooms, 213
  poultry, 129
  rib-eye steaks, with onions, 94
  scallops, with bacon, 187
  shrimp, Spanish, 190
  snapper, with dill, 164
  swordfish
    Japanese, 170
    steaks, with caper sauce, 171
  trout
    with herbs, 173
    with oregano, 174
  tuna, teriyaki, 179
  turkey, 129
  vegetables, 234
Guacamole, 249

H
Ham
  about, 116
  in farmer's supper, 108
  freezing, 118
  internal temperatures when roasting, 122
  roll-ups, 16
  steaks, grilled with pineapple, 109
  uses of, 109
Hamburgers, 99, 101
Herbs and spices. *See also specific herbs and spices*
  butter sauces, 134
  butter toppings, 86, 113
  dried, enhancing flavor, 21, 115
  fusilli with fresh herbs and ricotta, 210
  herbed rice pilaf, 250

mayonnaise, 161
trout, grilled with, 173, 174
for vegetables, 248, 263
yields, 82
Hummus, 217, 224

J
Julienne, how to, 32

K
Kebobs
grilled chicken, 133
turkey jerky, 147
Kitchen organization, 6

L
Lamb
butter toppings for, 113
internal temperatures when
roasting, 122
patties, Greek-style, 113
Lasagna, quick, 225
Leek and sausage sauce, with
lumache, 119
Leftovers
cooking for, 3
roasts, how to use, 25
safety precautions, 97
salad as, 40
Lemon(s)
with asparagus and carrots,
251
with chicken and broccoli,
simmered, 138
juice, bottled, 71
sole, with lemon and tarragon,
168
yields, 82

Lettuce
buying, 35
iceberg, 218
preparing, 36, 62
storing, 35–36, 40
Lime, with cumin, 151
Linguine
with salmon, cream, and
pistachios, 158
with sun-dried tomatoes, 214
with turkey, tomatoes, and
olives, 145
with white clam sauce, 181
Lobster
pike masquerading as, 157
seafood on English muffins,
180
Lumache, with leek and sausage
sauce, 119

M
Macaroni and chili, 87
Main courses
eggs as, 55
meat and vegetable
combinations, 90
salads as, 42
soups as, 35
vegetarian, 194–236
Marinades
about, 77
for chicken kebobs, 133
ginger, 134
Jamaican, 147
Marshmallow refrigerator squares,
310
Measuring, about, 11, 12
Meatloaf
individual portions, 96
Mom's, 96

Meats, 84–122. *See also* Beef;
Ham; Lamb; Pork; Prosciutto;
Sausage; Veal
broiling, tips for, 101
freezing, 89, 114
garnishes, 84
internal temperatures when
roasting, 122
reading labels, 121
roast, leftover, 25
safety precautions, 97, 114
thawing, 94, 97
and vegetable combinations, 90
Melon, quick fixes, 309
Menus
balancing, 19
planning strategies, 2–9
Mesclun and prosciutto, with
tortellini, 112
Microwaved foods
beef stew, 100
coconut, toasting, 297
desserts, thawing, 296–297
sauces, 297
shrimp in garlic and white
wine sauce, 189
sole Florentine, 169
tips, 203
Mince, how to, 32
Mint
in butter sauces for poultry, 134
in butter toppings for lamb,
113
and buttermilk shake, Middle
Eastern, 318
with peas or carrots, 240
Miso soup, 45
Mixers, electric, 7
Mousse
about, 312
chocolate, easy, 312

Muesli (cold Swiss oatmeal), 287
Muffins, basic, 285
Mushrooms
   London broil topped with, 95
   with pasta shells, prosciutto,
     and peas, 110
   portobello, grilled, 213
   sautéed, 254
   yields, 82
Mussels
   cleaning, 183
   French country, 183
Mustard
   dip, easy, 30
   glaze, honey mustard, 143
   pork chops Dijon, 116
   sauce, herbed, 153
   yields, 82

N

Noodles. *See* Pasta
Nuts
   almonds
     with broccoli, 263
     flounder amandine, 156
     with green beans, 241
   as appetizers, 14
   cashew curry, 203
   cashews, tamari, 26
   as fish toppers, 165
   peanut butter soup, 47
   pecan pie, classic, 306
   walnuts and prosciutto, with
     pasta, 111
   yields, 82

O

Oatmeal, cold Swiss (muesli),
   287

Oils
   about, 24
   to prevent boil-over, 220
   for sautéing, 201
   sesame, Asian, 74
Olives, yields, 82
Omelets
   basic, 282
   cheesy golden apple, 283
Onion(s)
   about, 54
   and cilantro relish, 254
   green, yields, 82
   grilled rib-eye steaks with, 94
   preparing, 67
   red, and chickpeas, 243
   sautéed, 201, 254
   soup, crock-pot, 273
   storing, 75
Orange(s)
   and curry, with carrots, 263
   and mixed green salad, with
     honey, 64
   yields, 82
Orzo, avgolemono with, 37
Oven-fry, defined, 294
Ovens, convection, 8
Oyster stew, coastal, 184

P

Paella, summer vegetable, 229
Pan-fry, defined, 294
Pancakes
   basic, with variations, 278
   buttermilk, 279
   cooking tips, 279, 280
   cornmeal, 280
   high-protein, 281
Pantries, stocking, 3, 11
Papaya, quick fix, 316

Parboil (blanch), defined, 294
Parsley
   about, 41
   and dill dressing, 58
Parsley, about, 41
Pasta
   angel hair, with smoked
     salmon and dill, 163
   bake, quickie, 259
   for baking, 228
   with basil and tomatoes, quick,
     226
   cappelletti carbonara, 107
   colorful avocado spirals,
     205
   easy no-cook sauce for,
     246
   farfalle, with turkey and
     sausage, 142
   fettuccine
     frittata á la pesto, 200
     with light Alfredo sauce,
      209
   fresh vs. dried, 222, 223
   fusilli, with fresh herbs and
     ricotta, 210
   with garlic and olive oil, 220
   gazpacho, with cannellini
     beans, 211
   gemelli, with eggplant and
     tomatoes, 207
   gorgonzola and fresh thyme
     sauce, 248
   how to cook, 209
   with jalapeño butter sauce, 221
   lasagna, quick, 225
   linguine
     with salmon, cream, and
      pistachios, 158
     with sun-dried tomatoes,
      214

with turkey, tomatoes, and
olives, 145
with white clam sauce, 181
as low-fat, 246
lumache, with leek and
sausage sauce, 119
macaroni and chili, 87
marinara sauce, 252
orzo, in avgolemono, 37
penne and chicken, with
garlic and sun-dried
tomatoes, 131
pepper pesto pasta, 98
preventing boil-over, 220
with prosciutto and walnuts,
111
Provençale, 135
rotelli, stovetop Greek, 192
salads
with chicken, 55
cooking pasta for, 70
Oriental noodle, 65
orzo, warm, 80
rotini, Alfredo, 68
salmon tortellini, 69
seafood, 70
Szechuan noodle, 74
with salsa verde (green
sauce), 223
shells, with prosciutto, peas,
and mushrooms, 110
spaghetti, summer vegetable,
230
and spinach frittata, 228
testing doneness, 222
tomato-basil, 233
tomato sauce, special
occasion, 263
tortellini, with prosciutto and
mesclun, 112
turkey tetrazzini, 148

yields, 82
ziti, crazy, 206
with zucchini sauce, 222
Peach(es)
crumble, 321
quick fixes, 321
and spinach salad, 66
yields, 82
Peanut butter soup, 47
Pear(s)
á la compote, 322
baked, 300
with brown rice, 256
with cheese, 300
poached, 322
spicy cold, 326
yields, 82
Pea(s)
minted, 240
with pasta shells, prosciutto,
and mushrooms, 110
soup, 46
Pecan pie, classic, 306
Penne, with chicken, garlic, and
sun-dried tomatoes, 131
Pepper(s)
and garlic dip, 30
pasta, with jalapeño butter
sauce, 221
yields, 82
Pesto
fettuccini frittata á la pesto,
200
pepper pesto pasta, 98
Pie(s)
cranberry apple, quick and
easy, 325
freezing and thawing, 296–297,
306
peach crumble, 321
pecan, classic, 306

pot, turkey, 141
tuna and tomato, 176
Pike, masquerading as lobster,
157
Pilaf, rice, herbed, 250
Pineapple
glaze, 324
grilled, with ham steaks, 109
quick fixes, 323
sherbet, milk, 323
stuffing, 324
Pita bread
about, 245
with baba ghanouj, 198
with hummus, 224
Polenta, 257
Popsicles, buttermilk, 302
Pork. *See also* Ham
chops
Dijon, 116
easy honey-herb, 115
in wine sauce, 117
cutlets, schnitzel, 118
internal temperatures when
roasting, 122
Potato(es)
oven wedges, 255
preparing, 255
salad, summertime, 265
storing, 100
yields, 82
Poultry, 124–148. *See also*
Chicken; Turkey
butter sauces for, 134
cooking temperatures, 125
Cornish hens, about, 132
garnishes for, 128
grilling, 129
substituting turkey for chicken,
144
thawing, 124

Poundcake, 296
  Estelle's cream cheese, 314
  old-fashioned, 319
Prosciutto
  in cappelletti carbonara, 107
  with pasta and walnuts, 111
  with pasta shells, peas, and
    mushrooms, 110
  with tortellini and mesclun, 112
Pudding
  eggnog mold, 313
  quick fixes, 302
  rice, one-minute, 320

Q

Quiche(s)
  broccoli, skillet, 196
  Lorraine, skillet, 290
  spinach, crustless, 195

R

Radishes, sautéed, 254
Rarebit
  California, 242
  Welsh, with vegetables, 267
Raspberry and cream cheese
  breakfast biscuits, 292
Recipes
  increasing quantity of, 271
  low-fat substitutes in, 287
Relish trays, 14, 15
Relishes
  onion-cilantro, 254
  salsa
    apricot, Southwestern, 262
    with black beans and rice,
      260
    verde (green sauce), with
      pasta, 223

Rhubarb
  sauce, 315
  yields, 82
Rice
  banana risotto, sweet, 328
  and black beans
    Caribbean, 202
    with ginger, 227
    with salsa, 260
    with tomatoes, 201
  brown, with pears, 256
  and chicken skillet,
    Guadalajara, 127
  cooking tips, 256, 260
  pilaf, herbed, 250
  preventing boil-over, 220
  pudding, one-minute, 320
  with tuna, peas, and cheese,
    175
  and tuna salad, 78
  yields, 82
Rice, wild
  and chicken salad, California,
    128
  and fresh tomato salad, 60
  salad, Minnesota, 63
Ricotta, with fusilli and fresh
  herbs, 210
Roast, defined, 294
Roll-ups
  ham, 16
  seafood, 20
  veggie, 28
Rotelli, stovetop Greek, 192

S

Safety
  eggs, 283, 291
  fish and seafood, 150
  in kitchen, 10–11

meat, 97, 114
poultry, 130
Salad dressings
  cilantro, 72
  dill parsley, creamy, 58
  lemon, spicy, 59
  vinaigrette, simple, 71
Salads, 36–81
  assembling, 79
  bean
    black bean, California, 54
    chickpea and black-eyed
      pea, 52
    chickpea and red onion,
      243
    cool, 58
    mixed bean, 253
    traditional three-bean, 77
  for buffets, 47
  Caesar, 53
  chicken, 127
    fruity, 61
    with pasta, 55
    with strawberries, 73
    with wild rice, California,
      128
    with wild rice, Minnesota,
      63
  coleslaw, Chinese, 56, 244
  cottage cheese, 53
  cream cheese wrap, 160
  fruit
    apple, 57
    five-cup, 59
    peach-spinach, 66
    red cabbage and apple, hot,
      62
    sweet potato and apple,
      warm, 81
  Waldorf, classic, 57
  Waldorf-style, 79

Greek, tangy, 76
green, 38, 44
   with honey and oranges, 64
   with spicy lemon dressing,
     59
ingredients for, 36, 56
lettuce, about, 35–36
as main course, 42
pasta
   with chicken, 55
   cooking pasta for, 70
   Oriental noodle, 65
   orzo, warm, 80
   rotini, Alfredo, 68
   salmon tortellini, 69
   seafood, 70
   with seafood, 70
   Szechuan noodle, 74
potato, summertime, 265
red cabbage and apple, hot,
   62
red-leafed Greek, 67
smoked fish, with cilantro
   dressing, 72
sweet potato and apple, warm,
   81
taco, 75
tomato and wild rice, 60
tuna, 50, 177
tuna rice, 78
wild rice, Minnesota, 63
Salmon
   with cream and pistachios, on
     herb linguine, 158
   one-pot dinner, 159
   in red wine, with apricots, 161
   sandwich, with herb
     mayonnaise, 161
   smoked, and dill in cream
     sauce, with angel hair pasta,
     163

and tortellini salad, 69
trout as substitute for, 173
Salsa
   apricot, Southwestern, 262
   with black beans and rice, 260
   verde (green sauce), with
     pasta, 223
Saltiness, reducing, 272
Sandwiches
   baba ghanouj spread for, 197
   barbecued beef, crock-pot, 276
   for buffets, 47
   chicken salad, 127
   egg salad, 219
   open-face beef stroganoff, 97
   pitas, with baba ghanouj, 198
   pitas, with hummus, 224
   Reuben, classic, 88
   salmon, with herb
     mayonnaise, 161
   seafood on English muffins,
     180
   tuna melt, 177
   tuna salad, 177, 178
Sauces
   Alfredo, light, 209
   berry, 316
   butter, for poultry, 134
   buttermilk, spicy, 154
   caper, 171
   cocoa, sweet, 329
   dill, 235
   gorgonzola and fresh thyme,
     248
   Indian, 191
   jalapeño butter, 221
   marinara, 252
   microwaving tips, 297
   pasta, easy no-cook, 246
   rhubarb, 315
   salsa verde (green sauce), 223

tomato, special occasion, 263
vanilla, sweet, 329
white clam, 181
zucchini, 222
Sausage
   sauce, with lumache and
     leeks, 119
   skillet, 120
   skillet supper, 121
   stew, crock-pot, 274
   with turkey and farfalle, 142
   and vegetable soup, very
     quick, 51
Sauté, defined, 294
Scald, defined, 294
Scallops
   Barbara's, 185
   coquilles St. Jacques
     Provençal, 186
   grilled, with bacon, 187
   preparing, 187
   spiced, 188
Scones, 293
Seafood. *See* Fish and seafood
Sear, defined, 294
Section, how to, 32
Shellfish. *See* Fish and seafood
Sherbet
   buttermilk fruit, 301
   pineapple milk, 323
Shopping
   for chicken, 139
   for fish and seafood, 171
   for lettuce, 35
   for meat, 114
   tips for, 4–6
   for vegetables, 28, 238
Shrimp
   about, 190, 192
   in garlic and white wine sauce
     (microwave), 189

Shrimp—*continued*
  grilled Spanish, 190
  in Indian sauce, 191
  seafood pasta salad, 70
  seafood roll-ups, 20
  stovetop Greek rotelli, 192
Simmer, defined, 294
Snapper
  with dill, grilled, 164
  red, á la Ritz, 165
Snip, how to, 32
Sole
  creamy baked, 166
  fillets, baked, 167
  Florentine, quick (microwave),
    169
  with lemon and tarragon, 168
Soups, 37–51
  avgolemono, with orzo, 37
  bean, hearty, 42
  beer, 38
  borscht, quick, 49
  broccoli, 39
  for buffets, 47
  canned, combinations, 35
  cheeseburger, 40
  chicken broth, crock-pot, 271
  chicken corn, Chinese, 41
  corn chowder, hearty, 42
  freezing, 34–35
  French onion, crock-pot, 273
  as main course, 35
  miso, 45
  pea, 46
  peanut butter, 47
  pinto bean, 48
  sausage and vegetable, very
    quick, 51
  strachiatella à la Romana
    (raggedy cheesy egg soup),
    49

toppings, 34
tuna chowder, 50
turkey and vegetable, hearty,
  44
Spaghetti, summer vegetable, 230
Spinach
  balls, appetizer, 22
  chard as substitute for, 261
  dip, 31
  with hard-boiled egg, 254
  and pasta frittata, 228
  and peach salad, 66
  quiche, crustless, 195
  sole Florentine (microwave),
    169
  wilted, 247
Steaming
  defined, 294
  tips for, 268
Stew
  beef, quick microwave, 100
  defined, 294
  gone-all-day, crock-pot, 272
  hearty smoked sausage, crock-
    pot, 274
  oyster, coastal, 184
  sloppy Joe, 102
Stir-fry
  chicken, stellar, 140
  defined, 294
  tofu, Szechuan, 232
Strachiatella à la Romana
  (raggedy cheesy egg soup), 49
Strawberry(ies)
  cake, angelic, 299
  and chicken salad, 73
  chocolate-covered, 299
  Devonshire, 315
  as garnish, 128
  whip, 327
  yields, 82

Stroganoff
  easy, 89
  open-face sandwiches, 97
  steak, 105
Substitutions, emergency, iv
Sugar, powdered, 82
Sweet potato and apple salad,
  warm, 81
Swordfish
  grilled Japanese, 170
  grilled steaks, with caper
    sauce, 171

T
Taco(s)
  meatless, 218
  salad, 75
  scoop, appetizer, 25
Tarragon
  and lemon, with sole, 168
Thawing
  casseroles, 194
  cheese, 259
  cookies, 303
  desserts, 296–297
  fish, 150
  meals, 18
  meat, 94, 97
  poultry, 124
  shrimp, 192
  vegetables, 252
Thermometers, meat, 122
Tofu
  sweet and sour, 231
  Szechuan stir-fry, 232
Tomato(es)
  and basil, with pasta, 226,
    233
  with black beans and rice,
    201

broiled, with breadcrumbs and cheese, 239
broth, eggs in, 247
bruschetta, 27
and eggplant, with gemelli, 207
plum, 233
sauce
marinara, 252
special occasion, 263
sun-dried
with linguine, 214
with penne, chicken, and garlic, 131
and tuna "pie", 176
and wild rice salad, 60
yields, 82
Tortellini, with prosciutto and mesclun, 112
Tortilla chips, low-fat, 18
Turkey
about, 143
breast
glazed, 143
herb-roasted, 144
butter sauces for, 134
cooking temperatures, 125
cutlets, Indian style, 146
with farfalle and sausage, 142
grilling, 129
jerky kebobs, 147
with linguine, tomatoes, and olives, 145
potpie, easy, 141
substituting for chicken, 144
tetrazzini, 148
and vegetable soup, hearty, 44

V

Vanilla sauce, sweet, 329
Veal
cube steaks, quick tangy, 114
internal temperatures when roasting, 122
Vegetable(s). See also specific vegetables
as appetizers, 14, 15
blanching, 60
buying and preparing, 28, 62, 236, 238, 243
combinations, 238
cream cheese coating, 265
dips for
black bean, 29
garlic-red pepper, creamy, 30
mustard, easy, 30
sour cream, 21
spinach, 31
yogurt, 31
and eggs, scramble, 291
grilling, 234
with herbs, 248
paella, summer, 229
roll-ups, 28
and sausage soup, very quick, 51
steaming, 268
stir-fried, 244
summer, with spaghetti, 230
thawing, 252
toppings, 251, 258
and turkey soup, hearty, 44

Welsh rarebit, with, 267
wrap, with dill sauce, 235
Vegetarian entrees, 194–236
Vinegar, about, 64

W

Waffles, basic, 286
Walnuts and prosciutto, with pasta, 111
Weights and measures, 10
Whipped cream
how to make, 296
yields, 82

Y

Yeast, yields, 82
Yields and equivalents, 82
Yogurt
dip, 31
frozen, with berry sauce, 316
fruit parfait, 307
and fruit, with couscous, 245

Z

Ziti, crazy, 206
Zucchini sauce for pasta, 222

Available wherever books are sold!

Everything® **Money Book**
$12.95, 1-58062-145-7

Everything® **Mother Goose Book**
$12.95, 1-58062-490-1

Everything® **Mutual Funds Book**
$12.95, 1-58062-419-7

Everything® **One-Pot Cookbook**
$12.95, 1-58062-186-4

Everything® **Online Business Book**
$12.95, 1-58062-320-4

Everything® **Online Genealogy Book**
$12.95, 1-58062-402-2

Everything® **Online Investing Book**
$12.95, 1-58062-338-7

Everything® **Online Job Search Book**
$12.95, 1-58062-365-4

Everything® **Pasta Book**
$12.95, 1-55850-719-1

Everything® **Pregnancy Book**
$12.95, 1-58062-146-5

Everything® **Pregnancy Organizer**
$15.00, 1-58062-336-0

Everything® **Quick Meals Cookbook**
$12.95, 1-58062-488-X

Everything® **Resume Book**
$12.95, 1-58062-311-5

Everything® **Sailing Book**
$12.95, 1-58062-187-2

Everything® **Selling Book**
$12.95, 1-58062-319-0

Everything® **Study Book**
$12.95, 1-55850-615-2

Everything® **Tall Tales, Legends, and Outrageous Lies Book**
$12.95, 1-58062-514-2

Everything® **Tarot Book**
$12.95, 1-58062-191-0

Everything® **Time Management Book**
$12.95, 1-58062-492-8

Everything® **Toasts Book**
$12.95, 1-58062-189-9

Everything® **Total Fitness Book**
$12.95, 1-58062-318-2

Everything® **Trivia Book**
$12.95, 1-58062-143-0

Everything® **Tropical Fish Book**
$12.95, 1-58062-343-3

Everything® **Vitamins, Minerals, and Nutritional Supplements Book**
$12.95, 1-58062-496-0

Everything® **Wedding Book, 2nd Edition**
$12.95, 1-58062-190-2

Everything® **Wedding Checklist**
$7.95, 1-58062-456-1

Everything® **Wedding Etiquette Book**
$7.95, 1-58062-454-5

Everything® **Wedding Organizer**
$15.00, 1-55850-828-7

Everything® **Wedding Shower Book**
$7.95, 1-58062-188-0

Everything® **Wedding Vows Book**
$7.95, 1-58062-455-3

Everything® **Wine Book**
$12.95, 1-55850-808-2

Everything® **Angels Mini Book**
$4.95, 1-58062-387-5

Everything® **Astrology Mini Book**
$4.95, 1-58062-385-9

Everything® **Baby Names Mini Book**
$4.95, 1-58062-391-3

Everything® **Bedtime Story Mini Book**
$4.95, 1-58062-390-5

Everything® **Dreams Mini Book**
$4.95, 1-58062-386-7

Everything® **Etiquette Mini Book**
$4.95, 1-58062-499-5

Everything® **Get Ready for Baby Mini Book**
$4.95, 1-58062-389-1

Everything® **Golf Mini Book**
$4.95, 1-58062-500-2

Everything® **Love Spells Mini Book**
$4.95, 1-58062-388-3

Everything® **Pregnancy Mini Book**
$4.95, 1-58062-392-1

Everything® **TV & Movie Trivia Mini Book**
$4.95, 1-58062-497-9

Everything® **Wine Mini Book**
$4.95, 1-58062-498-7

Everything® **Kids' Baseball Book**
$9.95, 1-58062-489-8

Everything® **Kids' Joke Book**
$9.95, 1-58062-495-2

Everything® **Kids' Money Book**
$9.95, 1-58062-322-0

Everything® **Kids' Nature Book**
$9.95, 1-58062-321-2

Everything® **Kids' Online Book**
$9.95, 1-58062-394-8

Everything® **Kids' Puzzle Book**
$9.95, 1-58062-323-9

Everything® **Kids' Space Book**
$9.95, 1-58062-395-6

Everything® **Kids' Witches and Wizards Book**
$9.95, 1-58062-396-4

Everything® is a registered trademark of Adams Media Corporation.

**For more information, or to order, call 800-872-5627
or visit everything.com**

Adams Media Corporation, 260 Center Street, Holbrook, MA 02343

We Have
EVERYTHING
KIDS'!®

Everything® Kids' Baseball Book
$9.95, 1-58062-489-8

Everything® Kids' Joke Book
$9.95, 1-58062-495-2

Everything® Kids' Money Book
$9.95, 1-58062-322-0

Everything® Kids' Nature Book
$9.95, 1-58062-321-2

Everything® Kids' Online Book
$9.95, 1-58062-394-8

Everything® Kids' Puzzle Book
$9.95, 1-58062-323-9

Everything® Kids' Space Book
$9.95, 1-58062-395-6

Everything® Kids' Witches and Wizards Book
$9.95, 1-58062-396-4

Available wherever books are sold!